PUBLIC RECORD OFFICE OF NORTHERN IRELAND

General Report on the Gosford Estates in County Armagh 1821

by

William Greig

with an introduction by
F. M. L. Thompson and D. Tierney

D1610550

BELFAST
HER MAJESTY'S STATIONERY OFFICE

Foreword

This book is one of a series intended both to show the range and type of archives available in the Northern Ireland Record Office and to present individual documents of intrinsic interest.

This 'Report' by William Greig was deposited in the Record Office in 1936 by the Earl of Gosford. Professor F. J. Fisher of the London School of Economics first suggested its publication, Professor F. M. L. Thompson of Bedford College, University of London kindly agreed to write a substantial introduction to what he describes as 'a document of absorbing interest to all students of pre-Famine Ireland' and Mr. D. Tierney of University College London has analysed the Tabular Reports in Part Two of the Introduction: the Record Office is greatly indebted to them all. The map of the Gosford estates was drawn by Miss E. Duncan of the Geography department in the Queen's University, Belfast. Mr. W. H. Crawford, an Assistant Keeper in the Public Record Office of Northern Ireland, has prepared the text and been responsible for the overall production of the book.

The manuscript was bound in a large volume 48 cm by 69 cm in half-leather of which now survive only the original boards with the nameplate and corners embossed in gold on red leather. It runs to 366 pages some of which are blank. The Report falls naturally into two sections. Of these the Prefatory Remarks and the General Report with its Appendix have been printed in this volume but the Tabular Reports and Additional Remarks have been omitted on the grounds of cost. Specimen pages only of the Tabular Reports and Additional Remarks have been included at the end of this volume but the whole is analysed by Mr. Tierney in his section of the Introduction.

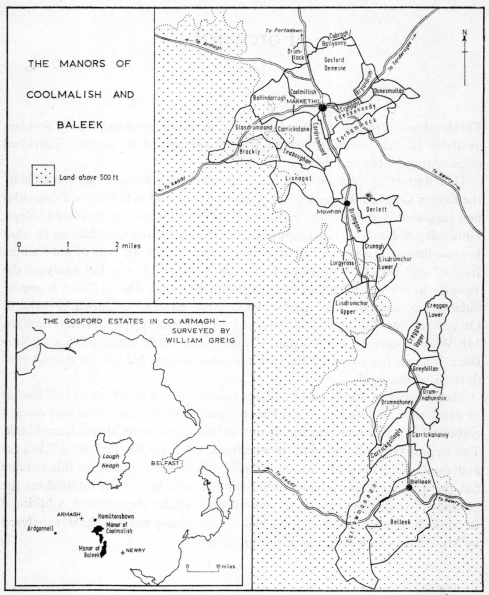

THE MANORS OF

COOLMALISH AND

BALEEK

::: Land above 500 ft

0   1   2 miles

To Portadown
To Armagh
Cabragh
Ballyanny
Drum-lack
Gosford
Demesne
Bryandrum
Dunesmullan
To Tanderagee
Ballindarragh
Coolmillish
MARKETHILL
Crunagh
Glasdrummond
Carrickalane
Lordrummond
Edenkennedy
Corhammock
Brackly
Seaboughan
To Newry
Lisnagat
To Keady
Mowhan
Drumgane
Derlett
Crunagh
Lurgyrass
Lisdrumchor
Lower
Lisdrumchor
Upper
Creggan
Lower
Creggan
Upper
Greyhillan
Drumnahoney
Drum-nahunshin
Carrickananny
Carrickgallogly
Carrowmananan
Belleek
To Keady
Belleek
To Newry

N

THE GOSFORD ESTATES IN CO. ARMAGH —
SURVEYED BY
WILLIAM GREIG

Lough
Neagh
BELFAST
ARMAGH
Hamiltonsbawn
Manor of
Coolmalish
Ardgonnell
Manor of
Baleek
NEWRY

0   10 miles

Crown copyright 1970

iv

BALEEK MANOR

Belleek — als *Baleek Upper and Baleek Lower*
Carrowmannan — als *Corromannon Upper, Corromunnon Lower and Corromannon Middle*
Carrickgallogly — als *Carrickgollogly, Carricgollogly, Carrickollogly*
Carrickananny — als *Carrickananey, Carrickanany, Carrickunnany*
Creggan Upper — als *Cregans Upper*
Creggan Lower — als *Cregans Lower*
Crunagh — als *Crunaght Upper and Crunaght Lower*
Drumnahunshin — als *Drumnahuncheon*
Drumnahoney — als *Drumhoney Upper and Drumhoney Lower*
Drumgane — als *Drumgean, Drumnegean*
Derlett — als *Dirlet*
Greyhillan — als *Greyhilla*
Lisdrumchor Upper — als *Lissdromchor Upper*
Lisdrumchor Lower — als *Lissdromchor Lower*
Lurgyross — als *Lurgiross*

COOLMALISH MANOR

Ballindarragh — als *Ballindaragh*
Ballyanny — als *Ballyany*
Brackly — als *Brackly Upper and Brackly Lower, Brackley*
Bryandrum
Cabragh — als *Cobragh*
Carrickalane — als *Carricklane*
Coolmillish
Cordrummond — als *Cordrumond*
Corhammock — als *Corhamock*
Crunaght
Drumlack
Dunesmullan — als *Dinnismullen or Dennismullen*
Edenkennedy — als *Ednekennedy*
Glasdrummond — als *Glassdrumond Upper and Glassdrumond Lower*
Lisnagat — als *Lisnegat*
Seaboughan — als *Sebochan*

HAMILTON'S BAWN

ARDGONNELL   als *Argonnell*

Contents

INTRODUCTION I

INTRODUCTION II

GENERAL REPORT ON THE MANORS OF COOLMALISH AND BALEEK,
WITH HAMILTON'S BAWN AND ARDGONNELL

BY WILLIAM GREIG

ILLUSTRATIONS

Tables

The Maps, Plans, &c.

EXECUTED BY

WILLIAM GREIG, AND JOHN HILL,

Being the result of their united exertions, contain a minute survey of every enclosure—specifying their description, quality, and contents; exhibiting the

Direction of water-courses, ridges, &c.

Natural features of the surface;

Kind of fences, buildings, and other circumstances capable of being so delineated; in a manner highly expressive;

Also, proposed alterations in roads, drains, and other improvements;

Sections or profiles of the grounds

being given, where requisite to further illustrate their curvature, comparative elevation of surface, and capability of improvement;

Also, the sub-soil, and mineral formation; with

Vignettes, being correct views of interesting passages of scenery, or to show the general aspect of the grounds.

W. G. flatters himself, that fourteen years' extensive practice in the improvement of Estates, and in Road Engineering, in these kingdoms, with sedulous attention to business, will continue to render his services satisfactory to his employers. Having frequent occasion to visit different parts of Ireland, gentlemen giving him timely notice, may avail themselves of his assistance, without travelling expenses. The most satisfactory references can be given, as to character, and professional abilities.

☞ Observations on improvements, &c. given in addition to considerable surveys, without any extra charge.

MAPS COPIED, ADDED TO LEASES, OR REDUCED FOR THE POCKET.

Letters addressed to No. 6, ... reet, Dublin; 1, Corn-Market, Belfast; or Cecil, Aughnacloy; will be immediately forwarded to W. G.

January 1st, 1819.

FINLAY, PRINTER, BELFAST.

WM. GREIG,

Rural Designer, and Surveyor in general,

IN returning his grateful acknowledgments to the Landed Proprietors, and Grand Juries, of Ireland, for their patronage since his arrival in this country, begs to inform them, that he has now made such arrangements, as will enable him to attend, with despatch and punctuality, to

Survey, Arrange, and Value Estates;

And to give designs and directions in various departments of RURAL IMPROVEMENT: particularly, for the ornamental and picturesque improvement of Residences, Grounds, and Villas; for Draining, Embanking, Planting, &c.: also, for laying out Roads, furnishing all the necessary plans, sections, estimates, &c. required by the Statutes.—The form of

GENERAL REPORTS

On Landed Estates, which he has invented, and which has been found so interesting and useful to Proprietors—presents at ONE VIEW, the

Contents, acreable rate, and rent of each holding;

Particulars of leases, and of portions of land occupied by sub-tenants, with the profit rent accruing to head-tenants;

Average annual amount, and acreable rate of tithe and cess;

Minute details of the population;

Cottagers;—Live stock;

Description of soil, as to surface, subsoil, and exposure;

Names and distance of markets, lime quarries, turbaries, and public roads, from each farm;

Improvements, kind of fences, and their state of repair;

Orchards, and forest trees planted by tenants;

Buildings, kind of covering, and their state of repair;

State of drainage and tillage;

Apparent character of tenants as to industry;

With observations on proposed arrangements, and means of improvement, &c.

The General Report

by F. M. L. Thompson

1 THE SIGNIFICANCE OF THE REPORT

The publication of this edition of Greig's Report by the Public Record Office of Northern Ireland is an event even more notable than the original submission of the Report to Lord Gosford in 1821. For, whatever Greig's own self-esteem and consciousness of his own originality may have led him to expect in 1821, it unhappily seems from the silence of contemporaries and of the subsequent estate documents that his vast Report was not so much bread cast upon the troubled waters of Irish agriculture, as a large stone which sank almost without trace in the pond of Gosford estate management. That this stone should be brought to the surface and exposed to the public gaze undoubtedly fulfils one of Greig's original intentions. But where he expected that immediate publication would make his Report not merely an instrument of instant improvements on the Gosford estate, but also an example which would contribute to a general regeneration of agriculture in Ireland and thus of the entire Irish economy, publication in 1976 may be expected to contribute to the advance of scholarship rather than the advance of national prosperity. The Report indeed constitutes a document of absorbing interest to all students of pre-Famine Ireland, of Irish agriculture, and Irish demography, of agricultural history in general, of estate management, and of contemporary applied economics; the aim of this Introduction is to elucidate some of these matters, by way of comment upon both the Report and the context in which it was set.

2 PROVENANCE

It is apparent both from the somewhat elaborate flourish with which he introduced his Report, and from some explicit remarks in the text (*pages* 12-13)*, that Greig felt he was introducing an instrument of estate management and aid to decision-making of some novelty. Indeed in the field reference book (for the estate map which accompanied the Report; printed for him by the same Belfast printer, F. D. Finlay, who produced the Report) Greig advertised his professional services to Irish landowners at large, offering to undertake surveys with his fellow-surveyor John Hill, and to present their results in 'the form of General Reports on Landed Estates, which he has invented, and which has been found so interesting and useful to Proprietors.' Now while it is true that the very idea of an estate survey accompanied by some description and estimation of its resources was far from novel by this date, it may well still be true that the Greig elaboration on a well-established mode of proceeding was an innovation. Should that be the case, it is worth while to establish in what the innovation consisted, and what factors led Greig to make it.

In English practice at any rate, the straightforward cadastral estate survey aimed at delineating and establishing the boundaries and location of the estate, its holdings, and their fields, had blossomed out into an exercise which was also intended to supply a valuation, and which therefore required some accompanying appraisal of the condition and resources of the estate, long before the beginning of the nineteenth century. The appraisal-and-valuation type estate survey was, for example, being advocated by John Norden as early as 1607, being practised by Edward Laurence in the 1720s, and being offered as a regular part of an organised consultancy service in land agency by the London firm of Nathaniel Kent, Claridge and Pearce in the 1780s.[1] While it was necessary for a surveyor to make some examination of the capabilities of an estate, both actual and potential, physical and human, in order to be able to arrive at a valuation, it did not follow that he committed the fruits of this examination to paper, in the

---

Pages 12–13 indicate that the reference is to pages 12 and 13 in the original manuscript version of Greig's Report. These page numbers have been placed in the margin against the published text of the Report.

1. F. M. L. Thompson, *Chartered Surveyors: the growth of a profession* (London, 1968), pp. 16-17, 28-9, 50. G. E. Mingay, 'The Eighteenth-century Land Steward', in *Land, Labour and Population in the Industrial Revolution*, ed. G. E. Mingay and E. L. Jones (London, 1967), pp. 9, 27; E. L. Jones, 'Industrial Capital and Landed Investment: the Arkwrights in Herefordshire, 1809-43', ibid. p. 60.

Greig fashion, and it might well be that in the earlier surveys much of the information on conditions and resources was simply carried in the surveyor's head—if indeed it was carried anywhere—and that only his specific recommendations for action ever got recorded. One valid claim for novelty for this Report is, therefore, that it actually recorded all the necessary details of a process of appraisal which, previously, had at least partially been conducted by memory, hunch and intuition. As a deliberate attempt to furnish all the relevant evidence on which managerial decisions could be based the Report could thus rank as an important step in the development of estate management towards a professionalized activity equipped with expressly formulated procedures.

The question whether, however, the Report did in fact supply all the evidence needed for fully-informed decisions—in spite of its sometimes pretentious air of comprehensiveness, and its often laborious detail—will be raised later. At the moment it will suffice to point out that there is indeed no known survey and report, on an exactly comparable scale of detail and thoroughness, for any British or Irish estate, for any earlier date than Greig.[1] In England, Scotland, and Ireland[2] there are estate documents of earlier dates which incorporate some, but not all, of the features of the Greig Report, particularly the enumeration of resident population, as in various Irish and Scottish estate censuses, and the discussion of rents and arrears, as in many eighteenth-century English estate papers.[3] But the earliest truly comprehensive report on a Scottish estate was probably James Loch's penetrating assessment of the Sutherland estate in his *Account of the Improvements on the Estates of the Marquess of Stafford*, which he published in 1820 as, in effect, a report on his management of the estate.[4] Possibly the *Report relative to the Lordship and Estate of*

1. This does not imply that some equivalent report does not, or did not at one time exist. No completely exhaustive search for such reports has been made.
2. And no doubt in Wales as well, though there appear to be no published works referring to them.
3. For example, *Inhabitants of the Argyll Estate, 1779*, ed. E. R. Cregeen, Scottish Record Society, 91 (1963); Irish estate censuses discussed in Joseph Lee, 'Marriage and Population in Pre-Famine Ireland', *Econ. Hist. Rev.*, 2nd ser. XXI (1968); English evidence discussed by G. E. Mingay, op. cit., and in *English Landed Society in the Eighteenth Century* (London, 1963), pp. 67-71; F. M. L. Thompson, *English Landed Society in the Nineteenth Century* (London, 1963), pp. 164-6, 224-5.
4. Discussed by D. Spring in *The English Landed Estate in the Nineteenth Century: its administration* (John Hopkins University Press, Baltimore, 1963), pp. 90-2. The absence of any mention of estate reports as a distinguishable and definable category of management practice, in this comprehensive study of estate management, is in itself indicative of the rarity of the Greig Report type of enterprise.

Marchmont, the Barony of Hume, etc., drawn up by David Low, later to acquire prominence as an agricultural writer, by order of Sir William Purves Hume Campbell, and published in 1819, ought to be ranked in the same category. Low's Report, indeed, commissioned by a landowner who had but recently built up his estate by inheritance and extensive purchases and who was desirous of obtaining an overall picture of what he had done, was in many respects similar to the Greig Report. It contained a detailed farm-by-farm description, and a series of reasoned recommendations for future management policy, though it lacked both the statistical recording of Greig and Greig's theoretical apparatus. In view of Greig's evident interest in Scottish affairs, and the fact that Low must have been working on the Marchmont estate at the same time as Greig was working on the Gosford estate, it is not impossible that the two men were aware of one another's existence. For England the first comparable report known to the writer was not made until 1829, when Edward Driver scrutinised the Scilly Isles for the Duchy of Cornwall estate, and submitted a Report which in mastery of detail, penetration, and sophistication of economic reasoning was at least the equal of Greig, and in lucidity and lack of prolixity clearly his superior.[1]

The primacy of Greig's General Report seems, therefore, to be credible, and it seems to lie in the scope of its generality, in its formal presentation as one single document. In this quality also seems to lie, not quite its uniqueness, but its rarity as the first of a species which never, in all the British Isles, became at all common. Both these features, originality and rarity, appear to stem from a single set of causes. Where the day-to-day management of an estate was reasonably competent and efficient by the standards of the times, occasions were unlikely to arise which called for a single, all embracing, searching look at all the manifold aspects of that estate. To be sure, occasions might, and did, arise which called for some special action to reduce debts, to curtail expenditure, to undertake improvements, to stimulate the tenantry to exertions, to tackle problems of mounting arrears, to rearrange fields or holdings, or in some other way to alter a previous course of management which had become congealed into an unimaginative and unenterprising routine. Such occasions, most commonly met with in the English experience when an estate fell into the

---

1.   Edward Driver, Report on the Scilly Isles, 1829, Drivers, Jonas and Co. MS, Charles II Street, London.

possession of a minor whose guardians stepped in to impose a regularised administration, or when an owner's debts piled up to a point where financial rationality became inescapably necessary, and most fruitful in administrative innovation when both these circumstances occurred at once, often resulted in a period of renewed vitality for an estate in which a leaner and tauter management produced a fatter income and a healthier tenantry.[1] The point, however, is that in most of these cases the preceding management had as a matter of course thrown up some, or perhaps a great deal, of the information about the estate—its holdings, tenures, rents, cropping and husbandry practices, and so forth—which was required for plotting these fresh courses for estate policy. Other relevant information—for instance about markets, local communications, labour supply, availability of tenants, or population pressures—either tended to be taken for granted in a settled, already developed, and not too rapidly changing country, or tended to be taken for granted by persons already familiar with the general situation on the estate in question. Thus it was that in the great majority of these English cases involving a more or less radical re-assessment of an estate's position, there was no need to assemble in one single document the whole array of data that is to be found in the Greig Report.

The general backwardness of Irish estate management, in comparison with English or Scottish practice, is therefore one main explanation for the appearance of the Greig Report. Edward Wakefield testified to this backwardness when he commented, in 1812, on the easy life led by Irish land agents: their work, he said, consisted of receiving the rents twice a year and setting out the turf-bogs in lots every spring, and that was it, apart from their social, political, and magisterial functions in representing their often absentee employers.[2] Such minimal routine duties do not suggest that Irish agents were at all likely to be active, energetic, or curious about the estates which they managed, nor do they suggest that Irish estates were at all likely to be supplied with any continuously or even intermittently collected economic data; while any systematic preservation of such information, should it have chanced to be casually acquired, in an accessible and

---

1. Instances of this are discussed in the works of G. E. Mingay and D. Spring already cited. See also F. M. L. Thompson, 'English Landownership: the Ailesbury Trust, 1832-56', *Econ. Hist. Rev.*, 2nd ser. XI (1958); and for Irish estates, O. Robinson, 'The London Companies as Progressive Landlords in Nineteenth-Century Ireland,' *Econ. Hist. Rev.*, 2nd ser. XV (1962).
2. Edward Wakefield, *An Account of Ireland, Statistical and Political*, 2 vols (London, 1812), I, 244.

intelligible form would appear to have been quite out of the question. Here was a virgin field into which Greig plunged with zest.

It is interesting to note that the only sphere in which Greig-type reports became at all common in England concerned estates where the owners did not possess any continuously-refreshed body of information about their estates, indeed did not possess any really relevant information at all. This ignorance, however, was due not to managerial indolence but to peculiar tenurial arrangements, and principally concerned the corporately-owned estates of the crown and the church. These estates had, in the main, been leased out for two or three hundred years before the nineteenth century on what were in effect perpetually-renewed leases, at merely nominal annual rents, to substantial men (usually already landowners in their own right) whose families became hereditary lessees, and who performed most of the functions of genuine landowners in finding the tenant-farmers who were the actual occupiers of the farms, and in collecting and appropriating to themselves the rents which represented the full annual values of those farms. The most usual form of such leases was the lease for three named lives, the lessee being by convention entitled to insert a new life into his lease every time an existing life died—or 'dropped' in the jargon of the lifehold world—on payment to the head-landowner of a renewal fine related to the actual current annual value of the estate. The head-landowner had thus only an intermittent and regular interest in knowing what the value of the estate was, and for all practical purposes it was the beneficial lessee who performed the landlord's functions in the landlord-tenant relationship and who had access to the sort of information which was generated by normal estate management.

If head-landowners with estates run under this arrangement of beneficial leases decided to terminate the system, and to resume full possession and control themselves, they had therefore to start more or less from scratch in putting themselves in the picture of where their estates were and what they were like. The crown decided to do just this; and with the establishment of the Ecclesiastical Commissioners for England and the formation of their Estates Committee so did the church on an even greater scale—in both cases in order to raise and make more regular the annual incomes from their properties. Hence such documents as the 1829 Report on the Scilly Isles, and the enormous collection of surveys and reports on church estates made by John Clutton and other professional surveyors from the late 1840s onwards, all of which may be classed as in the Greig category.[1]

To generalize about Irish land tenures would be exceedingly rash, but it is plausible to argue that some part of the seeming backwardness and indolence of Irish estate management may have been due to the way in which Irish tenures were a pale, and in some respects a bastardized, version of these English tenures for three lives. Until the end of the eighteenth century the commonest form of lease in Ireland seems to have been that for three lives, and it was certainly prevalent on the Gosford estate. In the Irish case, however, unlike the English, the lessee was almost invariably the actual occupier of the holding. Then from the early nineteenth century, and particularly after about 1810, it became usual to let holdings on the shorter, but still relatively long, leases of 21 years and one life, whichever should be the longer period. At the time of the Devon Commission this latter was still the most common type of lease, and its prevalence on the Gosford estate was noted by Greig.[2] This practice, in itself, meant that an owner possessed control of any given farm only at long—and of even greater importance, irregular—intervals. On top of this feature, subdivision of holdings, a process which appears to have begun on a significant scale from the 1780s, meant that an owner lost direct contact with a proportion—which was a growing proportion—of the actual occupiers of his lands; and this was so whether subdivision was of a commercial character, through middlemen, or simply familial in nature. The managerial implication of these two factors is that there was some justification for the absence, on Irish estates, of the sort of estate information which might be ready to hand and reasonably up to date on English estates; hence a partial explanation

1. Estate surveys and reports for the Ecclesiastical Commissioners are to be found in great quantity among the records of the Church Commissioners, and among the records of Messrs. Clutton, 5 Great College Street, London, S.W.1.
2. There are many references in the Devon Commission to 21 years and one life as the most common form of lease: the following references are all to the *Report of the commissioners into the state of the law and practice in respect to the occupation of land in Ireland, evidence:* hereafter cited as Devon Commission, Parts I, II, III, 1845, (606), 616), and (657) respectively, the sessional volume number being given in brackets. Antrim,W(itness) 96 Q(uestion) 30 (XIX): Armagh, W. 52 Q. 68, W. 77 Q. 45, W. 81 Q. 36, W. 73 Q. 24 (XIX); Cavan, W. 321 Q. 52 (XX); Clare, W. 579 Q. 13 (XX); Donegal, W. 97 Q. 45 (XIX); Kildare, W. 971 Q. 24 (XXI); King's County, W. 993 Q. 12 (XXI); Limerick, W. 628 Q. 40, W. 627 Q. 14 (XX); Meath, W. 20 Q. 51 (XIX); Queen's County, W. 979 Q. 24, W. 972 Q. 17, W. 866 Q. 13 (XXI); Roscommon, W. 7 Q. 171 (XIX); Sligo, W. 356 Q. 8 (XX); Tyrone, W. 199 Q. 6, W. 223 Q. 30, W. 213 Q. 14 (XIX); Waterford, W. 803 Q. 12, W. 812 Q. 38 (XXI); Westmeath, W. 419 Q. 29 (XX); Wexford, W. 941 Q. 11, W. 933 Q. 45, W. 938 Q. 17 (XXI); Wicklow, W. 953 Q. 44, W. 957 Q. 10, W. 1019 Q. 16 (XXI). In Cork and Tipperary 31 years and 3 lives was said to be the more usual term. Greig's own comments on leases are discussed below, pages 22 to 27.

for the appearance of one aspect of Greig-type activities—the data
collection on the scale of his 'Tabular Reports'—specifically in
Ireland.

It was noted earlier that in the English cases of radical re-appraisal
of an estate one expects to find that some particular occasion, a
minority or an alarming level of debts, served to set the process afoot.
It is difficult to establish whether anything in particular occasioned
the investigation of the Gosford estate, since no documents or
correspondence survive to indicate what led up to Greig's appointment or what terms of reference he was given. Negative arguments,
however, are possible. Greig began work on the survey in 1817 and
received his first payment in April 1818;[1] there was no minority at
this time, nor was there any recent succession that could have had a
new-broom effect, since the Earl of Gosford was then 41 and had
succeeded to the estates in 1807. The estate was certainly carrying a
load of debt, but this does not seem to have amounted to anything
out of the ordinary. In 1818 the debts outstanding on the security of
all Gosford's estates—not simply on those in County Armagh—
totalled some £45,000, on which the annual interest payment was
some £2,700; in addition there were annuities of £1,083 charged on
the estates, largely consisting of the dowager Lady Gosford's jointure
of £1,000. Interest and annuities together, £3,700, had to be met
from rents which nominally produced £10,476 a year; admittedly
arrears had been mounting sharply, and actual receipts in 1817, for
example, were only £6,600.[2] Even so, the debt burden though it may
look very large by bourgeois standards, was not exactly aristocrati-
cally alarming. In any case there is no sign at all in the Report itself
that Greig had been asked to consider the scope for retrenchment,
which would inevitably have enjoyed top priority if this had been a
debt-motivated enquiry.

A *post hoc* explanation lies temptingly close to hand, in that Lord
Gosford began building his large, moated, turreted, imposingly
baronial and lavishly appointed Castle at this time. The first recorded
payment for this crenellated extravaganza appears in the accounts for
1820, and it is therefore highly likely that the idea of building had been
forming in Lord Gosford's mind at about the time that Greig was

1. Gosford MS, D. 1606/7A/14 page 24. The records of the Gosford estate are held in the Public
    Record Office of Northern Ireland. The number of the collection is D.1606 and all references
    to items in the collection are prefixed with this number.
2. Gosford MS, Rentals 1816-18, D. 1606/7A/14.

commissioned. It is a possible inference, therefore, that the purpose of appointing Greig was to get him to see how much more revenue could be squeezed out of the estate in order to finance a fairy-castle dream. All that one can say is that, if so, the whole exercise must have been a sore disappointment to Greig's employer, since the reiterated theme of the Report on this matter is that less income should be drawn from the estate, that rents should be reduced, and that existing arrears should somehow be wiped out. A more positive point against such an interpretation of the origins of the Report is, perhaps, that the subject of castle-building is scarcely mentioned by Greig. In the light of Greig's character and opinions, this silence may indeed be taken as well nigh conclusive. The whole tone of the Report shows firstly that Greig had a proper respect for the principles of economy, efficiency and the encouragement of the tenantry, and secondly that however much he might wrap up his meaning in elaborate and sycophantic language he was still tolerably blunt in putting home-truths to his employer. If he had known about an expensive and flamboyant building project, he could scarcely have approved of it in the situation which he found on the estate, of a sharp and severe agricultural crisis which had revealed fundamental and most serious weaknesses, unless he had approved of it as a laudable local make-work scheme and symbol of the landlord's intention to reside and to exercise firm control. In either case he was not the man to forego lightly a chance of airing his views. That Gosford Castle was built in the course of the 1820s, at a cost probably in the region of £80,000, at a distressingly inappropriate time from the point of view of its effects both as an example to a struggling and impoverished tenantry, and as a grave misuse of the estate's resources, can scarcely have been with Greig's connivance and can hardly have any direct connection with the circumstance in which the Report came to be written.[1]

The views which Greig did wish to air come through loud and clear in the Report. Clearly, he was enamoured of the new political economy and eagerly seized an opportunity to impress an Irish land-owner with a didactic display of its lessons in a micro-application to the affairs of a single estate. Any reading of the Report suggests

---

1. Gosford Castle was still not complete by the mid 1830s, and by then was stated to have cost over £80,000; the architect was Thomas Hopper. See J. Binns, *The Miseries and Beauties of Ireland*, 2 vols (London, 1837), I, 195.

that Greig thought of himself as the teacher and Lord Gosford as his pupil, and through the layers of deferential language his tutorial role shows more clearly than his role as a professional adviser with any specific remit. It is of course quite possible that Greig was so ebullient that he ignored his original brief and was carried away into flights of ratiocination which no one had asked for. Certainty is impossible, since no documents or correspondence dealing with his original appointment have survived among the Gosford papers. On the one hand, a passage in one of Greig's subsequent letters, stating 'my business was only to return the farms as pointed out to me . . .' could imply that he was employed simply to survey and map the individual holdings, perhaps with the idea of establishing some systematic record of their location, tenants, and tenures.[1] On the other hand, a slightly earlier letter, written after he had already been at work for some considerable time, clearly implies that he had indeed been employed to make a general report as well as a physical survey of the whole estate of some 8,000 Irish acres and a set of individual maps for each separate lease.[2] Conceivably, from the estate's angle the main purpose of Greig was the highly practical one of obtaining reliable and up to date maps in order to execute fresh leases and reduce existing ones to some kind of order, while the main purpose from Greig's point of view was to execute a fundamental assessment of the condition of the estate and the factors which determined it. But it must remain unlikely that the entire investigating and reporting side of Greig's work was completely supererogatory and unsolicited.

In that case the reasons which led to the commissioning of the Report still remain to be established. It seems most plausible to associate this with the advent, not of a new owner, but of a new agent. William Blacker, who was later to achieve considerable renown as one of the foremost and most enlightened Irish land agents of the century, was already Lord Gosford's chief agent when Greig began work in 1817, but had not been long in that office. Indeed when he gave evidence to the Devon Commission in 1844, Blacker implied that he had become Gosford's agent in 1819, but that was clearly a slip of memory.[3] As the new man in charge, and one who had begun

1. Gosford MS, William Greig to William Blacker, 9 May 1819, D.1606/2/2, voucher 29.
2. Same to same, 19 October 1818, D.1606/2/2.
3. Devon Commission, Part I, 1845, XIX, W. 49 Q. 2, W. 52 Q. 14. A printed rent-roll for 1815 names William Blacker as agent, D.1606/7A/8.

his career 'as a mercantile man', Blacker may well have determined on a thorough overhaul of managerial methods. Moreover the calamities and disasters of the seasons of 1816 and 1817 lent urgency to the task of obtaining a systematic appraisal of the short-term prospects and underlying condition of the estate, although it seems that this acute distress occurred after Greig had embarked on some sort of work for the estate (*pages* 241-3). From the snippets of surviving correspondence, and from the absence of anything more than a lukewarm response after 1821 to Greig's recommendations, it does not look as though Blacker was ever over-enthusiastic about Greig's concept of a sweeping investigation and intellectualized diagnosis of the condition of the estate. But, with Greig on hand in County Tyrone offering to undertake such investigations, Blacker must have seen sufficient promise of concrete benefits to the estate from the more practical side of Greig's proposals to recommend that Lord Gosford should give Greig a chance to show what he could do. It remains to ask why Greig should have conceived his grand design of General Reports.

3 WILLIAM GREIG AND HIS REPORTING TECHNIQUE

Very little is known about the life or career of William Greig. The supposition that he was a Scotsman seems to be confirmed by the fact that he signed himself 'A Caledonian' in a series of articles which he contributed to the *Irish Farmers' Journal* in 1816 and 1817, to which he refers in the Report (*page* 254).[1] He claimed, in 1818, that he had then had fourteen years' extensive practice in the improvement of estates and in road engineering, which implies that his professional career began in 1804.[2] In the first of his *Irish Farmers' Journal* articles, datelined 2 December 1816, he stated that 'some seven or eight years ago I was induced to visit this kingdom', and since then had pursued his profession 'solely devoted to the general improvement of landed property and relative pursuits' in Ireland.[3] He may have begun his Irish practice, therefore, in 1808, after a spell of about four years' activity in Scotland. His interest in road engineering in Ireland—

1. *Irish Farmers' Journal and Weekly Intelligencer*, V, nos. XVII, XVIII, XXI, XXVIII, XXXI, 1816-17.
2. Advertisement dated 1 January 1819 in the field book to the maps of Coolmalish and Baleek (reproduced on pages x, xi), D.1606/6B/10.
3. *Irish Farmers' Journal*, V, no. XVII.

if not his technical proficiency in the subject—is well attested by his *Strictures on Road Police*, which was published in Dublin in 1818.[1] This work dedicated to Robert Peel who was then Chief Secretary for Ireland, concerned 'police' not in the sense associated with the later 'peelers' or 'bobbies', but in the older and wider sense of general civil administration, and is itself an absorbing display of many of Greig's qualities.

The internal evidence of the *Strictures* strongly suggests that Greig's time in Ireland up to this date had been largely, and perhaps exclusively, devoted to road surveying and engineering. He advances 'his practice as a Road Engineer, in Great Britain, and for the last nine years, in Ireland,' as his qualification for authorship; and states for example, that 'for many years I have been extensively employed in designing and taking levels, &c. for intended new roads, at the request of Grand Juries (of Irish counties)'; and that he had 'many years experience, while employed under the authority of his Majesty's Post-Masters General, in many counties of Ireland, in laying out new lines and improvements on the Post-roads.'[2] His remarks also suggest that before coming to Ireland he had been closely involved with road construction in Aberdeenshire.[3] Moreover a principal purpose of the book was to argue the case for the employment of none but properly trained and qualified professional men as full-time County Engineers to take charge of the road system of each county, and Greig clearly implies that road engineering is, or ought to be, a distinct sub-branch of civil engineering, and 'that a life-time will barely suffice to make a proficient.'[4] In association with the inference which the reader is obviously expected to draw, that Greig himself was 'a proficient' in this profession, this opinion if it is not to be taken as hypocritical dissembling means that Greig counted himself, at this date, as a road specialist—one who, in the course of his business might indeed have exceptional opportunities for observing agricultural practices and conditions, but one who was still basically a road man.

1. William Greig, *Strictures on Road Police, containing views of the present systems, by which Roads are Made and Repaired, together with Sketches of its Progress in Great Britain and Ireland from the Earliest to the Present Time, with an Appendix* (Dublin, 1818).

2. Ibid., pp. xi, 138, 182.

3. Ibid., p. 27, referring to his personal knowledge of roads made by landowners in Aberdeenshire within the last fifteen or twenty years. The Librarian of Aberdeen University, and Dr. I. H. Adams of the Scottish Record Office, Edinburgh, have most kindly searched the catalogues of their archives and the index of surveyors at Edinburgh, without discovering any reference to William Greig.

4. Ibid., p. 227.

If this is a correct reading of Greig's experience prior to the Gosford commission it explains the close attention which he paid to roads and communications on the estate, and the remorseless and pointless precision with which he recorded each holding's distance from market in the Tabular Reports;[1] it may also explain the complete absence of interest in the Report in certain matters, principally crops and yields, which an agricultural expert would have considered fundamental to any agricultural enquiry, but which a road man might overlook.

The structure of the *Strictures* shows that Greig had a strong bent for the historical method, and that he was widely read. The book contains a detailed account of the administrative arrangements for the care and upkeep of highways in Britain from the Romans onwards, and an enlarged treatment of the Irish institutions, both central and local, in the last two hundred years. In both sections he displays considerable knowledge of the relevant statutes and reports of parliamentary committees, and in the Irish section he reveals a close acquaintance with the published proceedings and accounts of local authorities, such as Grand Juries and County Assessment Committees, as well as close familiarity with the way in which Grand Juries actually discharged their road responsibilities in such matters as the appointment of overseers and conservators. He also draws on the works of many contemporaries who commented on the condition of roads, their economic importance, and their administration— from Arthur Young to William Jessop, the engineer; and he shows some knowledge of writing dealing with highway engineering and organization in foreign countries.[2] In addition, he had read Adam Smith and quotes from him on several occasions;[3] this was undoubtedly the source of the economics which he applied from time to time in his discourse. His observation that 'as the rent of land is the balance, after all expense of cultivation, including the taxes which are paid by the occupier; any increase of tax, &c. must ultimately be sustained by the proprietor of the land,' is a foretaste of his propensity for economic reasoning which is so fully displayed in the Report.[4]

If Greig had hopes that he himself would obtain secure and

1. The distance from markets of each townland, or group of holdings, was significant economic information; but to record this information for every individual holding was a waste of time.
2. *Strictures*, pp. 69-71, 222-7.
3. Ibid., pp. 64, 228.
4. Ibid., p. 124.

permanent employment as one of the County Engineers whose creation he was advocating, he was out of luck, and not for the last time in his career was sanguine, not to say naive, in his assessment of the readiness of those in authority to respond to his suggestions. It seems possible that his employment on the Irish post-roads under the general direction of the engineer officer Major Alexander Taylor may have come to an end, or at least dwindled away, by late 1816, for in the following months he had the time not only to write his *Striciures*, but also his contributions to the *Irish Farmers' Journal*. It is possibly significant that he apparently never completed this series, and that the final published instalment, at the end of which he promised to provide a continuation, was written on 5 March 1817.[1] This may indicate that his literary output was confined to a brief period in 1816-17 when his professional employment was both at a nadir and at a point of pronounced change of direction, and that he laid writing aside as his Gosford commission picked up to the level of a full-time operation.

Should this have been so, the interruption to his articles came at a fortunate moment for his reputation since the never-completed part of his announced brief was the most specialised and technically demanding section of the whole exercise: the fulfilment of his pledge to provide a blueprint of the means of promoting the further improvement of the agricultural interest of Ireland. His agricultural expertise was thus never put to the test in the *Journal*. It is tempting to think that not merely was it put to the test in the Gosford Report instead, but that it was also to some extent acquired on the job in the course of preparing that Report. For it is possible to see in many of the features of the Report—in its style, its inexhaustible fascination with detail, its didactic quality, and in its omissions—the joyful zest of a person who has thought and read about a subject, revelling in his first chance to apply his ideas in practice. In other respects the *Journal* articles appear as a dress rehearsal for the Report, or the Report appears as a recapitulation and enlargement of themes broached in the *Journal*.

The articles set out to furnish 'a sketch of the progress of domestic improvement, (or in other words) domestic economy in Ireland, with an enquiry into the effects of the late war, and of the present peace,

---

1. *Irish Farmers' Journal*, V, no. XXXI.

on the agricultural interest of that kingdom—and on the means of promoting its further improvement.' The method of doing this was to provide an economic history of Ireland 'from the epoch of the modern prosperity of Ireland—the peace of Aix-la-Chapelle in 1748', based on a fairly close use of the Irish trade statistics, which he handled with some sophistication, pointing out the errors of those who forgot about, or did not even realise, the difference between official and current values.[1] It is plain that he had read some of the works of Arthur Young, Chalmers, Colquhoun and d'Ivernois, as well as Adam Smith, and that he was an effective controversialist who had fully grasped many of the teachings of political economy. Such evidence of intellectual ability might lead one to wonder whether Greig was a university man, but the idiosyncratic spelling, syntax and punctuation of the Report militate against this, though some of these quirks may fairly be laid at the door of Greig's clerk who wrote up the Report. The comparative regularity and acceptability of these matters in his published works are probably to be credited to his publishers' proof readers. His own habit, in the articles, of being unable to resist temptations to slip in the odd few lines 'of the poetic effusions of Pope', and from 'honest Milton' or 'the satiric Swift', indicates the enthusiasm of a largely self-educated man rather than the discipline of a university training.

This enthusiasm led him, in the articles, into a lively discussion of the growing prosperity of Ireland in the later eighteenth century in which he showed his sound economic sense by giving great weight to market factors which increased the demand for Irish produce—or which, in the case of the American War, served to damp down this demand—and which led to a shift in Irish exports from the products of pasturage to those of tillage; and by allowing only a minor (and possibly negative) role to the political 'independence' of 1782 which most Irish writers at this time regarded as the origin of economic advances. This took him on to an examination of the great wartime prosperity of Irish agriculture, particularly after 1806 and particularly in its grain export sector, in which he aired the theme of Irish advantages in the British market while competition from other suppliers was suspended, that he later developed in the Report (*pages* 237-9). He imagined that this temporary Irish monopoly

1. Ibid., no. XXI.

position in the British market was equally advantageous to Irish linen exports: for although he was aware of the steep rise in the price of the raw material, flax, between 1800 and 1810 (repeated in Report, *page* 237), and was aware of the cost-reducing effects of innovations in British industry, particularly in cotton—'for there were many articles of British manufacture which had increased little in price, nay some had even diminished (from the advantages derived from that economy of labour which is produced by the substitution of machinery in place of manual labour, and the strength of animals)'[1]—he did not put these two pieces of information together and reason that because linen and cotton goods were in competition with each other the linen manufacturers were not able to pass on to the consumer all the rise in raw material costs, so that the war was in fact a period of some difficulty for the Irish linen industry. The state of the linen industry was indeed of critical importance on the Gosford estate, as the Report makes clear, and by the time of writing it Greig had formed a much less rosy view of its future and of its competitive position in the market for textiles in general (*pages* 251-2 and Appendix *pages* 298-304).

In the articles, Greig advanced the view that 'proofs of a growing prosperity were to be found . . . among the inhabitants of the most remote recesses of the country' during the thirty or so years before 1815. 'The female inmate of the lowly cabin' he stated, 'who formerly went to market and to mass with a covering of homely household manufacture, at length found herself bedecked in the more gaudy productions of Manchester or Glasgow—the husband, who formerly on holidays, concealed his rags under the flowing robe of his ancestors, was enabled to procure his broadcloth from Leeds or the Liberty, with a beaver hat and boots as necessary accompaniments, and in process of time, spurs and a silver-plated whip were added, to grace the saddle and bridle, which now occupied the places of the primeval suggan and branks. The livestock began less commonly to occupy the same apartment with their owner—cabins more generally received the comfortable and convenient appendage of a chimney, and the luxury of glass windows, and internal furniture of the simplest and rudest construction was changed for articles of more convenient or ornamental structure.'[2] By the time of the Report he seems to have thought

1. Ibid., no. XXII.
2. Ibid., no. XXVIII.

better of this optimistic view, for even in Armagh which was accepted as the most advanced and prosperous of Irish counties, he found that 'among the mere occupying tenants . . . their comforts and opulence have not augmented in any considerable degree; on the contrary it is most certain that in a great proportion of instances they are much lessened, even before the late calamitous events occurred' (*page* 19). Nevertheless the high consumption and increased expectations theory which he espoused in the articles—'that the introduction of new wants and new luxuries would rouse to exertion that part of her population whose previous indolence was connected with her poverty'[1]—was retained in the Report as a favoured device for energising the slothful and sustaining the efforts of those who were trying to increase their productivity and their incomes (*pages* 236, 238).

The Report was to deal acutely with the relationship between price levels and rents, and with the factors which produced sharp changes in price levels between 1800 and 1818, in the course of sustaining one of its central arguments: that rents fixed in relation to wartime prices had become wholly unrealistic and ought to be sharply abated. In the articles, Greig had already looked approvingly at inflationary measures—'whatever evils have resulted, and may yet be dreaded, to result from the excessive issue of paper money, it was owing, probably, to the invigorating effects of augmented circulation, thereby promoted, that our agriculture and manufactures, our commerce and navigation not only flourished, but gradually increased amidst our additional taxes and accumulating debts'.[2] He returned to this theme in the Report—'one of the many remarkable occurrences of modern times is the wonderful operation of a paper currency, which seems to have the all-powerful forces of steam'—and, insofar as re-inflation was a solution for Irish difficulties which he did not dare to advocate openly, he may be considered an Attwood *manqué* (*page* 248). It is not perhaps surprising, in view of what has been conjectured about Greig's career up to this point, that the articles show none of that detailed knowledge of agricultural practices and tenurial arrangements which is exhibited in the Report. It is more striking that they do not reveal any concern at all with the problems of population growth and subdivision of holdings, and the looming nightmare of

1. Ibid., no. XXII.
2. Ibid., no. XXXI.

falling production, profits and rents, which were to form the central pre-occupation of the Report.

These extremely important matters were, for Greig, personal discoveries made as a result of his Gosford experience. They were also discoveries which he could not easily have made simply by more extensive reading of contemporary literature, since it seems that it was only in the post-war period that the opinion began to be at all widely advanced that subdivision had proceeded dangerously far.[1] Quite aside from any question of the novelty of his general technique of inquiry and report, it is the freshness, cogency and pungency of his analysis of the mechanism of population pressure and the ruinous effects of the subdivision which accompanied it, that make the publication of his Report worth while. The main elements of his diagnosis (*pages* 262-9) were not themselves novel, as he acknowledged, for others had already commented on the connection between population growth and subdivision. But if not the first, he was certainly among the earliest of those who warned Irish landlords that the relationship was dangerous and that subdivision was a 'ruinous system' which would lead to untold disasters if not checked. His warnings, if not exactly bald and blunt, on account of his feeling that views especially if unpalatable needed to be well packed in cotton wool before being presented to a person of rank, were still plain and had the great merit of resting on detailed observation and precisely recorded evidence. Herein perhaps lies his essential originality, for empirically-validated theories were worth any number of Malthusian-inspired speculations.

His penchant for the empirical method had already been shown in his published writings, but the scope for its employment in agricultural matters must also have been suggested to Greig by the contemporary vogue for detailed agricultural reports, of which he can scarcely have contrived to remain ignorant even though he nowhere refers to them explicitly. Sir John Sinclair was the father of all these reports, and his existence is acknowledged, as an afterthought, when Greig claimed that after completing his own labours he stumbled upon Sinclair's advocacy of detailed estate reports (*page* 24). It may well have been true that by this date Sinclair was widely regarded as a tiresome nuisance,[2] but even so this recognition of a debt to the man who had largely organised the *First Statistical Account of*

---

1. K. H. Connell, *The Population of Ireland, 1750-1845* (Oxford, 1950), pp. 168-71.
2. Rosalind Mitchison, *Agricultural Sir John* (London, 1962), chap. 18.

Scotland between 1790 and 1797, and who had used the Board of Agriculture—for whose establishment he was chiefly responsible—to collect and publish the series of *County Reports* on the agriculture of the English and Scottish counties, was something short of handsome. The urge to assemble detailed information on population, resources and activities had been transmitted to Ireland, and under the aegis of the Dublin Society a series of *Statistical Surveys*, of several Irish counties, was published in the first few years of the nineteenth century. With a pleasantly Irish touch these *Statistical Surveys* contained practically everything but hard statistics, but they were arranged systematically so that for each county the surveyor set out with a long list of headings on which he was to seek information, headings which provided him with a set of categories for analysing in particular the evidence on agricultural resources, organisation and methods, should he be diligent enough to collect it.

It would have been astonishing if anyone who claimed to be familiar with Ireland and its agriculture, as Greig did, had been unfamiliar with such a prime source for his subject, especially with Sir Charles Coote's *Statistical Survey of the County of Armagh* (Dublin, 1804) which was the most recent and detailed account available of the county in which the Gosford estate lay. To attempt to see any direct influence of Coote on the shape of the Report would be a doubtful business, since although Greig deals with most of the matters listed in Coote's master plan for conducting surveys, he does not take them in the same order, and he very nearly fails to mention crops at all, while Coote had given them a prominent place in his scheme. On the other hand an indirect influence seems exceedingly likely. The county surveys—and the national ones, such as Edward Wakefield's *Account* of 1812—had created an appetite, even if they had not wholly satisfied it, for hard facts and for counting things, and they had done much to establish an expectation that the decisions and policies alike of private individuals and of public authorities should be grounded on observed and recorded evidence. In this respect Greig's micro-study of an estate was in the same category as Wakefield's macro-study of an economy, and it was at this point that the line of inquiries sired by Sinclair coupled with the intellectual equipment and the experience of Greig's earlier career to produce the Gosford Report as its offspring.[1]

---

1.   Besides the accounts mentioned in the text, see also W. Shaw Mason, *A Statistical Account or Parochial Survey of Ireland*, 3 vols (Dublin, 1814-19).

4 THE REPORT

The Report and Survey set out to treat the whole of the Earl of Gosford's property in County Armagh at this time, which, as already stated amounted to some 8,000 acres. Lord Gosford also had another Irish estate, in County Cavan, of perhaps 3,000 acres with a rental of £2,700 and an English estate at Worlingham, Suffolk which he acquired by marrying the heiress of Robert Sparrow, and it was never intended that Greig should deal with these other properties. The County Armagh estate was subsequently considerably expanded, particularly by the purchase of the Graham estate in 1829; by 1873 it extended to over 12,000 acres. Greig in fact never reported on, or rather never valued, the whole of the estate, since he provided no valuations for the two towns which Lord Gosford owned, Markethill and Hamilton's Bawn. It will be seen that the omission makes his valuation rather more than puzzling when read in conjunction with his opinions on rent levels.

The Report consists of an introduction of 25 pages, five pages of discussion in detail of the possible improvement of Markethill which is the central town of the estate, 58 pages of general observations on the estate, and an appendix of some 35 pages dealing with some of the techniques of the linen industry, forestry—which apart from the parkland was not of much importance on the estate—an elaborate receipt for composting bog or peat earth with farmyard manure in order to spin out the supplies of dung, together with instructions for analysing the quality of marls, a scheme of premiums for encouraging improvements by tenants, and plans for improved cabins and farm-houses. This textual matter was based, in large part, on the field work and observations which Greig set out to make holding by holding, and whose results he recorded in nearly 200 pages of 'Tabular Reports' and 'Additional Remarks' on the manors of Baleek and Coolmalish, and the detached townlands of Hamilton's Bawn and Argonell. Only specimen pages of these tables and notes on individual holdings and tenants have been included in the present edition. The nature of the data which he collected is described by Greig in his introduction (*pages* 8-12). The evidence actually recorded has been analysed by David Tierney, in the second part of this Introduction, in order to show the statements and conclusions which can be derived from it about the estate and its inhabitants. The distribution of holdings by size and by value, the extent and timing of sub-division, the provision of farm buildings and the possession of livestock, the occupations and religion of the tenantry, and some key demographic information on size of household and relative ages of husband and wife—all this, as Tierney shows, can be calculated with reasonable precision for the Gosford estate from Greig's data. Where these calculations can be checked against an independent source, such as the 1821 Census, the correspondence is sufficiently close to buttress confidence in the general reliability of Greig's observations, and thus in the types of agricultural and demographic data for which no other contemporary statistical source exists. Students who require more detailed information, on individual tenants or individual holdings, will in any case wish to use the original manuscript and maps (see Foreword).

It is clear from Tierney's discussion that Greig himself did not make sustained or systematic use of his own raw material, and that some of his statements in the main body of the Report would have been modified by close attention to his own figures. It is also clear that Greig never completed the full programme of the statistical part of his enquiry. The occupational information, for example, is much more complete for Baleek than for Coolmalish; while the columns which he designed in his report-sheets for recording the holdings and rents of sub-tenants before his new valuation, in order to estimate the profit-rents of the head-tenants (*page* 9), have in no instance been completed. Similarly the quantity of 'spent bog' for which a column was provided on the printed sheets, was never entered, although there must have been a considerable acreage of it particularly in Coolmalish whose turf supplies were nearly exhausted (*page* 235), and although Greig regarded the possible rehabilitation of these worked-out bogs as a worthwhile source of new agricultural land (*page* 9). The column for entering the area and rental of turf bogs was clearly more appropriate for Baleek, which still had a moderate supply of unexhausted turf, than for Coolmalish, but the absence of entries in the latter manor may indicate some actual failure to record.[1] The provision for recording orchards and forest trees Greig knew in advance to be largely superfluous, because few existed or could be expected to exist under the soil conditions prevalent, but the categories were included because eighteenth-century landlords had tried to promote orchard

---

1. Columns 9 and 10 in the Tabular Reports are transposed in the General Report, which refers to them as Columns 10 and 9.

planting by including covenants in leases; the lack of entries for orchards, therefore, may represent faithful recording (*page* 11). On the other hand the fact that entries for tithe and cess payments were made throughout the sheets for Coolmalish, while these columns have been left blank after the first quarter of Baleek had been covered, indicates that Greig had wearied of his labours.

Fortunately for historians, doubts about the completeness of Greig's recording affect, in the main, areas of little interest, and the obvious omissions do not make the inclusions unusable. The partial nature of the statistical record, however, suggests not merely that Greig lost heart and got tired, but that this entire side of the enquiry was a self-imposed task and not part of the function he was being paid to perform. This suggestion is supported by what can be discovered about the payment to Greig, for even by including all payments made for Greig's assistant, Hill, for the chainmen's wages, and for board and lodging, these do not add up to more than £308; of this, by Greig's own reckoning, scarcely £100 can have been left for his own income after meeting all the expenses of the survey, which was slender reward for three or four years' work.[1] The total cost to the estate, however, for the 8,000 or so acres covered represents a cost of barely 9d. per acre; this would be, at contemporary rates, a normal charge for surveying, mapping and valuation alone, and no ordinary professional surveyor would have dreamt of throwing in as well a written description and analysis, let alone a statistical return, for the same price. It is hardly surprising that in one of his letters to Blacker, Greig protested that 'I have denied myself and family every dispensable necessary to struggle thro this to me ruinous engagement'.[2] It seems, indeed, from the context of these letters that he had been employed to ascertain the contents of the estate and the precise boundaries of the existing holdings, so that Blacker could get on with new leases; and that from the end of 1818 he concentrated on finishing this surveying and valuing task, at times at the expense of completing 'the whole in a manner correspondent with the part already done'.[3]

Alongside the theorising and generalisations of the Report the dominant theme of the Additional Remarks is the practical business of granting new leases at a new valuation. Unfortunately none of the

1. Gosford MS, vouchers 1818-21, D.1606/2/2-5.
2. Ibid., Greig to Blacker, 19 Oct. 1818, D.1606/2/2.
3. Ibid., Greig to Blacker, 19 Oct. 1818, 9 May 1819, D.1606/2/2.

documents make it absolutely clear how many leases, covering what proportion of the estate, were in force at the time of Greig's survey. Since a long lease at a fixed rent determines the distribution of income between landlord and tenant, this is a crucial matter, of central importance in assessing the economic and social effects of a period of rising agricultural prices such as the quarter century before 1815. Greig, indeed, asserted that 'a very considerable portion of the best land on the estate is held under old leases, generally at low rates' (*page* 246). His own detailed evidence, which records only in an incomplete and somewhat haphazard manner cases in which pre-war rent levels and pre-war leases were still in force, did not enable him to back up this assertion with any precision. In fact there was only one townland, out of the total of thirty agricultural townlands on the estate, for which the rental remained constant between 1792 and 1815, and was indeed still unchanged in 1823; this suggests that only one major lease or group of leases did not fall in at some time during the wars. The rental of this townland, Glassdrummond in Coolmalish manor, was 3% of the total estate rental in 1792, but because it stayed still while all around it rents went up it had fallen to 1.8% of the comparable total estate rental in 1815.[1] The gross rent of the estate moved from £3,770 in 1792 to £7,354 in 1815, but the rental of 1815 included several townlands which had not been present in 1792, and which had presumably been acquired in the interval. When these new acquisitions are deducted, the total 1815 rental of those town-lands which were included in the 1792 rental amounted to £6,108, showing a wartime increase of about 60%. This is significantly lower than the average rise in English rents in the same period, and is mainly accounted for by the existence of the very long leases on the Irish estates. The normal duration of a lease for three lives may be taken as about sixty years; a count of twenty-six such leases whose expiry dates are known, comprising all the surviving leases from four townlands on the estate, yields an average duration of sixty-four years.[2] With such a long life, it is clear that many of these leases would not have fallen in at any time during the wars, and that many

---

1. Ibid., estate accounts 1793, 1815, 1818, 1823, D.1606/7A/4, 7, 8, 19, 21, 32.
2. All the surviving leases of the four townlands of Lisdrumchor and Baleek—in Baleek manor—and Bryandrum and Corhamock—in Coolmalish manor—have been analysed by Mr. Crawford to whom I am greatly indebted. There were 96 individual rent-payers in these four town-lands in 1818, and among them 34 leases for three lives are known to have been still in force then.

were still in force at the time of Greig's survey. On the other hand, if all, or the great bulk, of the holdings had been held under such leases at the start of the wars, in 1792, then unless a significant proportion of them had terminated during the wars there would have been no chance of raising the rents in the way in which the rentals indicate they were raised. Indeed if we assume a normal time-distribution of leases in force at the start of any twenty-five year period, then in the course of those twenty-five years something like forty per cent of the leases will expire and provide opportunities for re-letting at enchanced rents. If something like this did occur, then the actual rise in rents between 1792 and 1815 of £2,333 was not spread over the estate at large, but was produced entirely by that fraction of the estate—perhaps two-fifths of it—which alone became subject to re-letting in the period. On those holdings whose rents were altered at all, in other words, the increase may have been of the order of 150%. This at once puts the Irish situation into a more intelligible light. Those Irish tenants who experienced any rent increases, experienced a very sharp rise, much above the English average; but they co-existed with a larger body of Irish tenants who experienced no rent increases at all, and who were therefore able to appropriate to themselves in the shape of increased profits all the benefits of the rise in agricultural prices. A paradoxical situation eminently suited to Ireland, but one obviously fraught with difficulties and dangers as a contrast between the fortunes of different groups of tenants became ever more marked. In particular as the margin grew between fixed rents and the current annual value of the holdings of those in the fortunate group, the temptation to go in for sub-division and sub-letting at full rack rents must have become irresistible.

When leases for three lives did fall in during the wars, it seems that very few were renewed for the same term, even at enhanced rents. Among the leases of the sample four townlands there are only two instances of leases for three lives granted after 1788. Judging from the same sample it seems that of the new or renewed lettings made after 1792, in about two-thirds of the cases the term was for one life or 21 years, and in the remaining one-third no lease was given, implying occupancy either 'at will' or from 'year to year'.[1] Thus in contrast to England, long agricultural leases did not fall entirely out

---

1. Ibid.

of favour during the war period, though the leases which were granted were shorter ones than formerly, presumably because neither land-lords nor tenants were anxious to commit themselves to really long period fixed rents at a time of rapidly altering price levels. When the future course of prices became most erratically unpredictable, after 1815, the annual tenancies seem to have begun to creep in as tenants in Ireland, as in England, declined to accept leases. Certainly Greig noted that tenants in Ireland 'at present' very generally refused to take leases, because the rents were considered too high (*page* 259).

Greig was a persistent advocate of leases as the best means of stimulating improvement by providing security of tenure, and regarded them as particularly necessary in Ireland because the tenant there was expected to provide the buildings and much of the other permanent equipment of the farm, which in England would have been supplied by the landlord (*pages* 256, 260). His entire valuation was based on the assumption that all the holdings would be leased at 'realistic' rents fixed in relation to current and expected prices at a level which, while not exorbitant, was still sufficiently 'smart' to sting the naturally indolent Irish tenants into some sort of exertion (*page* 257). His leasing policy was intended to halt what he regarded as the recent rot, of refusal to take leases, and to stabilise the post-1792 situation of leases for one life or 21 years. It was also intended to stabilise the existing structure of holdings, and halt the process of subdivision. It has already been remarked that he regarded this as the supreme task of Irish landowners and of Irish estate management if disaster and catastrophe were to be avoided. The main remedy which he proposed was first, to recognise the subdivision which had already taken place by granting leases direct to the great majority of the existing occupiers rather than to their head-tenants, and then to enforce clauses prohibiting any further subdivision. Constant pub-licity, by printing this clause on every rent receipt, was expected to do the trick (*pages* 271, 286). His other remedy, to discourage improvi-dent and premature marriages, by education and by providing more schools, would necessarily only take effect slowly (*pages* 272, 286). His faith in the efficacy of leases and the enforcement of their condi-tions was touching, but hardly justified by his own analysis of the force of population pressure and social habits, or his own observation of the extent to which the existing subdivision had occurred under leaseholders (*page* 265), whose leases already contained covenants prohibiting alienation and subletting.

The type of lease which Greig advocated, that for 21 years and one life, was the most usual form of lease in Ireland in the pre-Famine period, but was virtually unknown in Britain, where when farm leases were granted at all they were for definite terms of years.[1] Contemporary Irish writers do not seem to have felt it necessary to comment on this peculiar form of lease, beyond remarking on the political importance of the lifehold element, which was sufficient to give the leaseholder a county vote if his holding had an annual value of forty shillings. Although the electoral motive for granting these leases was undoubtedly strong in many cases, it is unlikely that it was so strong and so prevalent as to account for the widespread presence of this type of lease. Greig's additional explanation, cryptic as it is, is therefore welcome (*page* 260). It seems that 21 years was too short a term to call forth, in Irish conditions, all that was necessary in the way of tenant's outlays on buildings and fences, but that landowners were reluctant to make a definite surrender of control of their property for any longer period. The solution was to introduce the unpredictable element of a life as the final determinant of the lease's duration. The life nominated might well live longer than 21 years from the date of the grant, in which case the tenant reaped his returns on investment over the longer period; but it might die before the 21 years was up, in which event the tenant still enjoyed the minimum term. As a gamble loaded in the tenant's favour the arrangement no doubt had its attractions. But as a device for giving an extra fillip to investment by tenants it must have had an extremely limited effect, since prolongation of occupation at the old rent must have appeared a precarious business in every year after the twenty-first.

In England when leases for lives were granted it was quite common practice by this time for the named lives to be prominent local or national figures, whose deaths could hardly escape notice; members of the royal family were often named, though some lessees clearly doubted their chances of longevity and kept clear of royal dukes. But in Ireland glorious liberty reigned, and from the point of view of estate management this was mere licence, for with each tenant backing his own fancy in picking a 'life' it could become a nightmarish task

---

1. See above, p. 7 n. 2.

distinguishing between 'lives' with similar surnames, chasing after emigrants to procure certificates that they were alive, and proving death in the face of plausibly mendacious tenants.[1] Greig's suggestion that the tenants' choice of lives should be strictly controlled, and that there should be but one life used in all the leases of one townland, was therefore a highly practical recommendation (*page* 260). Equally businesslike was his discussion, at the same point, which weighed the managerial advantages of having a large block of contiguous holdings falling out of lease at the same moment, which furnished an opportunity for re-arranging fields and boundaries, against the disadvantages of providing an invitation to combinations of tenants to resist rent increases.

It is thus a little disappointing that his discussion of tenant right is not more perceptive. It is true that he produces an interesting formula for using the amount paid for tenant right as a gauge of the fairness of rents (*page* 256). But his only other remarks on the matter are not very helpful, since they amount to bewilderment at the Irishness of the whole thing—'a claim of tenant right where no lease exists and where no improvements have been made is unknown in any other country'—and denunciation of the doleful effects of this in diverting tenant capital away from productive uses (*page* 277). This ignores the point that willingness to make such payments presumably arose because in this way the incomer could obtain rights which were valuable to him and not obtainable direct from the owner. These would be either the right to enjoy a holding, for a time at least, at a preferential rent inherited from the seller, below the going rate; or more probably, the chance to have some sort of holding at all, there being no other means of getting one. A market-sensitive rent policy would curb this 'unjustified' tenant right in the first case; in the second case it could be eradicated only if landlords became willing to gratify the whole of the demand for holdings. Though Greig wished for the gradual elimination of 'unjustified' tenant right, he did not specify the means for achieving this. Moreover, although he approved of 'justified' tenant right, as payment for tenant's improvements or for unexpired portions of leases, he did not note that it could act as a direct substitute for long leases, and one which tended to be preferred by tenants at a time when rents were changing rapidly. Further,

---

1. W. A. Maguire, *The Downshire estates in Ireland*, 1801-45 (Oxford, 1972), pp. 133-8. Royal lives were sometimes used in Irish leases after 1750, but only occasionally.

if the estate administration could establish general control over the custom, it could be used to curb subdivision by scrutiny and regulation of all transactions, that is by the prevention of 'free sale' (*pages* 262, 271).[1] Tenant right could thus play a part in fighting for the cause which Greig had most at heart.

Greig held that the fixing of rents at a proper and fair level was next only in importance to arresting, and if possible reversing, the process of subdivision. As a matter of urgency the rent question had priority, for here instant results could be achieved, whereas in all else he looked only for gradual changes. The curious thing is that although he regarded rents as so crucial, he provided so little information on his precise method of fixing them. True, he gave a general account of Irish agricultural history since 1782, as he had done in his earlier works (*pages* 237-40); and to this he now added a description of the seasons since 1815, particularly of the harvest failures of 1816 and 1817 and the bitter distress of the winter of 1817-8, disasters which wiped out the farmers' savings and forced them to sell off a large part of their livestock (*pages* 240-45). This added up to a sufficiently convincing general explanation of the trend of rents during the wars, of the circumstances which by 1818 had made these rents totally out of gear with the post-war price level, and of the reasons for rapidly mounting arrears since 1816. But Greig's argument rested at this level of generality, which was indeed an adequate basis for his repeated insistence that an abatement of rents was the essential first step, without which it was vain to look for any improvement, any reduction of arrears, any access of spirit or skill in farming, any change in methods, any relief from the atmosphere of dejection. The actual size of the abatement which he considered necessary he did not, however, disclose; nor did he reveal except in the most general way the processes by which he arrived at his new valuation. His test of a valuation by the ratio between rent and tenant right payments was one that could only be applied in the future to his own valuation, as transfers of holdings occurred, and could not be used in arriving at that valuation. Later evidence suggests, in any case, that his ideal ratio of two years' purchase for tenant right was never achieved, and that a great deal more than this was customarily paid.[2] Greig points out, what was surely abundantly true, that it was extremely vexing to

1. Ibid., p. 249.
2. Devon Commission, Part I, 1845, XIX, W.52 Q. 73-6.

'fix a fair and equitable rent on lands in this country' (*page* 247),
because so many tenants were only partly dependent on farming, and
partly on domestic industry, and were therefore willing to pay something like an accommodation rent for land, rather than being obliged
to consider fairly closely what they thought its basic farm rental
value might be. Even more tenants, presumably, were so anxious
for land that they would recklessly, if not cheerfully, offer any old
rent for the sake of getting their feet in the door, without ever having
any intention of actually paying it. To valuers accustomed to thinking
that rent had some relation to the productive capacity of the particular
piece of land and the cost of procuring that output, or even some
connection with what a willing tenant would freely offer for a plot,
the situation was understandably confusing and irregular.

All this, however, sheds little light on Greig's own methods of
valuation, and his further remarks that the business of valuation is
'one of the most difficult duties which can engage the attention of a
professional person . . . and also unpleasant' (*page* 255) are no more
enlightening. That he was most meticulous in going round and valuing
field by field, and from this arrived at an average rent per acre for
each farm (*page* 256) we can readily credit. But his conversion of all
his observations on soil type, location, state of drainage and of cultivation, and all the factors which contributed to forming a view of the
fertility of different fields and farms, into a figure of rent per acre,
was something which went on in his head; a process of making a
judgment which all valuers necessarily use, but of whose nature he
left fewer recorded traces than some. In particular it would have
been interesting if he had left some record of the range of yields, of
which crops or animals, which he attributed to different qualities of
land; and if he had noted the prices of the marketable produce used
in translating his view of rent-bearing capacity into money terms.
For he must have made some such calculations in order to produce
a ranking order, in rent terms, of all the farms on the estate. And from
the point of view of the estate the greatest merit of his valuation may
have been simply that it was a comprehensive valuation carried out
for all the farms at a single point in time, so that the relative value of
the farms to each other was rationally determined. Certainly Greig
notices that his valuation produced a re-shuffling of farms in relation
to their rental values (*page* 256), and he rightly felt that this introduction of orderliness was one of the benefits of a professional valuation,

with the fixing of a 'fair' absolute level of rents as the other main advantage.

With his emphasis on the need for immediate rent reductions Greig's cryptic treatment of the recording of the actual current rents of each holding is also curious. What he recorded were the rents 'by former surveys', which meant the rents fixed at the time when the subsisting leases had been first granted. Many of these rents had, therefore, been fixed in the 1780s, and Greig did not trouble to point out that the rents he was proposing were in many cases steep increases over these eighteenth-century levels. Thus his valuation produced a total rental of £8,292 against the actual 1816 rental of £7,676, an increase which he can hardly have expected to have been paid, in view of the rapidly mounting arrears of the previous few years. In his conclusion to the Report, Greig indeed acknowledged that the outlook, by May 1821, had deteriorated a good deal since his valuation was made in 1818, and that its rents could not be paid (*page* 288). The true comparison of existing rents and Greig's valuation is even more startling, since Greig did not make any valuation for the two towns on the estate, Markethill and Hamilton's Bawn, nor for the detached, but agricultural, townland of Argonell. The actual rent of these three in 1815 was £1,426 and in 1818 it was £1,439. The area for which Greig proposed a valuation of £8,292 was, therefore, charged with a rent of £5,811 in 1815 and £5,646 in 1818. These figures can only be reconciled with Greig's persistent talk of rent reductions on the assumption that his valuation was intended to apply to a situation in which all the actual occupiers of holdings had become direct tenants of Lord Gosford paying their rents direct to him, a future state in which head tenants and subletting had been eliminated. In that case it is not merely sad for historians, but a grave weakness in his own argument, that Greig did not collect the information which he at one time intended to collect, on the rents actually being paid by sub-tenants to their immediate superiors, for without this evidence he could not prove that his valuation represented a net reduction of rents paid by occupiers, though a net increase in rents received by Gosford.[1] If we are disposed to credit his assertions that he was indeed recommending reductions, then we can conclude that at the least the profit-rents of head-tenants amounted to the difference

---

1. See p. 22, n.1. At the end of 1828 an abatement of 10 per cent was allowed to all tenants who held at Greig's valuation: Gosford MS, D.1606/11B/9.

between the valuation and the actual rental, some £2,500 a year, or something like half the landlord's rents.

If he was over-optimistic about rents, he came to feel that he had been almost equally so about the prospects of working off existing arrears. These had more than doubled between November 1815 and November 1816, by which time they amounted to £4,454 or over half a year's rent. Greig strongly disapproved of any attempt to get this arrear paid up in cash, on the grounds that this would inevitably divert tenants' resources from current farming operations, and if these were curtailed, further fresh arrears would soon appear. At the same time he argued that to ignore these arrears, even though they were due to abnormal seasons, would look like weakness to the tenants and would undermine all habits of punctuality in rent payments, which were a necessary spur to industry. He therefore proposed that the arrears should be worked off in labour, on which a value would be set, either in making approved permanent improvements on their own farms, or in work and cartage for building the new castle (*pages* 257-8). This proposal, however, ignored the fact that such labour services would also tend to be at the expense of current farming operations, and by the time he composed his conclusion in 1821 Greig had come round to the view, expressed with much circumlocution and obfuscation, that past arrears ought to be wiped clean off the slate (*page* 289).

If his financial recommendations were not entirely practical, Greig more than made up for this by the extreme sobriety and caution of the rest of his observations. Unlike some pedlars of nostrums for Irish troubles who imagined that a few bold managerial decisions plus a dose of landlords' capital could transform Irish peasant farming into English-style agriculture, Greig always had in the forefront of his mind a vivid picture of the constraints which available resources, particularly human resources, placed on all schemes for promoting agrarian change. Thus, although he held that most of the holdings on the estate were already too small to be economically viable, and although he discussed the desirable size of farms—in terms of capacity to furnish adequate supplies of animal manure for crops, especially potatoes, which implied holdings of one-cow or two-cow standard; and in terms of ability to afford constant profitable work for a horse or a pair of horses, which implied a 30 or 50 acre minimum (*pages* 274-5)—he held out no hope that the existing size pattern could be altered at all speedily. This was partly on humanitarian and political grounds, because dispossession of small tenants would cause inconceivable 'heartbreakings and calamities', and because with 'so many helpless wretches without house, without food, and deprived of all prospect of obtaining them any more, . . . a rebellion would be unavoidable of a new description'. But it was also partly on the more strictly economic ground that even if the lands could be thrown together to form larger farms, there existed no supply of substantial tenants capable of occupying them to advantage (*pages* 270-1).

The same awareness that, because of her previous agricultural history, Ireland simply did not possess any considerable body of men with the skill and capital necessary to make enterprising English-type tenants, led to well-grounded scepticism on the prospects of breaking the grip of backward and slovenly farming practices. It was for this reason that Greig argued that it was pointless to prescribe any particular course of husbandry in the covenants of leases, the tenants having neither the wit nor the means to follow any regular course (*page* 261). He was thinking perhaps of the Holkham model of the use of leases to promote new crop rotations, though his acquaintance with what he referred to as 'Mr. Coke of Holkburn in the County of Suffolk' was plainly limited (*page* 18). The common form of tillage farming, he noted, was one of bleeding the land to death by taking successive grain crops, with no manuring, until the land was exhausted, whereupon it was allowed to recuperate for some years by being thrown down to pasture, the cycle then being repeated. The 'improved' form of farming on the estate appears to have consisted of the same process, plus some manuring of the first grain crop in the series.[1] Greig did not suppose that it was possible to eradicate this vicious system all at once. His highly ingenious remedy was to propagate the doctrine that larger crops of potatoes could be procured by heavier manuring, tenants being sure to heed advice and encouragement which resulted in more potatoes; the larger supplies of manure would, however, need to come from better feeding of the livestock, and this better feeding would have to come from the introduction of artificial grasses or green crops. In this devious way a direct appeal to the bellies of the tenants could lead to the end of continuous cropping and the introduction of some element of rotation (*page* 278).

---

1. Coote, *A Statistical Survey of the County of Armagh* (Dublin, 1804), pp. 172-3 had noted this system of excessive cropping, without considering that it merited any severe strictures.

A small and gradual improvement in the standard of farming, a halt to the process of further subdivision, and perhaps a slow and piecemeal enlargement of farms as here and there an opportunity for consolidation might offer itself as a more opulent tenant could be encouraged to take over a holding vacated by an indigent tenant (*pages* 272, 275), these were the modest expectations which at the end of the day Greig held out to Lord Gosford. If these things could be achieved, and if Lord Gosford could succeed in entering into direct tenurial relations with the existing sub-tenants, either by granting them leases or by making tenancy agreements directly with them, then some increase in the gross rental of the estate could be looked for. Otherwise Gosford would be fortunate if he could hold his gross rental at something near its 1818 level, and would certainly have to accept a lower net income after meeting some new expenses in aiding the tenants in liming, draining, providing some building materials, and financing prizes for good farming (*pages* 280-5, 316-20). But if they were not realised, he could expect before very long a crisis of subsistence, which would wipe out his tenants in agonies of misery, but which would also wipe out his rents (*page* 268).

5 THE CONSEQUENCES OF THE REPORT

Even these modest expectations do not seem to have been modest enough, judging by the history of the estate between Greig and the Famine. The main purpose of the Report, the new valuation, does indeed appear to have been partially fulfilled, and in accordance with Greig's 1821 recommendation, for those tenants who were paying on his valuation in 1823 were allowed a ten per cent abatement.[1] But although his valuation was thus put into effect it was certainly not fully applied, since throughout the remainder of the decade the nominal rental of the estate stayed well below the full Greig level, at first tending to fall year by year, and being stabilised by 1825 at around £7,000, nineteen per cent under Greig's par.[2] After 1830 further comparisons become difficult, since the Gosford estate was then rapidly enlarged by extensive purchases, from the 8,000 acres of Greig's day to the 20,000 acres which Binns reported at his 1836

---

1. Gosford MS, estate account for 1823, D.1606/11B/3.
2. Ibid., estate accounts 1821-9, D.1606/7A/28-38.

visit, or the more reliable 16,000 acres which Blacker recorded in 1845.[1] If he had been misleading about rents, Greig apparently erred the other way over arrears, becoming prematurely despondent. The 1816 figure of £4,454 turned out, in the event, to be the peak in outstanding arrears, and the amount gradually declined to some £2,725 by 1827, and then—with the accounts of the critical intervening year unfortunately missing—had virtually been wiped off by 1829, when only £370 of arrears were left.[2] It is clear that some portion of the arrears built up in the disastrous years had been written off as bad debts, the debtors presumably having left the estate; but in view of Blacker's generally stern line on the collection of arrears—'I never excuse arrears, but by an annual deduction'[3]—it seems unlikely that any part were deliberately forgiven as an act of policy, so that something like £3,500 was probably either paid off in cash or worked off in labour in the course of ten years, without producing the damaging effects on farming which Greig had feared.

There is conceivably some trace of Greig's influence behind the appearance for the first time, in the estate accounts for 1820, of a small expenditure on 'lime bounties' which was an allowance to tenants of half the cost of carting lime to their farms, and of an equally small disbursement for providing slates for farm buildings.[4] But apart from these straws there is no indication that the Report had any other impact on the management of the estate. It is of course possible that the agent, William Blacker, was influenced by some of Greig's arguments and recommendations; but on the whole the Blacker of the *Prize Essay* and the evidence to the Devon Commission emerges as an independent and forceful man who at any rate gave the impression that his views and policies derived only from his own experience. Blacker became famous for the system of management which he introduced on to the Gosford estate, and on to other estates of which he became agent, notably that of Colonel Close of Drumbanagher, and the Dungannon School Lands estate in County Tyrone, a system which was quite widely copied throughout Armagh.[5] The system

---

1. Binns, *Miseries and Beauties*, I, 153; Devon Commission, Part I, 1845, XIX, W. 52 (Blacker) Q. 7.
2. Gosford MS, estate accounts 1821-9.
3. Devon Commission, Part I, 1845, XIX, W. 52 Q. 14.
4. Gosford MS, estate account 1820, D.1606/11B/2.
5. *Third Report of the Commissioners appointed to inquire into the condition of the Poorer Classes . . . in Ireland* (hereafter cited as Poor Inquiry, Ireland), Appendix F, pp. 417-8, H.C. 1836, XXXIII, 419-20, which gives a good, concise, description of the system.

involved the encouragement of green crop farming—mainly of clover, tares, and rape; turnips seemed to be beyond the capacity of the tenants—and stall-feeding of the cattle. By this method one acre was said to be able to support as many cows as three had done formerly, and since no stock was any longer depastured many hedges and fences were removed, leading to further economies in land. 'The country,' it was said, 'when seen from any elevation, is one continuous patchwork of grain and potatoes, densely crowded with habitations. This has a more striking appearance to an Englishman, as there are no hedgerow trees to intercept the profuse exhibition of fields of grain now ripe for harvest.'[1] The introduction of these new methods was encouraged by supplying the farmers with lime and seeds on interest-free loans, by providing the services of an estate bull at nominal charges—this Greig had specifically recommended (*page* 285)—and above all by the educative and supervisory work of expert bailiffs, termed 'agriculturalists', whom Blacker imported from Scotland and put in charge of sub-districts of the estate. By 1836 he had apparently procured some sixty of these Scottish trouble-shooters or peasant-chasers, but they had been scattered over Ireland to many landowners who had asked Blacker to find them one, and were not all employed on the Gosford estate.[2]

There is nothing in Greig's Report which foreshadows this scheme, unless it be his very general advocacy of the introduction of artificial grasses; but this was such an obvious point to anyone who was interested in farming at this time, that one can hardly suppose that Blacker was in need of any prompting from Greig before the thought of clover occurred to him. Moreover the emphasis of Blacker's system on more intensive cultivation, and on making the small holding of three to ten acres into a viable farm, indicates that he disagreed with Greig on the desirable size of farms, or at least disagreed on the practical possibility of ever achieving such a size in Irish demographic circumstances. Though Blacker no doubt disapproved of further subdivision as much as Greig did, it seems that he recognised that he was not in fact able to prevent it.[3] By how much subdivision had progressed on the Gosford estate between 1818 and 1830 it is not at present possible to say, although further research

1. Ibid.
2. Binns, *Miseries and Beauties*, I, 153-4.
3. Devon Commission, Part I, 1845, XIX, Witness 52 Q. 15.

might produce an answer; but at least it seems most unlikely that the gradual consolidation, which Greig looked for, had made any headway at all.[1] In effect it looks as though Blacker evolved his system because he recognised that increasing subdivision and ever smaller holdings were there to stay, and that it was necessary to make the best of a bad job. If so, the central core of Greig's recommendations had no practical effect on the estate at all. His maps and valuation were of real service in the estate office; but the Report as such was less a working estate document than an ornamental set-piece to be consigned to the estate archives which Greig desired to see established, until it should one day be discovered by the historians.

---

1. The figures in the estate accounts of the number of individuals who paid rent, which show a fairly steady increase, are not a sure guide to the process of subdivision since the number of actual occupiers who did not pay rent direct to the estate may have varied considerably over time.

The Tabular Reports

by D. Tierney

Greig collected a mass of information, holding by holding, for the manors of Baleek and Coolmalish and the detached townland of Ardgonell: there are no entries under the other detached townland of Hamilton's Bawn (see map on page iv). It was based in large part on his own field work and personal observation. He entered this information on specially printed forms which he called Tabular Reports, and accompanied the numerical data with observations recorded on separate sheets of Additional Remarks, the two together occupying nearly two hundred large folio pages. Sample pages of the manuscript are illustrated at the back of this volume. In the following subsections an attempt has been made to summarise, analyse and interpret the chief features of this body of information.

1 POPULATION

In his Tabular Report Greig provides information on:
a. the number of people living on the estate (analysed in Table 1);
b. the ages of the holders of land and their spouses (analysed in Tables 2 and 3);
c. the number of children in each family resident on the estate (analysed in Table 4), and divided into male and female (analysed in Table 1);
d. the number of male and female servants (analysed in Table 1); and
e. the number of cottiers (analysed in Table 1).

4

Table 1

Population

	Adults		Children		Servants		Cottiers	Total Pop.
	M	F	M	F	M	F		
BALEEK MANOR								
Upper Baleek	21	21	31	30	1	1	—	105
Lower Baleek Village	7	6	12	13	—	—	—	38
Lower Baleek	16	16	36	38	2	3	2	113
Upper Corromannon	18	22	38	42	—	—	—	120
Mid Corromannon	12	12	27	23	—	—	—	74
Lower Corromannon	20	22	37	31	2	5	1	118
Carrickollogly	22	23	32	48	3	1	—	129
Carrickananey	10	11	30	19	—	—	—	70
Upper Cregans	16	16	39	32	5	4	3	115
Lower Cregans	19	16	29	25	1	1	—	91
Upper Crunaght	5	3	12	2	2	1	1	26
Lower Crunaght	5	5	13	11	1	4	—	39
Upper Drumhoney	8	8	10	24	—	—	—	50
Lower Drumhoney	12	13	21	27	1	1	—	75
Drumnahuncheon	12	11	22	24	2	2	—	73
Drumgean	6	9	20	17	1	2	—	55
Dirlet	15	10	15	22	7	5	5	79
Greyhilla	17	14	28	23	3	1	—	86
Upper Lisdrumchor	27	27	58	48	7	7	4	178
Lower Lisdrumchor	6	6	7	5	2	2	—	28
Lurgiross	17	19	36	32	1	3	—	108
Total of Baleek Manor	291	290	553	536	41	43	16	1,770
COOLMALISH MANOR								
Lisnegat	17	17	41	34	1	1	—	111
Upper Brackley	14	16	22	43	—	—	—	95
Lower Brackley	15	16	26	32	—	—	—	89
Upper Glassdrummond	13	11	22	30	1	1	—	78
Lower Glassdrummond	7	3	1	2	4	3	1	21
Sebochan	9	8	12	20	—	—	2	51
Carricklane	16	16	22	24	2	2	3	85
Cordrumond	8	5	13	20	1	1	—	48
Ballindaragh	25	27	47	32	1	1	2	135
Corhamock	21	21	36	45	1	1	—	125
Dennismullen	9	11	27	29	—	—	—	76
Ednekennedy	7	8	23	11	—	—	—	49
Drumlack	7	7	16	11	—	—	—	41
Cobragh	1	2	5	4	—	—	—	12
Ballyanny	10	9	25	25	1	1	—	71
Bryandrum	9	9	20	14	4	4	2	62
Total of Coolmalish Manor	188	186	358	376	16	15	10	1,149
Argonnell	15	15	28	28	3	1	—	90
ESTATE TOTAL	494	491	939	940	60	59	26	3,009

Note: Of the total number of holders whose marital status is known (554): 30 (5.4%) are unmarried (one of them female), 59 (10.7%) are widows and 34 (6.1%) are widowers.

TABLE 2

Ages of Holders of Land and their Spouses

	MALES												FEMALES											
	under 21	21-25	26-30	31-35	36-40	41-45	46-50	51-55	56-60	61-65	66-70	over 70	under 21	21-25	26-30	31-35	36-40	41-45	46-50	51-55	56-60	61-65	66-70	over 70
BALEEK MANOR																								
Upper Baleek	1	2	4	5	3	0	2	0	1	1	0	0	0	2	7	2	1	2	3	1	1	1	1	0
Lower Baleek	0	0	4	2	3	4	5	1	2	1	0	1	0	1	7	1	5	3	7	0	1	0	1	0
Upper Corromannon	1	0	5	5	5	0	3	2	1	0	0	0	0	5	6	1	5	3	0	0	3	0	0	0
Middle Corromannon	0	1	2	3	1	2	1	1	0	0	0	1	1	5	3	3	4	0	2	0	0	0	0	0
Lower Corromannon	0	2	2	1	2	2	3	2	2	0	0	3	3	1	1	0	5	2	2	3	1	3	0	0
Carrickollogly	0	2	2	4	6	6	2	0	1	2	0	0	0	6	7	3	3	1	3	1	0	1	0	0
Carrickananey	1	3	0	1	1	1	0	0	0	0	0	0	1	2	2	2	1	0	1	0	1	0	0	0
Upper Cregans	0	0	1	2	1	0	4	1	3	0	0	0	1	0	1	2	2	3	2	1	2	1	0	0
Lower Cregans	0	1	3	4	5	0	2	2	1	1	0	2	2	2	2	2	3	1	1	0	1	1	0	0
Upper Crunaght	0	0	0	0	0	2	0	0	0	0	0	3	1	0	5	5	0	0	0	0	0	1	0	0
Lower Crunaght	0	0	0	0	0	1	2	1	1	1	0	0	0	0	0	0	1	0	0	1	0	0	0	0
Upper Drumhoney	0	0	1	1	2	4	0	0	0	0	0	0	0	0	0	2	2	2	2	0	2	0	0	0
Lower Drumhoney	0	0	2	3	3	4	3	0	1	0	0	0	0	0	3	5	2	1	0	2	2	0	0	0
Drummahuncheon]	0	0	1	2	2	0	1	0	0	1	0	0	0	0	3	3	2	0	2	2	1	0	0	0
Drumgean	0	0	0	1	1	2	0	1	0	0	0	0	0	0	0	0	0	2	0	1	0	0	0	0
Dirlet	0	2	1	2	4	1	2	0	0	0	0	1	1	2	1	1	4	1	1	0	0	1	1	1
Greyhilla	0	3	3	0	5	0	4	4	0	0	1	1	0	0	0	6	1	1	0	0	1	0	0	0
Upper Lisdrumchor	0	1	1	0	0	4	5	1	2	1	2	0	0	1	2	3	3	4	3	1	3	0	0	0
Lower Lisdrumchor	0	0	0	0	2	0	0	2	0	2	1	0	0	0	1	1	4	1	0	1	3	0	0	0
Lurgiross	0	0	1	2	2	3	3	1	1	0	2	1	1	1	0	1	1	1	1	2	4	1	0	1
Total of Baleek Manor	3	12	35	34	55	34	43	20	19	9	17	10	8	15	49	30	64	22	29	16	27	6	10	2
Percentage of total	1.0	47 16.2		89 30.6		77 26.5		39 13.4		26 8.9		10 3.4	2.9	64 23.0		94 33.8		51 18.3		43 15.5		16 5.8		2 0.7

TABLE 2—(contd.)

Ages of Holders of Land and their Spouses

	MALES												FEMALES											
	under 21	21-25	26-30	31-35	36-40	41-45	46-50	51-55	56-60	61-65	66-70	over 70	under 21	21-25	26-30	31-35	36-40	41-45	46-50	51-55	56-60	61-65	66-70	over 70
COOLMALISH MANOR																								
Lisnegat	0	0	1	0	2	2	2	2	5	1	1	1	1	0	3	0	0	1	6	4	1	1	0	0
Upper Brackley	0	0	1	3	1	2	3	0	3	0	1	0	0	2	1	1	5	2	2	1	0	0	1	1
Lower Brackley	0	1	2	3	1	1	3	0	3	1	1	0	1	1	4	2	1	2	1	1	3	1	0	0
Upper Glassdrummond	0	0	2	0	0	1	3	3	1	0	3	0	0	0	0	1	0	1	4	1	0	1	0	0
Lower Glassdrummond	0	0	0	1	0	1	1	1	0	0	1	0	0	0	3	0	2	2	0	1	0	0	0	0
Sebochan	0	0	3	1	2	0	1	0	1	0	1	1	0	2	0	0	1	1	0	1	0	0	0	0
Carricklane	0	0	1	3	0	3	1	3	1	2	0	0	0	3	5	0	3	0	2	1	0	0	0	1
Cordrumond	0	1	0	1	0	4	0	1	1	0	0	0	0	2	0	1	0	4	2	2	0	1	0	0
Ballindaragh	0	0	3	0	4	2	2	1	2	2	4	4	0	0	3	3	2	3	2	0	6	0	3	3
Corhamock	0	4	3	2	2	2	2	2	2	0	1	1	0	3	3	3	5	1	1	1	0	1	0	1
Dennismullen	0	0	0	0	1	3	0	1	1	0	0	0	0	1	1	0	3	3	3	1	0	0	0	0
Ednekennedy	0	0	1	1	0	0	0	2	2	2	0	1	0	0	0	1	0	1	3	0	2	1	0	0
Drumlack	0	0	0	1	0	1	2	0	0	0	0	0	0	0	0	1	1	2	1	1	1	0	0	0
Cabragh	0	0	0	0	0	2	0	2	0	0	1	0	0	0	0	0	0	0	0	0	1	0	0	0
Bryandrum	0	1	2	2	0	0	1	1	0	1	0	2	0	2	2	2	0	1	1	1	1	0	0	1
Total of Coolmalish Manor	0	6	18	18	17	18	27	18	23	8	13	10	2	13	29	13	25	18	28	14	15	7	4	7
Percentage of total	0	24	24	35	35	45	45	41	41	21	21	10	2	42	42	38	38	46	46	29	29	11	11	7
	0	13.6	13.6	19.9	19.9	25.6	25.6	23.3	23.3	11.9	11.9	5.7	1.1	24.0	24.0	21.7	21.7	26.3	26.3	16.6	16.6	6.3	6.3	4.0
Argonnell	2	0	5	2	0	1	3	0	1	0	0	1	0	2	5	1	0	3	1	0	3	0	0	0
ESTATE TOTAL	5	76	76	126	126	126	126	81	81	47	47	21	10	113	113	133	133	101	101	75	75	27	27	9
Percentage of total	1.0	15.8	15.8	26.1	26.1	26.1	26.1	16.8	16.8	9.8	9.8	4.4	2.1	24.2	24.2	28.4	28.4	21.6	21.6	16.0	16.0	5.8	5.8	1.9

TABLE 3

Age gap between husbands and wives

Wife older than Husband:	Number in each group	
15—11 yrs.	1	0.3%
10— 6 ,,	9	2.6%
5— 1 ,,	18	5.2%
Same Age	24	6.9%
Husband older than Wife:		
1— 5 yrs.	174	50.0%
6—10 ,,	77	22.1%
11—15 ,,	33	9.5%
16—20 ,,	8	2.3%
21 and over	4	1.1%
	348	100.0%

Note: Greig did not provide the information for every household.

TABLE 4

Number of children per family

	0	1	2	3	4	5	6	7	8	9	10	11	Total no. of families
BALEEK MANOR													
Upper Baleek	4	5	4	0	2	2	0	2	2	0	0	0	21
Lower Baleek Village	0	1	1	0	0	0	1	0	2	0	0	0	5
Lower Baleek	1	1	4	0	2	2	2	0	2	1	1	0	16
Upper Corromannon	1	2	3	4	3	2	4	1	1	0	0	0	21
Mid Corromannon	0	1	2	4	0	2	2	0	1	0	0	0	12
Lower Corromannon	2	2	2	5	2	2	1	1	1	0	0	0	18
Carrickollogly	4	0	3	4	6	3	1	2	0	0	0	0	23
Carrickananey	0	1	2	2	1	1	0	1	0	0	0	0	8
Upper Cregans	0	2	1	2	1	1	2	3	1	0	0	1	14
Lower Cregans	3	3	1	1	6	1	0	1	0	0	1	0	17
Upper Crunaght	0	1	1	0	1	0	0	1	0	0	0	0	4
Lower Crunaght	1	0	0	0	1	0	1	1	1	0	0	0	5
Upper Drumhoney	0	0	0	1	0	1	2	1	1	0	0	0	6
Lower Drumhoney	0	2	3	1	1	2	2	1	0	0	0	0	12
Drumnahuncheon	0	2	4	3	0	1	2	0	1	0	0	0	13
Drumgean	0	0	1	2	2	1	0	0	2	0	0	0	8
Dirlet	2	1	2	1	0	3	0	1	1	0	0	0	11
Greyhilla	1	2	2	4	1	4	1	1	0	0	0	0	16
Upper Lisdrumchor	0	2	4	3	4	2	4	0	2	1	1	0	23
Lower Lisdrumchor	3	1	0	0	0	1	0	1	0	0	0	0	6
Lurgiross	1	3	5	2	3	1	1	0	1	2	0	0	19
Baleek: total number of families	23	32	45	39	36	32	26	18	19	4	3	1	278
Baleek: total number of children	0	32	90	117	144	160	156	126	152	36	30	11	1,054
Percentage of families in each category	8.3	11.5	16.2	14.0	13.0	11.5	9.4	6.5	6.8	1.4	1.1	0.3	

TABLE 4—(*contd.*)

COOLMALISH MANOR

Lisnegat	1	1	0	3	3	2	3	2	1	0	0	0	16
Upper Brackley	0	1	2	0	4	4	4	0	0	0	0	0	15
Lower Brackley	0	3	2	4	1	2	0	1	1	0	0	1	15
Upper Glassdrummond	2	0	2	1	2	2	2	1	0	1	0	0	13
Lower Glassdrummond	1	1	1	1	1	1	1	0	1	0	0	0	8
Sebochan	2	1	0	1	0	0	0	0	0	0	0	0	4
Carricklane	1	4	6	3	1	2	0	1	0	0	0	0	18
Cordrumond	0	0	1	1	1	1	2	1	0	0	0	0	7
Ballindaragh	5	4	3	4	7	4	0	0	0	1	0	0	28
Corhamock	3	3	4	2	2	3	3	1	0	1	0	0	22
Dennismullen	0	2	0	1	2	1	4	2	0	0	0	0	12
Ednekennedy	0	1	0	1	3	2	0	1	0	0	0	0	8
Drumlack	1	0	1	1	2	1	0	0	0	1	0	0	7
Cabragh	0	0	1	0	0	0	0	1	0	0	0	0	2
Ballyanny	0	0	0	2	2	3	1	0	1	0	1	0	10
Bryandrum	2	0	2	2	1	0	1	2	0	0	0	0	10
Coolmalish: total number of families	18	21	25	27	32	28	21	13	4	4	1	1	195
Coolmalish: total number of children	0	21	50	81	128	140	126	91	32	36	10	11	726
Percentage of families in each category	9.2	10.8	12.8	13.8	16.4	14.3	10.8	6.7	2.1	2.1	0.5	0.5	
Both manors: total number of families	41	53	70	66	68	60	47	31	23	8	4	2	473
total number of children	0	53	140	198	272	300	282	217	184	72	40	22	1,780
Percentage of families in each category	8.7	11.2	14.8	13.9	14.4	12.7	9.9	6.6	4.9	1.7	0.8	0.4	

Note: Because Greig did not always provide information about the family as a unit, 43 of the 1,823 children on these two manors have not been included in this analysis.

The table can refer only to children living on the estate: it is not possible to determine whether children were born to these marriages.

2 OCCUPATIONS

Greig's enumeration of occupations is much more complete for Baleek manor than for Coolmalish manor. Not only are the occupational details missing for some tenants in the latter manor, but he made no attempt to list the trades of children resident on the farms. In Baleek, however, the occupations both of holders and their children are reasonably complete, only the townlands of Drumgean and Lower Lisdrumchor being at all seriously defective.

TABLE 5

Occupations of holders of land and male children

	Holders of land	*Male children* (Manor of Baleek only)*
Weaver	288	138
Mason	7	0
Tailor	6	2
Carpenter	5	0
Wheelwright	3	0
Flax Dresser	3	1
Brogue Maker	2	1
Millwright	2	0
Reedmaker	2	0
Miller	2	0
Constable	2	0
'Armagh Staff'	2	0
Blacksmith	2	3
Flax Drier	1	0
Coppersmith	1	0
Cooper	1	1
Surveyor	1	0
Grocer	1	0
Linen Buyer	1	0
Linen Merchant	1	0
Innkeeper	1	0
Parish Priest	1	0
Hatter	1	0
Cotton Spinner	0	7†
	336	153

* Children's occupations are noted for Baleek manor only.
   The total number of male children in Baleek was 553.

† The child cotton spinners worked on William Atkinson's cotton manufactory at Glenanne. Although Greig does not include details of girls' occupations it is likely from his remark on page 299 of the report that many of them were also employed as cotton spinners there.

The analysis of holders' occupations is given in Table 5. Linen-weavers account for 85.7% of the occupations listed, whilst if the

flax dressers, reedmakers, flax drier, linen buyer and linen merchant
are included, 88.1% of the occupations relate to the linen trade.[1]
Although weavers form such a large majority of those giving an
alternative occupation, they comprise a much smaller proportion of
the total number of land-holders on the whole estate: 45.2%. Due to
the omissions in Coolmalish, it is probably more realistic to take the
percentage figure for Baleek: 48.6%. Even if all other occupations
are taken into account, this still leaves nearly half the tenants without
an alternative occupation to farming. In 1804 Sir Charles Coote had
written: '[In County Armagh] agriculture is but a secondary motive;
it is merely pursued as a means of supply of provisions, rather than
of trade from which any profit may be gained'[2] but in the fourteen
years which followed, changes in demand and supply had undermined
the importance of the domestic linen industry. It might be expected
that, in cases where the father was wholly engaged in farming, the
children's occupations would provide an alternative source of income.
This, however, was not the case. In almost every instance where
children had a trade it was that of the father—and in Baleek manor[3]
there are only five instances of children described as weavers whilst
the fathers had no occupation.[4] The other 133 were themselves the
children of weavers.

The number of looms is obviously relevant to the ability of weavers
to carry on their trade. From Greig's enumeration it is not possible
to calculate the number owned, as opposed to hired, on the estate.
He seems to have included in his reckoning all the looms that he
found in the cottages. There were 337 occupied looms on the estate,
195 in Baleek and 142 in Coolmalish with the higher valued townlands

---

1. All the weavers appear to be linen weavers: only in the case of a couple of children is cotton
    weaving engaged in.
2. Coote, *County Armagh*, p. 3. See also Conrad Gill, *The Rise of the Irish Linen Industry* (Oxford,
    1925), p. 41. By 1818 Gill's comment is a more accurate description of the Gosford estate
    weavers: 'The craftsman was primarily a farmer or farm-labourer and manufacture was a
    bijwerk . . .' The full extent of the changed importance of the domestic linen industry, already
    obvious when Greig was reporting in 1818, may be seen from the later comment of the
    Assistant Poor Law Commissioners on the barony of Lower Fews (containing the Gosford
    estate): 'Among the small farmers of this district there does not appear to be the least idea of
    bringing up any of their sons to any other mode of life than agriculture; for, though some are
    taught weaving, yet that trade is never looked on as an exclusive mode of support. The weaver
    is also a farmer, and still retains the same anxiety for a small portion of land.' (Poor Inquiry,
    Ireland, Appendix F, footnote on p. 72, H.C. 1836, XXXIII, 74).
3. Children's trades were not entered in the Tabular Report for Coolmalish.
4. This close association of the child's trade with that of the father can also be seen in some of
    the other occupations; two of the tailors have children working at the trade, whilst the two
    blacksmiths (brothers) have three of their sons with them. Two masons, two tailors, a brogue-
    maker, a millwright, and a hatter give weaving as the only trade of one or more of their
    children.

TABLE 6

Linenweavers and looms

TOWNLAND	WEAVERS		LOOMS	
	Landholders	Children	Occupied	Unoccupied
BALEEK MANOR				
Upper Baleek	11	6	8	0
Lower Baleek Village	2	0	2	0
Lower Baleek	7	4	7	0
Upper Corromannon	8	8	14	0
Middle Corromannon	1	4	4	0
Lower Corromannon	13	18	25	0
Carrickollogly	10	8	12	0
Carrickananey	4	7	5	0
Upper Cregans	9	11	11	2
Lower Cregans	13	8	11	2
Upper Crunaght	4	6	5	0
Lower Crunaght	2	3	2	0
Upper Drumhoney	4	2	5	0
Lower Drumhoney	7	10	12	0
Drumnahuncheon	12	6	12	0
Drumgean	10	0	10	0
Dirlet	2	2	3	0
Greyhilla	12	8	10	1
Upper Lisdrumchor	25	15	20	3
Lower Lisdrumchor	5	3	5	0
Lurgiross	12	9	12	2
Total on Baleek manor	173	138	195	10
COOLMALISH MANOR				
Lisnegat	17	—	14	3
Upper Brackley	6	—	4	5
Lower Brackley	11	—	17	2
Upper Glassdrummond	4	—	11	1
Lower Glassdrummond	7	—	9	1
Sebochan	2	—	6	0
Carricklane	3	—	6	1
Cordrumond	7	—	3	2
Ballindaragh	12	—	15	4
Corhamock	15	—	15	4
Dennismullen	5	—	12	1
Ednekennedy	3	—	4	4
Drumlack	0	—	0	0
Cabragh	0	—	0	0
Ballyanny	4	—	5	0
Bryandrum	7	—	9	0
Total on Coolmalish manor	103	a	130	28
Argonnell	12	a	12	1
ESTATE TOTAL	288	a	337	39

a Greig did not enter children's occupations for Coolmalish manor or Argonnell townland.

having slightly more in relation to their population than the poorer (see Table 8). Eighty-five tenants had two looms, three had three, and one tenant had four.[1]

Multiple ownership of looms is no necessary indication of industry. William Rolston (*pages* 39, 93), a tailor holding fourteen and a half acres who had three looms with three sons weaving, is described as 'most industrious': Widow Hall (*pages* 45, 96) had nine acres, three looms, four adult sons and one adult daughter, but only one of the sons described himself as a weaver and Greig characterised them as 'not industrious', adding that they had recently been ejected though put into possession again. The solitary case of the four-loom tenant is a little puzzling (*page* 152). Besides the problem of finding space in his cottage for four looms plus eight persons (he has no workshop), no clue is given by Greig as to why he alone should possess so many.

The difference in the number of unoccupied looms as between Baleek and Coolmalish is striking. Only 5% of Baleek's looms are so described, as against 17% in Coolmalish. Although the difference in general levels of prosperity is presumably a partial explanation of this, nevertheless the only townland in Coolmalish with an average rent of under £1 per acre (Upper Brackley) has proportionately the highest number of looms unoccupied.[2]

There were a few cotton weavers on the estate employed by William Atkinson who had established an extensive cotton spinning works at Glenanne in Lisdrumchor to supply his weavers in the Portadown area.[3] Greig believed 'that considerable advantage would accrue from a more intensive introduction of cotton weaving among the tenantry' (*page* 299) because it would provide employment for the rapidly increasing population, particularly since the linen trade appeared to be in decline. He urged that 'some cotton looms might be procured and given out . . . . and every inducement held out to

1. Coote was not accurate as regards the Gosford estate when he wrote of County Armagh: 'The number of looms exceeds the number of houses, as most houses have two or three looms . . .' (*County Armagh*, p. 269).

2. Coote (ibid., p. 269) commented ' . . . when the demand for linens is brisk . . . many new looms are made . . .'. Taking into account the difficulties faced by the linen trade during the previous decade (see Gill, *Ir. Linen Industry*, pp. 221-226) it may be true that, in general, the tenants holding the higher-valued land found themselves with looms built or bought during the earlier prosperity of the industry that no longer repaid use.

3. According to a valuation survey the cotton works in 1838 contained two spinning factories, one with 3,216 spindles and the other with 1,200, and a weaving factory with 167 looms. The machinery was driven by water power for nine months of the year but when the water level dropped too low an eight-horse-power engine was used (PRONI, First Valuation field book VAL IB/212 Parish of Loughgilly, townlands of Upper and Lower Lisdrumchor).

tenants having several sons to encourage one or more being learned
to weave cotton.' (*page* 301).

The occupations other than weaver are much as one might expect
on a rural estate containing no large town. Although there was a
parish priest, there were no Presbyterian ministers or priests of the
established church: the latter, of course, resided on their own glebe
lands. There was no teacher (though there is some suggestion of a
school to be built in Baleek[1]). There were only two blacksmiths with
three assistants, which, having regard to the 311 horses, let alone all
the other repair work undertaken by a smith, seems quite inadequate.
Markethill, Hamilton's Bawn and perhaps even Armagh and Newry,
may have provided many of the essential services such as saddle and
harness making, inns (there was only one on the estate), glazing, etc.[2]

The wealthiest tenants on the estate were the linen merchant, linen
buyer and innkeeper.[3] All three are described as 'opulent' (the only
occasions when Greig extends his classification of varying degrees of
industry and sloth). William Beard, the linen buyer (*pages* 65, 120),
although he farmed only seventeen acres, had a full complement of
farm buildings, all slated (including two stores), three cows, one horse,
two servants and a cottier weaver. The linen merchant, James Stewart
(*pages* 69, 111), had over fifty acres, seven cows, four other cattle, four
horses, six sheep and two pigs, five servants and a cottier weaver. In
addition, according to Greig, he had built 'a substantial and even an
elegant house and offices . . . at an expenses of from £1,200 to £1,500'.
Interestingly, Stewart was unmarried while Beard had no children.
The innkeeper, Bernard O'Heare (*pages* 31, 83) had a total of eighty-
five acres, all the usual out-buildings, six cows, four other cattle, two
horses and two pigs, as well as four servants and two cottiers.[4] The

1. According to the Ordnance Survey Memoir for Mullaghbrack parish, Gosford school in
Markethill had been established in 1815 (Royal Irish Academy, Dublin, O.S. Memoirs box 18,
Armagh I/xix). The census report of 1821 seems to indicate that there were several schools in
Baleek Village: '. . . one of the schools in this village (Baleek) is a Sunday school of 179 boys
and 173 girls. It is supported by the Earl of Gosford'. (*Abstract of the answers and returns
made pursuant to . . . 'an act to provide for taking an account of the population of Ireland and for
ascertaining the increase or diminution thereof'*: hereafter cited as 1821 Census of Ireland,
p. 249, H.C.1824, (577), XXII, 683).
2. The Ordnance Survey Memoir for Mullaghbrack parish contains a list of occupations for the
town of Markethill in 1838: 2 surgeons, 8 grocers, 4 haberdashers, 22 spirit dealers, 1 painter
and glazier, 1 watchmaker, 2 bakers, 1 tailor, 3 shoemakers, 1 reedmaker, 1 nailer, 1 wheel-
wright, 2 smiths, 1 pawnbroker, 1 ironmonger, 1 chandler, 1 gunpowder dealer, and two
butchers. It also notes 2 hotels, 1 hardware shop and 2 delf shops.
3. William Atkinson, the cotton manufacturer, is not resident on the estate (*page* 113) and in any
case Greig apparently feels, as he does with the parish priest (*page* 68), that comment on his
character, means, or industry would be impertinent.
4. See also page 66.

grocer, John McParlan, Senior (*pages* 59, 105), though Greig does not call him opulent, had a degree of prosperity nearly as marked as the tenants described above: he had twenty-eight acres, all the necessary farmbuildings, six cows, two other cattle, two horses and two pigs, He employed three servants and a 'boy'.

The presence of servants, although in the above cases obviously, to some degree, an indication of affluence, is also accounted for by the nature of their business. Where other tenants engaged in occupations other than weaving, they, too, had servants. In most other cases, however, servants can be seen as filling gaps left in the family, due to the age or extreme youth of the holder or his children or when the holder was unmarried or childless.[1]

3 LIVESTOCK

(analysed in Table 7)

According to Greig, the totals of livestock are less than was usual on the estate. Because of the bad seasons of 1816 and 1817 and the fever that accompanied them 'very many of the tenants on the Gosford estates are much reduced in their stock and capital' (*page* 243). In any case, as one might expect from the small average size of holdings '. . . the management of live stock does not form a very prominent feature in the rural economy of the district' (*page* 11). Nevertheless the possession 'of a cow or two' was characteristic of the Ulster small farmer,[2] and according to Greig, 'a cow forms the chief treasure, the butter paying a large portion of rent' (*page* 266). Doubtless some of the tenants entered as having no stock, and usually described as indigent, may themselves have had a cow in the better times. Most tenants have one or two; more than three is usually an indication of a lucrative subsidiary occupation or income.[3]

1. An example of this, though an extreme one, is the townland of lower Glassdrummond in Coolmalish manor. There is a total population of twenty-one of whom seven are servants and one a cottier. Of the seven households, five have unmarried holders or couples without children (*page* 136).
2. E.R.R. Green, 'Agriculture' in *The Great Famine* ed. R. D. Edwards and T. D. Williams (Dublin, 1956), p. 108.
3. The innkeeper, linen buyer, and grocer all carry more stock per acre than the average farmer or farmer-weaver. A contrast is provided in the case of the Markey brothers. They 'for a long time enjoyed a profit-rent out of the greater part of Carrickollogly townland from a lease . . . taken out by (their) father' and between them they had forty-eight acres carrying a stock of thirteen cows, three other cattle, four horses, seven sheep, and three pigs (*pages* 43, 44, 97).

TABLE 7

Livestock

TOWNLAND	Cows	Cattle	Horses	Sheep	Pigs
BALEEK MANOR					
Upper Baleek	30	4	5	4	3
Lower Baleek Village	12	1	4	0	2
Lower Baleek	38	7	8	2	6
Upper Corromannon	27	2	6	0	3
Middle Corromannon	20	1	5	0	5
Lower Corromannon	43	0	15	3	0
Carrickollogly	44	6	14	7	8
Carrickananey	17	0	5	0	0
Upper Cregans	27	8	10	0	12
Lower Cregans	21	2	10	0	3
Upper Crunaght	8	3	3	0	3
Lower Crunaght	17	6	6	7	4
Upper Drumhoney	15	2	6	0	2
Lower Drumhoney	14	1	3	0	3
Drumnahuncheon	23	2	7	2	2
Drumgean	22	6	10	0	9
Dirlet	27	10	11	3	11
Greyhilla	32	6	12	0	1
Upper Lisdrumchor	56	12	20	12	10
Lower Lisdrumchor	5	1	2	0	3
Lurgiross	26	2	8	0	4
Total on Baleek manor	524	82	170	40	94
COOLMALISH MANOR					
Lisnegat	44	2	17	0	18
Upper Brackley	17	0	8	0	6
Lower Brackley	21	1	7	0	7
Upper Glassdrummond	17	3	5	0	15
Lower Glassdrummond	17	0	5	0	8
Sebochan	12	2	5	0	7
Carricklane	35	2	13	0	16
Cordrumond	11	0	5	0	6
Ballindaragh	37	0	18	0	13
Corhamock	26	0	10	0	12
Dennismullen	14	0	8	0	6
Ednekennedy	13	0	6	0	7
Drumlack	7	0	5	0	0
Cabragh	4	0	2	0	1
Ballyanny	21	1	8	0	12
Bryandrum	19	0	7	0	7
Total on Coolmalish manor	315	11	129	0	141
Argonnell	23	5	12	0	17
ESTATE TOTAL	862	98	311	40	252

Livestock would especially be a help to the tenant on less fertile land, increasing the viability of the holding, and in Baleek one finds proportionately more cows and cattle to the acre than in Coolmalish. Baleek's superiority in cattle is especially marked, eighty-two of the estate total of ninety-eight being found there.

Greig's tabular column devoted to sheep is largely superfluous: there are only forty on the whole estate, all in Baleek and over half of them owned by five tenants.[1]

Greig comments especially on the 'small number of pigs entered in the tabular report of an animal which was so numerous everywhere in Ireland' (*page* 244). They had been sold off during 1816 and 1817, due to the lack of feeding. Although the potato crop of 1818 made it feasible to replenish stock, the high prices then obtaining for lean pigs allowed only those whom Greig termed the 'more substantial farmers' to purchase them.

A horse (or the use of one) was essential not only for farm labour, but also for 'drawing home turf, carrying produce to market' (*page* 267) and for the drawing of lime. Nevertheless, nearly one in every two tenants was without a horse of his own, although a few tenants had a pair. Not having one's own horse undoubtedly led to inconvenience and perhaps some loss. As Greig explains, 'Those who cannot keep a horse or horses must of course want until those who do possess them have their own lands tilled, and thereby lose the best part of the season, and the crops rendered later and more uncertain than those of their neighbours round them.' (*page* 267). Yet, with a figure of about one horse to every thirty acres, the estate cannot be said to suffer from being 'under-horsed'.[2]

Examining the percentage of stock held in townlands of differing valuation reveals how the bad seasons had affected the richer and poorer areas (see Table 8). Those valued at under £1 per acre, although

1. Coote (*County Armagh*, p. 292) had commented on their absence in 1804: 'I do not know that this County [Armagh] has ever been a sheep country . . . . Sheep-feeding is not pursued by the small farmer.'

2. William Blacker, in evidence to the Devon Commission, answering a question about the area of land he thought necessary for the employment of one horse, answered that 'from twenty to twenty-five acres would reasonably keep a horse for farming purposes . . .' (Devon Commission, Part I, H.C. 1845, XIX, W. 52 Q.22). There is a complete absence of asses, although elsewhere in Ireland the animal was gradually replacing the horse (see G. O'Brien, *The Economic History of Ireland from the Union to the Famine* (London, 1921), p. 33). It would appear from Coote that horse-breeding was not a feature of County Armagh—pressure of tillage, on the one hand, and the competition of other animals for fodder would scarcely permit it and horses were bought as three-year-olds from Connaught and Fermanagh dealers (Coote, *County Armagh*, p. 290).

they account for 29.1% of the acreage have only 13.9% of the pigs.
In order to pay the rent or realise some capital or through inability
to spare feed, holders in these townlands had apparently sold their
pigs. Although their stocks of cattle and horses are also proportionately lower than those of tenants in the higher-valued townlands
(cattle 23.5% and horses 22.8% respectively,) their stock of cows is
roughly proportionate to acreage (28.5%), an indication that the
greatest effort was made to retain this animal, serving as it did to
help pay the rent, feed the family and manure the holding. Greig
spells out the consequences for the tenant of parting with the cow:
'he must then be satisfied with the potato crop alone, the grain and
flax being barely sufficient to pay his rent; and as from want of animal
manure they are yearly becoming worse and at length from the
exhausted state of the lands prove inadequate to pay rents, particularly in bad seasons, beyond this stage misery and ruin are rarely
avoidable.' (*page* 266).

TABLE 8

Relationship between the valuation of townlands and the population, looms,
farm-buildings and stock on them

	Percentage of Townlands valued at		
	Under £1 *per acre*	£1 *to* £1 10s *per acre*	*Over* £1 10s *per acre*
Acreage	29.1	63.0	7.9
Rental	16.1	72.1	11.8
Population	28.0	63.5	8.5
Protestants	24.8	67.5	7.7
Catholics	41.5	51.1	7.4
Looms	23.3	69.8	6.9
Workshops	17.6	61.8	20.6
Cows	28.5	63.8	7.7
Cattle	23.5	74.0	2.0
Horses	22.8	69.5	7.7
Pigs	13.9	77.0	9.1
Houses	24.7	68.6	6.7
Barns	17.6	75.2	7.2
Byres	22.6	68.9	8.5
Stables	20.7	67.9	11.4
Car houses	22.2	68.7	9.1

Note: See Table 12 (Rents proposed by Greig).

4 BUILDINGS

(analysed in Table 9)

TABLE 9

Houses, farm buildings and workshops

TOWNLAND	Houses	Byres	Barns	Stables	Car Houses	Work Shops
Upper Baleek	22	11	1	1	1	0
Lower Baleek Village	7	4	2	2	1	0
Lower Baleek	17	13	3	2	1	1
Upper Corromannon	24	11	0	0	0	0
Middle Corromannon	15	10	2	2	2	2
Lower Corromannon	24	18	12	9	8	1
Carrickollogly	30	22	12	5	5	1
Carrickananey	14	13	4	4	3	6
Upper Cregans	19	15	8	9	7	0
Lower Cregans	18	14	9	4	1	1
Upper Crunaght	5	4	3	3	2	1
Lower Crunaght	5	5	5	4	4	1
Upper Drumhoney	9	7	3	4	1	0
Lower Drumhoney	17	13	3	3	2	0
Drumnahuncheon	17	12	5	4	1	1
Drumgean	12	11	7	6	4	3
Dirlet	15	13	9	7	7	1
Greyhilla	19	17	9	7	4	3
Upper Lisdrumchor	33	25	12	8	5	3
Lower Lisdrumchor	4	4	2	2	2	1
Lurgiross	20	18	6	4	3	3
Total of Baleek manor	346	260	117	90	64	29
Lisnegat	26	24	20	5	6	2
Upper Brackley	20	15	6	4	3	1
Lower Brackley	17	11	6	2	1	0
Upper Glassdrummond	21	12	7	2	2	1
Lower Glassdrummond	7	7	5	3	2	0
Sebochan	16	11	2	0	0	0
Carricklane	19	17	10	7	4	0
Cordrumond	9	9	4	2	1	1
Ballindarragh	34	29	14	3	3	1
Corhamock	30	24	13	6	5	0
Dennismullen	12	11	6	2	3	0
Ednekennedy	9	9	4	2	2	0
Drumlack	10	7	0	1	0	0
Cabragh	3	3	1	2	0	0
Ballyanny	12	11	3	3	2	1
Bryandrum	10	10	7	5	2	1
Total of Coolmalish manor	255	210	108	49	36	8
Argonnell	21	16	9	2	0	0
ESTATE TOTAL	622	486	234	141	100	37

'The farm buildings and cottages in this part of the county of Armagh are much more substantial and comfortable than in many other parts of Ireland.' (*page* 284).

In his enumeration of buildings Greig includes dwelling houses, barns, byres, stables, workshops and carhouses. Not all the holdings have a dwelling house, usually because the holder resides elsewhere on the estate or outside it. Usually all the houses (and the buildings in general) are thatched. Out of a total of 622 houses, only 48 are slated or partly slated. Greig attempts a classification of buildings into very good, good, tolerable, bad and ruinous or in ruins. It is at best a very subjective yardstick (he gives no indication of his criteria) and in a few places it appears a little absentminded—one set of buildings are described as 'Protestant' (and on a Catholic's holding!) and he sometimes omits a classification. Further, there seems a possibility that he modified his categories to suit the different town-lands and, for example, what was dismissed as 'bad' in the richer townlands may have passed as tolerable elsewhere. However, a summation of his judgments shows a clear enough picture: reducing his categories to two, 'tolerable or better' and 'less than tolerable', the first accounts for 80% of all types of farm building, with only 20% described as bad or ruinous. From his remarks in the General Report it seems clear that this represents a very recent improvement (*page* 245). It is difficult to learn much from Greig about the average accommodation or of what materials the houses were built. Although he shows an elevation and plan of what he calls 'the best description of common cottages or cabins in this part of the country' (*pages* 329, 330), this suggests that the average cottage was smaller or less well-built than the model illustrated. What the average may have been like is perhaps better indicated by the following description written some twenty years later: 'These (poorer) tenants build their own houses of clay and straw, or rushes. They make the walls solid, and raise them two feet high at a time with mud and rushes, allowing them ten days to dry between the layers . . . These dwellings, including windows, cost the tenant fifty shillings . . . They contain two bays or rooms, each fourteen feet square. Most of the poor people prefer these thatched mud cabins to a house of stone and slate . . .'[1] Fifty shillings would appear to be an under-estimate, especially since thirty years

1. Binns, *Miseries and Beauties*, I, 154. The passage quoted was written after his visit to the Gosford estates as an Assistant Poor Law Commissioner and describes conditions there.

5

earlier Coote had noted that 'some cottages are put together at the cost of from three pounds to five pounds but are of very inferior materials', and gone on to estimate what he regarded as the 'expense of building a comfortable cottage'.[1] The figure he arrived at (£7 19s. 3d.) clearly relates to a building built to standards very much beyond those of the tenants above. However, it would probably be more correct to lean towards the higher figure. Greig himself rarely quotes a figure for building costs. When he does it is obviously because the instance is sufficiently singular to merit special mention. In Greyhilla, Baleek manor, he remarks on a house costing £24, (*page* 68) whilst the linen merchant's and innkeeper's are noted as having cost hundreds of pounds.[2]

Of farm buildings, only a byre is found attached to the majority of houses: 78.1% of houses have a byre, whilst only 37.6% have a barn, 22.7% a stable, 16.1% a carhouse and 5.6% a workshop.[3] From the very common presence of the byres (on some parts of the estate over 80% of houses have them) they seem to have fulfilled many of the roles carried out by other buildings on larger farmyards. Presumably they could function as a cowhouse or piggery or a stable. The term 'workshop' covers not only a weaver's shed, but is often used by Greig to describe the place of business of the tenant: it may be the inn, or the flaxmill or the forge, etc. Thus the already small number of workshops becomes an even smaller number of weavers' sheds, a position Greig is especially anxious to improve as a workshop will, he thinks, induce weavers to keep another loom (*page* 299).[4]

---

1. Coote, *County Armagh*, p. 251. Coote's bill is made up as follows:

Mudwork and plastering	..	..	..	£3 8	3
Roofing	..	..	..	1 14	1½
Thatching	..	..	..	2 5	6
Door and Leaded Windows	..	..	..	0 11	4½
				£7 19	3

2. For a study of the evolution of houses in County Armagh see T. G. F. Paterson, 'Housing and house types in County Armagh', *Ulster Folklife*, VI (1960), pp. 8-17.
3. The percentage figures for farm buildings have been calculated as percentages of the total number of houses. This is a more reliable indicator than the total number of holdings or holders. Some holdings are multiple, with farm buildings on one holding only, whilst a few holders do not reside on the estate and have their buildings elsewhere. Since, however, the latter are so few, the calculation on the *houses* basis may be taken as a tolerably accurate guide to *holders'* possessions also.
4. He is by no means correct, however, when he goes on to argue that 'those having two or more looms employ apprentices or journeymen in addition to their own family . . .' This is not the picture revealed in the Tabular Report where there is no correlation between the numbers employed outside the family and the number of occupied looms. Servants substitute for a missing family rather than augment an existing one. (See note 1 on page 48).

When one compares those townlands valued at under one pound per acre and those over that figure, in every case there is seen to be a smaller percentage of each kind of farm building on the poorer holdings: 70.3% have byres, 26.8% barns, 18.4% stables, 7.6% car-houses and 3.8% workshops. As one might expect, if these houses have a building at all it will be the all-purpose 'byre'.

5 NUMBER OF PEOPLE PER INHABITED HOUSE

To obtain an average figure for the whole estate, the following method has been used. The total population of each townland (less the number of cottiers, but including the male and female servants) has been divided by the number of inhabited houses. This figure for houses may differ from the *total* number of houses in any particular townland because some holders are resident elsewhere on the estate or outside it. An average figure for each townland thus obtained, an average for each manor and the whole estate may be calculated. Since the 'spread' may be, exceptionally, wide (eg. 8.00 in Upper Crunnaght and 3.00 in Lower Glassdrummond) a median measurement is likely to be a more accurate estimate of density. Unfortunately, however, all other contemporary information on household densities is either based on an arithmetic mean or presents the data in such a form that only an arithmetic mean can be calculated.

On the whole Gosford estate the average number of persons per household is 5.67. There is a considerable variation in density between Baleek and Coolmalish manors. For Baleek the figure is 5.88; for Coolmalish 5.39. For those townlands valued at under £1 per acre, the household density is 6.01, and for those over £1, 5.56. This difference is further emphasised when it is considered that there are proportionately fewer servants in the poorer than in the richer townlands.

There are many estimates of the number of persons per house in Ireland during the late eighteenth and early nineteenth centuries, though they are of widely varying worth. Most of them have been very fully discussed by Professor Connell.[1] The estimates of the

---

1. Connell, *Population*, pp. 14-25.

compilers of the county surveys[1] appear to be based on little more than informed guesses, but both the incomplete 'census' of 1813 and the first decennial census of 1821 yield figures based on an enumeration of both population and houses.[2] Thus, although they must both be treated with some degree of caution (particularly that of 1813), they may be used as a yardstick for comparing the Gosford figures based on Greig's fieldwork of 1816. The 1813 census produces a figure of 5.8 persons per house, that of 1821, 5.95.[3] Even if one accepts the accuracy of the enumeration, these figures include the very different household densities of the urban and rural areas—the large towns showing a much higher figure per household.[4] Certainly the figures calculated from the 1813 census for the barony of Lower Fews (which includes the Gosford estate) and for the county of Armagh are lower than the average for the country as a whole.[5] The density in Lower Fews was 5.42 and in County Armagh 5.54. The figures in the 1821 census for the Lower Fews barony show surprisingly little change over those for 1813.[6] Although population had risen, the number of houses had kept pace with it, so that the average number of persons per house is 5.43, an increase of only 0.01 in nearly eight years. The Gosford estate figure of 1818 (5.67) is so much higher that greater fragmentation in a period of less than five years can scarcely account for the difference. It is quite possible that surrounding estates in the barony show a somewhat different pattern, or it may be more simply explained by less painstaking work on the part of the census enumerators.

---

1. Ibid. p. 20. Sir Charles Coote ventured no estimate of population density per household, merely quoting Bushe's (1788) figure of 'more than six to each house' (Coote, *County Armagh*, p. 246).
2. That of 1813 was 'carelessly and incompletely taken', while the 1821 census, though not seriously defective, was regarded by the 1841 census commissioners as likely to be an under-estimate of population (Connell, *Population*, pp. 20, 21, and p. 2).
3. Connell, *Population*, p. 17.
4. The wide variations in density as between town and country are discussed at length in T. Newenham, *A Statistical and Historical Inquiry into the Progress and Magnitude of the Population of Ireland* (London, 1805), pp. 249-51.
5. Reproduced in Mason, *Statistical Account*, II, Table III, p. xli. The figure for County Armagh is based upon returns from six of the eight baronies.
6. 1821 Census of Ireland, p. 248, H.C. 1824, XXII, 682.

6 RELIGION

Greig notes the religions of the tenants 'not with any view to perpetuate any invidious distinctions but because the subject is interesting from so frequently being taken into account in political calculations and reasoning.' (*page* 11).

He did not on all occasions make a note of the holder's religion, but more than 90% of them were given an affiliation. Of these, 64.8% were entered as Protestant, and 35.2% as Catholic.[1] The Catholics are found heavily concentrated in the poorer rented lands. The townlands valued at under £1 an acre, although they contain only 29.1% of the population, have 41.5% of the Catholics. However, Greig remarks: 'Perhaps there are few situations in which there is less difference to be remarked between the industry of the two persuasions when placed in similar circumstances than in this country. Very many instances occur of Catholic occupiers being industrious and consequently comfortable and there are many instances of Protestant occupiers even with all the advantage of old leases held at very low rents, from their sloth and improvidence very truly disgraceful'. (*page* 11).

The proportion of Protestants on the estate is higher than in the region at large. Shaw Mason's figures for the diocese of Armagh in May 1814 give Roman Catholics as 57% of the total population.[2]

Greig does not divide Protestants into members of the Established Church and Dissenters; however, the figures cited in the previous footnote suggest that the Presbyterians were the more numerous.

---

1. In 1834 the proportions for the four parishes which contain the Gosford estate—Baleek, Loughgilly, Mullaghbrack, and Kilclooney—were Church of Ireland 22%, Presbyterian 44% and Roman Catholic 34% (First report of the commissioners of public instruction, Ireland, pp. 150a, 152a, 160a, 164a, H.C. 1835, XXXIII. 202, 204, 212, 216).
2. Mason *Statistical Account*, II, p. xlix. It may be noted, however, that Armagh diocese includes not only that country, but also parts of Counties Tyrone, Londonderry and Louth. By 1838 according to the figures for Church and Chapel attendance, Roman Catholics in Loughgilly parish amounted to 50.2% of the population (Ordnance Survey Memoirs, box 8, Armagh I/xvii): the parish included the manor of Baleek. See also Binns, *Miseries and Beauties*, I, 193, where he notes the preponderance of Roman Catholics in the barony of Lower Fews.

7 SUBDIVISION OF HOLDINGS

(*pages* 263-275)

Greig's Tabular Report is much more detailed for Baleek manor than for Coolmalish. Each holding in the former is given a detailed comment, whilst in the latter even extensive subdivision is only cursorily mentioned.

By comparing the entries in the columns 'contents, etc., by former surveys' and 'contents, etc., by new surveys' and by comparing them both with the numbers entered as paying head rents in the surviving rentals, one can approach an estimate of the extent of subdivision. Except in the case of Upper Baleek, Lower Baleek and Upper Corromannon it is impossible to date the drawing up of these former surveys (*page* 313).[1] However, several factors suggest that the impetus towards subdivision can be dated at least from the 1780s. There is, firstly, the evidence surviving in Greig's Appendix to his General Report (*page* 313); secondly, in almost all cases of family subdivision the original lessee is the father or (more rarely) the grandfather of the holding subtenants; and thirdly, the acreage held by the original lessees makes it unlikely that their holdings were themselves the product of subdivision.[2] There is, however, the possibility that the poorest townlands, such as Baleek, Corromannon, Carrickgollogly and Drumhoney were parcelled out by middlemen some time before the pressure towards fragmentation was effective on the rest of the estates (*page* 264).[3] This appears to have been a once-for-all process, in that the holdings on these lands, as originally sublet, were too small and too poor to permit further extensive subdivision.

The greatest proportion of holdings in both manors is concentrated in the over 5 and under 15 acre class: in Baleek 55.9% and in Coolmalish 62.0%, the average for the whole estate being 58.4%. Holdings of less than an acre are very few (0.5% of the estate) whilst holdings of over 30 acres (1.9%) are hardly less rare (see Table 8). Coote's average

---

1. It appears that Greig intended to make this appendix a comprehensive survey of the extent and reasons for subdivision. As completed, however, it included only ten cases from the first two townlands of Baleek manor. Of the ten, eight were surveyed in 1801 and two in 1788.
2. Connell dates the process 'after the 1780s' and 'during the years before 1815' (*Population*, pp. 165 and 167).
3. In these four townlands there were 40 head-tenants paying rent in 1793; in 1818 there were 160. The increase in headrent payers was consequent on the lands falling out of lease. It is, however, probable that many of these holders were already subtenants in the 1790s.

for Armagh County is somewhat lower than for the Gosford estate;[1] this, and the 1841 census figures for rural Ulster[2] suggests that the possibilities for subdivision had not yet been fully worked out. Greig, too, suggests as much: 'The subdivision of lands has not in every instance advanced so far on the Gosford estates as in many other parts of this country . . .' (*page* 263).

Inter-familial subdivision, either between sons or as marriage portions for daughters, is by far the commonest cause of subdivision. An example combining both causes may be cited from the townland

TABLE 10

Size of holdings

	Baleek		Coolmalish		Total	
	Number	%	*Number*	%	*Number*	%
under 1 acre	0	0	4	1.4	4	0.5
1 acre and under 5 acres	86	20.1	63	21.6	149	20.7
5 acres ,, ,, 15 ,,	240	55.9	181	62.0	421	58.4
15 ,, ,, ,, 30 ,,	92	21.4	43	14.7	135	18.7
30 ,, ,, ,, 50 ,,	9	2.1	1	0.3	10	1.4
over 50 acres	2	0.5	0	0	2	0.3
	429	100.0	292	100.0	721	100.0

of Upper Drumhoney (*pages* 55 *and* 102). Andrew Boyde 'the former tenant' held a total of 32a. 2r. 14p. He left one part (14a. 2r. 37p) 'to his daughter married to (John) Edgar and the remainder to his son David Boyde and his other two daughters married to Robert Good-fellow and William Courtney. David Boyde sold his share to James Patterson who lives immediately adjoining on another estate (a share

1. Coote (*County Armagh*, p. 232) considered that 'the average size of farms may be five acres . . .'
2. *Report of the Commissioners appointed to take the census of Ireland for the year* 1841: hereafter cited as 1841 Census of Ireland; p. 454, H.C. 1843, XXIV, 566. In rural Ulster holdings of one to five acres comprised 43% of the total number while those of five to fifteen acres made up another 42%.

amounting to 10a. 2r. 6p.)—William Courtney holds 4a. 3r. 10p. and Goodfellow still less 2a. 2r. 6p.; perhaps there is now no alternative but grant a lease to each of their own portions as now surveyed unless Courtney's and Goodfellow's could be joined under one tenant.'

On two occasions Greig draws special attention to the 'ruinous system' of subdividing. In one, from Carrickgollogly townland, the original holding was 9a. 1r. 15p, now divided into three portions

TABLE 11

Rental value of holdings as proposed by Greig

Rent (in shillings)	Baleek			Coolmalish			Total		
	Acres	%	%	*Acres*	%	%	*Acres*	%	%
1s. and under 6s.	0	0	} 21.7	0	0	} 0.0	0	0	} 13.2
6s. „ „ 11s.	996	21.7		0	0		996	13.2	
11s. „ „ 16s.	332	7.2	} 32.6	0	0	} 6.0	332	4.4	} 22.2
16s. „ „ 21s.	1,166	25.4		169	6.0		1,335	17.8	
21s. „ „ 26s.	1,048	22.8	} 40.0	678	23.9	} 87.6	1,726	22.9	} 58.7
26s. „ „ 31s.	789	17.2		1,805	63.7		2,694	35.8	
31s. „ „ 36s.	0	0	} 5.7	181	6.4	} 6.4	181	2.4	} 5.9
36s. „ „ 41s.	264	5.7		0	0		264	3.5	
	4,595	100.0	100.0	2,833	100.0	100.0	7,528	100.0	100.0

3a. 0r. 15p., 2a. 3r. 23p., and 3a. 2r. 17p. respectively (*pages* 43 *and* 96). 'Widow Brady the former tenant had three daughters and the farm was divided amongst them for marriage portions. Margaret Brady or widow Troy has been left with four children, one boy a helpless cripple. Widow Brady or rather widow McKeown was deserted by her husband and left with three children. John Quinn married the third daughter. They are all very poor. Quinn has a cow, ought to be able to pay rent. It is presumed the females, particularly Widow Troy, have also endeavoured to pay although in the midst of great poverty. The hardships of turning out so many persons is distressing. To grant a lease jointly would be to perpetuate discord and further distress yet the reporter would demur at recommending leases being granted for so small portions of land under such circumstances. Yet perhaps after all it may be the safest mode to grant them and he requests particular attention. The situation of this farm is an illustration of the ruinous consequences of allowing subdivision.'

This comment is not an isolated example of Greig's apparent reluctance or inability to consolidate holdings obviously uneconomic and fraught with future difficulty for the estate. The following comment makes this reluctance even clearer: 'John and Joseph Watson's lease containing twelve acres is now divided in the most numerous manner among Hugh McAlden, Joseph McKenzie and John Andrews. McAlden is a pensioner and got his part as a marriage portion with a daughter of John Watson. John Andrews has his in like manner with the daughter of Joseph Watson and McKenzie has his from his mother who was a daughter of Joseph Watson. He gave her a house and garden. If possible this should not be let in three divisions when the lease expires yet the claims which the present occupiers have are not easily obviated—but no smaller division ought to be allowed.' (*page* 110).

It is difficult to see what claims these sub-tenants would have at the expiration of head-leases especially since clauses against alienation had been inserted in Gosford estate leases since the 1760s.[1] The examples quoted have been instances of family subdivision, and in the following example, where sub-letting outside the family has occurred, Greig is more certain that consolidation may be possible, though even here its feasibility is by no means certain: 'William Hughes son of Edward the lessee pays double to his father—Edward sold part to James Stenson and he again sold to John Stewart for about £70 six years ago and William McKenzie holds from Stewart at a high rent. If possible the entire should again be let in one when the present lease expires.' (*pages* 69, 111).

---

1. Devon Commission, Part I, H.C. 1845, XIX, W. 52 (Blacker) Q. 15: 'Lord Gosford's leases for these eighty years back were all made with a covenant for non-alienation . . .' It has, however, been noted that in the linen-producing counties in the late eighteenth century 'ever-rising rent-rolls made landlords less eager to enforce restrictive clauses in leases. . .' (W. H. Crawford, 'The rise of the linen industry' in L. M. Cullen (ed.), *The Formation of the Irish Economy* (Cork, 1969), p. 33).

When considered alongside Greig's remarks in his General Report (*page* 271), these examples seem an implicit recognition of tenant right in the fullest sense of that term.[1]

The subdivision of a holding so as to realise part of the tenant right was very rare. This might seem surprising since the windfall gains to be made would have been extremely lucrative during the first decade of the century.[2] For instance: '6a. 3r. 0p. were left to Warnock's daughters as a fortune. They sold it to Alex Hocks about twelve years ago who paid £80 and in the two years after he sold it for £100 to Cornet the present occupier . . .' (*page* 109). However, the opportunities for alienating in this way would obviously be gravely limited by the claims of sons and daughters (or nephews) for future inheritance.

A number of instances do occur of the outright sale of an interest already acquired by descent or as a marriage portion. In some of the cases the reason is given explicitly as emigration, and since sale would involve leaving the estate it is probably the most common motive, providing as it would both passage money and some capital. 'William and John Geary's lease . . . John sold his part to Patrick McParlane

---

1. L. M. Cullen has recently questioned the existence of, or at least the extent of, tenant right in the eighteenth century ('Problems in the Interpretation and Revision of Eighteenth Century Irish Economic History' in *Trans. Royal Hist. Soc.* 5th ser. XVII (1967). Although the Greig report belongs to the second decade of the nineteenth century, in his discussion of the subject (*page* 277) Greig takes it for granted as a long-established custom. Cullen suggested that 'What is sometimes described as a tenant right by later writers referring to this period (the eighteenth century) was simply the right of a tenant to sell his interest in a lease' (p. 9). Lord Lurgan's agent, in his evidence to the Devon Commission defined it as ' . . . the claim of the tenant and his heirs to continue in undisturbed possession of the farm, so long as the rent is paid; and in the case of an ejectment, or in the event of a change of occupancy, whether at the wish of the landlord or tenant, it is the sum of money which the new occupier must pay to the old one for the peaceable enjoyment of his holding. It is the system which has more or less prevailed since the settlement of Ulster by James I' (Devon Commission, H.C. 1845, XIX, W. 92 Q. 38). Greig, although reluctantly, recognises the existence of a right based on the second part of this definition and from his comments on the difficulty of removing subtenants especially those related by blood to the original lessee—he implicitly recognises a right embracing security of tenure also.

2. Greig (*page* 256) says ' . . . Formerly when lands were constantly rising in value and money abundant, this (the goodwill or tenant right which could be obtained) was often very high even for farms by no means cheap, viz. from five to ten and even fifteen pounds per acre, . . .' Of three holdings sold in Lower Drumhoney, Baleek Manor, in the first decade of the century the tenant right was valued at about £10 per acre or, at Greig's valuation of rents, at something less than ten years purchase (*page* 103). Greig (*page* 256) suggests a drastic postwar drop in the value of tenant right: 'If the occupier can obtain two years' rent for his goodwill the bargain is to be considered a fair one and if more can be obtained it is either very favourable or the purchaser has more than a common command of money or anxiety to obtain land, ...' In 1845, evidence about County Armagh given to the Devon Commission put the figure of tenant right purchase at about nine and a half years purchase for lands out of lease and 'something more' for a leasehold interest (Devon Commission, H.C. 1845, XIX, W. 92 Q. 38).

for 125 guineas (10a. 0r. 20p.) and went to America with nine children . . .' (*page* 110).[1]

The middleman, so often cast as the villain (though sometimes the victim[2]) of the Irish land system, occupies only a minor role on the estates, and this seems to have been true of the whole county.[3] There are a few examples of large old leaseholds extensively sublet, more common in Coolmalish than in Baleek, although in total acreage they amount to no more than 10% of the estate.[4] Greig was not alone when he painted a somewhat lurid picture of the middleman's effect on the countryside: 'It is, in general, the interest of middlemen to apportion the lands which they hold, into small-holdings. This ruinous system is now almost entirely given up in Ulster. About fifty or sixty years ago it seems to have been difficult to find tenants to occupy large tracts, particularly of unreclaimed or partially improved uplands, and they were frequently leased to opulent individuals who procured sub-tenants for them (Doctor Robinson's and Bell's leases in Glassdrumond, Brackley, etc., are instances of this kind on the Gosford estates) . . .' (*page* 264). In spite of Greig's remarks about middlemen taking less well-endowed land, the surviving middlemen on the Gosford estates all held land valued at about the average for the estate as a whole;[5] nor is there any evidence that the middlemen were prone to permit excessive subdivision. 31% of holdings on middlemens' lands were between one and five acres as against 20.7% for the whole estate, but the latter percentage includes much land inferior in quality to that held by middlemen and so less able to sustain extensive subdividing. Moreover, 13.4% of their tenants held

---

1. Although this tenant was a Roman Catholic, Wakefield had written of County Armagh in 1812: 'No Roman Catholic was ever known to emigrate from this part of Ireland.' (Wakefield, *Account of Ireland*, II, 597). Even by 1837, according to Binns, the position had not greatly altered: 'Many of the inhabitants of this barony (Lower Fews) have emigrated . . . . [but] the Roman Catholics have not emigrated to any considerable extent.' (Binns, *Miseries and Beauties*, I, 193).

2. F. S. L. Lyons, 'Vicissitudes of a middleman in County Leitrim, 1810-1827' in *Irish Historical Studies*, IX (1955) especially pp. 309 ff.

3. Coote (*County Armagh*, p. 119) asserts that in County Armagh 'the occupying tenant has no lazy middleman between him and his landlord.' Middlemen had, however, held extensive holdings in the poorer townlands. By 1818 their leases, had, for the most part, long expired. It is to them presumably that Greig refers in the passage quoted above. See also L. M. Cullen, 'The Irish economy in the eighteenth century' in Cullen, *Formation of the Irish economy*.

4. Only two of the middlemen held more than 100 acres. Dr. Robinson had four holdings amounting to 165 acres (*pages* 133, 135, 154, 155, 157) and John Reed held the whole townland of Lower Drumhoney of 147 acres (*pages* 57, 103). There are less than half a dozen other middlemen on the estate, usually holding between forty and sixty acres.

5. There is, however, evidence from the surviving estate rentals that the poorest townlands of Upper and Lower Baleek, Upper, Middle and Lower Corromannon and Carrickollogly were held by extensive middlemen at least as late as 1793.

between fifteen and thirty acres (compared with 18.7% in the same category on the whole estate).

The middlemen held at the rents entered in the 'former surveys'; these are only one-half to one-third of Greig's valuation so that considerable profit-rent would have been amassed in the years prior to 1815 (see Table 12).[1]

Greig is understandably reticent on how far the desire to enlarge the franchise has contributed to Gosford sub-division: 'The desire to acquire political influence or the apparent necessity to follow the same procedure, has encouraged the sub-division of lands as the number of freeholders have too often been considered paramount to any other interest or consideration.' (*page* 264).

Though he does not deny that such base motives would sway the earl of Gosford (as one might expect him to do if they didn't), Wakefield's comment probably includes County Armagh: 'In the north the people seem to be more slightly held by this connexion and to depend more on their own individual exertion, which may be owing, in some measure to the inhabitants of these northern districts having little or nothing to do with the return of members of parliament'.[2]

---

1. This proposition assumes that experience on the Gosford estate differed from that in County Leitrim (see p. 63, n. 2) where a theoretical profit became a large loss through inability to collect arrears. In the Leitrim experience, however, the middleman was already paying substantial head-rent to the landlord, which was not the case on the Gosford estate.
2. Wakefield, *Account of Ireland*, II, 743.

TABLE 12

Rents proposed by Greig

TOWNLAND	ACREAGE to nearest acre	RENTAL to nearest 25p	AVERAGE RENT per acre
		£	£
BALEEK MANOR			
Upper Baleek	363	118.25	0.33
Lower Baleek Village	95	72.0	0.76
Lower Baleek	237	152.75	0.65
Upper Corromannon	393	130.0	0.33
Middle Corromannon	240	111.75	0.46
Lower Corromannon	311	263.5	0.82
Carrickollogly	254	228.5	0.89
Carrickananey	111	201.25	1.81
Upper Cregans	191	245.5	1.29
Lower Cregans	215	266.75	1.24
Upper Crunaght	111	125.25	1.13
Lower Crunaght	138	197.5	1.43
Upper Drumhoney	163	149.5	0.92
Lower Drumhoney	147	153.0	1.05
Drumnahuncheon	182	206.5	1.13
Drumgean	247	355.25	1.44
Dirlet	211	305.5	1.45
Greyhilla	202	238.0	1.18
Upper Lisdrumchor	438	450.25	1.03
Lower Lisdrumchor	153	279.75	1.83
Lurgiross	193	257.5	1.33
Total of Baleek manor	4,595	4508.25	0.98
COOLMALISH MANOR			
Lisnegat	355	462.5	1.30
Upper Brackley	169	163.75	0.97
Lower Brackley	172	208.25	1.21
Upper Glassdrummond	192	236.5	1.23
Lower Glassdrummond	87	118.75	1.36
Sebochan	134	174.5	1.39
Carricklane	230	316.25	1.37
Cordrumond	121	168.75	1.39
Ballindaragh	328	412.5	1.26
Corhamock	319	425.75	1.33
Dennismullen	145	206.75	1.43
Ednekennedy	144	213.0	1.48
Drumlack	99	143.25	1.45
Cabragh	51	80.25	1.57
Ballyanny	115	184.0	1.60
Bryandrum	171	269.0	1.57
Total on Coolmalish manor	2,832	3783.75	1.34
Argonnell	217	303.5	1.40
ESTATE TOTAL	7,644	8595.5	1.12

TABLE 13

Number of holdings and their holders

		Baleek	*Coolmalish*	*Total*
1.	Number of holders	356	280	636
2.	Number of holdings	429	308	737
3.	Excess of holdings	73	28	101
4.	3 as a percentage of 2	17.0	9.1	13.7

From the above table it can be seen that consolidation was not entirely absent from the estate, and, in the case of Baleek, joint holdings account for just over 17% of the total. They are rarely adjoining holdings in the same townland, the additional holding often being acquired as grazing land when the resources of the existing holding were inadequate to maintain increased stock. There are only a few examples of large or multiple holdings. Not many could hope to combine acquisitiveness, bravery and charity as effectively as the local Baleek innkeeper, Bernard O'Heare. Described by Greig as 'opulent', he held eighty-five acres in four lots. In Middle Corromannon (where his family probably originated) he held two farms of approximately eleven and twenty-two acres respectively, one as grazing land, the other recently acquired, it having 'been given up by the former tenants'. A holding of eleven acres in Upper Corromannon was given him by 'Mr. Tuft, the former tenant . . . for having personally defended Tuft's house very bravely and with great risk when attacked by bandits'. Finally, in Lower Baleek, he had a holding of nearly thirty-nine acres where he 'built two tenements . . . on which a very considerable sum has been expended (say from four hundred to six hundred pounds) . . . So improving and substantial a tenant is seldom found in so upland a situation and cannot have too much land as rents will be sure and the grounds improved . . . His liberal assistance to numbers of the poor tenants in 1816 and 1817 was a principal means of enabling them to retain their holdings until the return of better times . . .' (*pages* 31, 35, 37, 83, 89, 91).

William Atkinson, also, held a number of separate lots, about seventy-two acres in total, all in the townlands of Upper and Lower Lisdrumchor. He was the cotton manufacturer who had established an 'extensive cotton manufacture' at Glenanne (*page* 300). Of his lands in Lower Lisdrumchor, about fifty-one acres were held as a perpetuity (the only tenant appearing to hold in this way),[1] while a further seventeen acres were held from a middleman. A further four acres were held, again as a sub-tenant in upper Lisdrumchor. About his qualities as a tenant, Greig is even more enthusiastic than in the case of O'Heare: '. . . without any personal intimacy with Mr. Atkinson the reporter considers it but justice to remark that in the whole course of his observations in Ireland he has not met with a more spirited improver or a tenant who better merits every encouragement from a landlord . . . Mr. Atkinson has expended considerable sums on the judicious and permanent improvement of the lands he holds at will or under determinable leases, and to which he ought to get every addition which can be granted and which he may require because under his management they will be rendered more valuable than in the occupation of common tenants'. (*pages* 71, 73, 113).

The cottier is a rare figure indeed on the Gosford estate. There are less than thirty of them, somewhat more in Baleek than in Coolmalish (see Table 1). Although the cottier, the middleman and the landlord have formed the traditional trinity of the Irish land system, there has been serious confusion as to the precise definition of cottier status.[2] To the nineteenth century English economist the cottier was usually synonymous with any small tenant holding at will, although as Dr. E. R. R. Green points out, both the witnesses before the Poor Commissioners and the compilers of the agricultural statistics follow the 'normal Irish usage' in regarding a cottier as 'primarily the tenant of a cabin and a small portion of land, holding at will and bound to labour for his landlord whenever required.'[3] Greig, also, uses 'cottier' in this sense. He enters them under the heading 'servants', and where their precise occupation is defined it is either as weavers or labourers. Only in some cases does he separately classify their 'houses and gardens' with the rent paid. This does suggest that perhaps not all the cottiers possessed a portion of land in addition to their cabins and that their distinctiveness from the other servants lay in their living-out. Where a

---

1. John Hancock, agent to Lord Lurgan, in evidence to the Devon Commission defined a perpetuity in land as 'a lease for lives renewable for ever' with normally a fine of a year's rent on renewal (Devon Commission, H.C. 1845, XIX, W. 92 Q. 36).
2. As Cullen has pointed out especially in the article cited above (p. 62, n. 1) and his *Anglo-Irish Trade 1660-1800* (Manchester, 1968), p. 6.
3. Both J. S. Mill and J. E. Cairnes regarded all tenants 'whose rents are determined by competition' as cottiers: see Green in Edwards and Williams, *Great Famine*, p. 92 and especially footnote 8, p. 444. Dr. Collison Black in *Economic Thought and the Irish Question 1817-1870* (Cambridge 1960), pp. 87 and 88 appears to use the term in the same sense as the classical economists whose thought he is discussing. O'Brien in *Econ. hist. Ireland, Union to Famine*, pp. 9-10 cites the Devon Commission definition as 'those who hold, in addition to their cabin, a small lot of ground at a fixed rate, generally payable in labour. . .'

house and garden is mentioned separately, the rent is between thirty and fifty shillings for half a rood or less, and presumably paid in money, because in two instances the rent is mentioned specifically as being paid in labour (*pages* 146, 162). The presence of cottiers (as indeed the presence of servants in general) is closely related to the peculiar needs of the households employing them. They are to be found where the holder is unmarried, or without children, or where the family is very young; where the tenant is old or, as in the case of the ubiquitous Bernard O'Heare, follows a full-time occupation other than farming.[1]

8 TITHE AND CESS

In Armagh tithe was levied on grain, hay and flax.[2] These were the crops commonly liable to tithe in the rest of Ulster—only in Donegal, Derry and Tyrone were potatoes added. In comparison with other counties in Ireland, those in Ulster appear to have escaped relatively lightly.[3] Tithe and cess rates levied for the parish were paid together, a practice leading, says Coote, to 'the weakest too often (paying) the greatest share.'[4]

Greig, unfortunately, compiled tithe and cess details for six only of the twenty townlands in Baleek manor, but Coolmalish manor is complete with the exception of the single townland of Ballindaragh. Except on the poorer lands (where tithe and cess payments are almost equal) cess normally amounts to something approaching two-thirds of the total rates. Calculating tithe and cess rates paid as a percentage of rent paid, one finds a tendency for the poorer townlands to pay a greater proportionate share. In those townlands valued at under £1 tithe and cess amount to 10.4% of rents; for those over £1 the proportion is 8.8%.

1. See also page 47. Wakefield (*Account of Ireland*, II, 740) referring to the north of Ireland: says 'It is common for a manufacturing farmer who occupies not more than ten acres of land, to let a part of his "take" to a sub-tenant at will, who erects thereon a wretched cabin, and employs one or more looms for the benefit of the landlord . . .' It was not common on the Gosford estate: Greig mentions the occupation of a minority only of the cottiers, but just over half of them he describes as weavers, and presuming that the same proportion applied to those whose work is undefined, this would leave little more than a dozen weaver-cottiers on the whole estate.
2. *Second report from the select committee appointed to inquire into the collection and payment of tithes in Ireland*, Appendix XIV, p. 580, H.C. 1831-2, XXI 594.
3. In Roscommon, for example, tithe was levied on grain, hay, flax, wool, lambs and there was '. . . . a small charge for every married couple, every milch cow and brood mare, but it does not appear to be collected' (*ibid*, p. 611). As regards the level per acre, too, Loughgilly and Mullaghbrack parishes seem to have paid less than other parts of Ireland. See W. Shaw Mason, *A Survey, Valuation, and Census of the Barony of Portnehinch* [then Queen's County now County Laois] *compiled in the year* 1819 (Dublin 1821), Table I where tithe per acre ranged from 8¾d. to 2/4½d. In only one townland on the Gosford estate does the tithe per acre exceed 1/6, while the average lies between 8d. and 1/- per acre.
4. Coote, *County Armagh*, p. 234.

GENERAL REPORT

ON THE MANORS OF

COOLMALISH AND BALEEK,

WITH

HAMILTON'S BAWN, AND ARGONNELL;

PART OF THE PROPERTY

OF THE

RIGHT HON. ARCHIBALD, EARL OF GOSFORD,

IN THE

COUNTY OF ARMAGH;

CONTAINING MINUTE DETAILS OF THEIR CIRCUMSTANCES,

VIZ.:

NAMES OF TENANTS, LESSEES, AND SUB-TENANTS;
CONTENTS, ACREABLE AND GROSS RENT OF EACH HOLDING;
DESCRIPTION OF SOIL, AS TO SURFACE, SUB-SOIL, AND EXPOSURE;
DISTANCE FROM ROADS, MARKETS, TURF-BOGS, MILLS, AND LIME-QUARRIES;
IMPROVEMENTS, ORCHARDS, PLANTATIONS OF FOREST TREES, KIND OF FENCES;
STATE OF DRAINAGE, TILLAGE, BUILDINGS;

LIVE-STOCK, POPULATION, COTTAGERS;
APPARENT CHARACTER OF THE OCCUPIERS, AS TO INDUSTRY;
THEIR RELIGION AND TRADE, BESIDE FARMING;
THE NUMBER OF LOOMS THEY HAVE, OCCUPIED AND UNOCCUPIED;
ACREABLE RATE; ANNUAL AMOUNT OF TITHE; COUNTY AND VESTRY CESS;

WITH OBSERVATIONS ON PROPOSED ARRANGEMENTS, AND THE MEANS OF IMPROVEMENT.

DRAWN UP FROM ACTUAL SURVEYS, &c. BY

WILLIAM GREIG,

Rural Designer, and Surveyor in general,

NOVEMBER, 1818.

BELFAST:

PRINTED BY F. D. FINLAY, 1, CORN-MARKET.
1818.

6

EDITOR'S NOTE

In this printed text the punctuation and spelling (except for proper names) of the original have been modernised and the syntax tidied: wherever a sentence is capable of various interpretations or simply incomprehensible it has been left to the reader's judgement. This rather extensive revision was essential because Greig never revised the text he had dictated to an amanuensis who spelt phonetically, punctuated haphazardly in his own fashion, and faithfully wrote down Greig's grammatical errors. Initially many words were underlined but as Greig's exuberance gave way to a growing disillusion with the project this practice was abandoned: the underlining has been translated into italics. The page numbers of the original manuscript appear in small type in the margin along with Greig's own marginal headings. The running headings he devised for the Report have been adapted with the minimum of alterations to form the running headings in this volume. His rudimentary index has been incorporated into a more comprehensive index.

I PREFATORY REMARKS

William Greig having been employed to make a survey and p. 8 valuation of the Gosford estates in the County of Armagh and to furnish a report etc., of their present circumstances and means of improvement, has lost no time in fulfilling the intended object to the best of his ability. The minuteness and detail with which the whole have been executed, will, it is hoped, account for the length of time which has unavoidably elapsed since the date of the engagement.

The survey and maps which have been accordingly executed exhibit an exact view of the natural features and surface of the grounds, viz. the hills, rocky grounds, lakes, rivers, streams, roads, lanes; arable, meadow and reclaimable lands; bogs, turbaries, plantations, orchards, gardens and every enclosure; the direction of water courses and plough ridges; dwelling and office houses, mills, lime-kilns, Danish raths, etc.; the boundaries of townlands and of the respective holdings held at will, also of those under lease and of the portions held by subtenants.

From the circumstance in many cases of several leases being held by persons of the same name or their descendants—also from the same individuals holding mixed portions of those and of lands at will—was the cause of very considerable trouble and delay. But by frequent recurrence to the ground with the counterparts of such leases the particulars have at length been ascertained.

The numbers in black on the maps refer to the book of contents and valuations in which is specified the quantity of arable, meadow, pasture, spent-bog, turf-bog, water, roads, and waste in each enclosure; with the valuation, description, and quality annexed; also showing the total contents and average value of each holding. Other particulars are explained in the notes annexed to the maps, book of contents, etc.

The mineral formation throughout the estate is in general very uniform. Had it been otherwise it might have been desirable and of sufficient importance to incur the expense of making *sections* of the stratification from an actual series of levels etc., with views of their different aspects. The sections and outlines which are given in a separate appendix to the following reports, are taken from such *eye*-sketches etc., as the more obvious appearances pointed out, and may serve better than written descriptions to illustrate what more particularly relates to the natural arrangement of soil and sub-stratum, as connected with the present inquiry, and to assist in illustrating the utility of draining etc., and some other improvements suggested. The

view which is added to the maps, taken from a favourable
point east of Mowhan Bridge will convey an idea of the general
appearance of the lands at the northern extremity of Baleek
manor.

The General Report has been a work of much greater difficulty and consideration—which is confidently anticipated will
be found proportionally satisfactory and important—for the
remarkable and almost instantaneous change which had in the
meantime taken place in the *value of lands* and the circumstances
of the tenantry, from a sudden fall in the price of produce and
also from the calamitous effects of adverse seasons and contagion, rendered a most particular investigation obviously
necessary, in order to obtain *data* sufficiently correct, not
merely to assist in making a fair and equitable valuation of the
lands but also in devising the most practicable means of
improvement. This could only be effected by going over the
lands repeatedly in every direction for the purpose of making
and recording observations and in order to procure information
at once correct and diffusive. To digest and arrange materials
necessarily so multifidous and to present them in a view at *once*
comprehensive and yet sufficiently minute and extensive has
been a labour little less arduous.

p. 9   A tabular form on a plan in some respects entirely new, after
much study has been adopted as being considered best calculated for this purpose, and the following remarks are given
to illustrate the contents and utility of registering the different
subjects included in the columns thereof.

The classification which has been adopted of circumstances
so different and numerous, may not be the best which might
have been selected but while no important circumstance has
been omitted it is hoped none too insignificant has been
included.

As the report can only be fully understood and appreciated
by a reference to the maps the number of each farm or holding
(as marked in *red* on the maps) is inserted in column first.

In column second the numbers of the fields etc. included in
each farm or holding (as marked in *black* on the maps) are
referred to. The same numbers also refer to the book of contents and valuations.

In column third the tenant's number in the agent's books is
referred to—in order to connect and compare the investigation
of each tenant or farm with the state of their accounts, etc.

In column fourth the number of the lease is likewise referred
to when it may be necessary to recur to the same.

In column fifth is inserted the names of lessees and of the present tenants who are in the occupation.

In column sixth is inserted the names of subtenants of those who do not hold the entire of one lease.

In column seventh it was considered important to show the contents and valuations by former surveys etc.; the total acres, rate per acre, and total acreable rent of each holding.

In column eighth is inserted the quantity held by each subtenant, at what rate per acre, and the total rent paid by them, in order to ascertain the profit rent accruing to the head tenant. And this is the only part of the report which is given with a considerable degree of diffidence, owing to the *artifices* with which profit rents are generally concealed, both by the *head* tenants and their *subtenants:* being frequently exorbitant but paid with difficulty and obtained by ways and means which a proprietor or his agent could not and ought not to attempt, viz. in labour, produce, etc. Although the information in this particular is not of very high importance, where it was not considered correct a blank is left rather than hazard what might mislead.

In column ninth is given the quantity of *turf bog* held by each tenant; rate and rent of the same; in what townland it is situated; distance from the farm; the number of the bog and of the individual lot in that bog, as referring to the maps etc., in the separate surveys of the bogs. Turf bog or turbary whether considered as a source of income to the proprietor or of convenience to the tenant, is a subject of increasing importance and its remoteness or vicinity is to be considered as affecting the value of the lands, in a district generally more or less engaged in the linen manufacture.

In column tenth is given the total acres in each lease and of the portions occupied by subtenants also of each holding at will; the rate per acre; and total rent from the new survey and valuations.

In column eleventh is given the quantity and rent with reference to the number of the bog etc., as above; of the spent or cut out bog held in addition to the lease that its improvement may be promoted or enforced.

In column twelfth is inserted the *tithe* as paid in common being one of the chief taxes which affect the occupation of tillage lands or perhaps, as it ought more properly be considered, a portion of rent. In either view it affects the rent paid to the proprietor. Tithe has been latterly subject in many cases to considerable fluctuation and the rate per acre and annual amount is therefore to be considered as the average of a few years.

In column thirteenth is inserted the *cess* both *county* and p. 10 *vestry,* paid in common, and is also to be considered as affecting the ability of the tenant to pay rent, particularly for lands of a ,poor and inferior quality, for which the acreable rate of cess is frequently as high as for lands of the best quality.

In column fourteenth is inserted the *mills* bound to grind at, the distance from the farm and toll paid; all of which are of importance, as affecting the value of the farm, either as an *item* of rent, being so bound, or the convenience afforded. Where the farms are bound to the manor mills only generally the distance to the nearest is inserted.

In column fifteenth the names of the nearest *lime quarries* and their distance are inserted, as the facility of obtaining this valuable means of improvement is one of the important circumstances which affect lands situated in a district naturally deficient in calcareous matter.

In column sixteenth is inserted the names of *three* of the *principal markets* nearest to each farm, with their respective distances. The vicinity to good markets is a circumstance too important to be omitted, being one of the chief causes of promoting industry and improvement and, of course, materially affecting the value of lands.

In column seventeenth the distance from public roads and what markets or places of *note* they lead to, are inserted as well as the general accommodation of the farms as to the lanes or *by-roads* which connect them with the public or leading roads; for without sufficient accommodation in this respect neither can improvements be easily affected or rendered valuable.

In column eighteenth an *epitome* is given of the circumstance of the *soil* of each farm as to *surface, subsoil,* and *exposure,* as a difference in those more or less considerable frequently exists in the same farm, sometimes in the same field. Nothing farther than the generally prevailing kind or quality can be given, and the arrangements of culturable or surface soil admits of such an endless variety and gradation and have been so differently classed by agriculturists, that it is difficult to adopt suitable designations or to render those always sufficiently explicit by brief explanations. Suffice it to mention that the term *loam* is employed to designate soils which contain such due proportions of *clay, sand, gravel,* etc., as to constitute in a considerable degree a superior quality of soil. And where either of those *three* predominate they are termed *clayey, sandy* or *gravelly loam*, etc. Those which are chiefly composed of *clay* and its varieties and modifications are termed stiff clay, wet or cold clay, gravelly clay, and those approaching to loam are termed clayey loam etc., as the case may warrant.

It has been considered of importance to insert the *general subsoil*, either *earthy* or *rocky strata*, on which the surface or vegetable *soil* immediately rests, as the productiveness of the latter must be much influenced by the *nature* of the *substratum*. Thus a *sandy soil* may sometimes owe its *fertility* to the *power* of the *subsoil* to retain *water* and an *absorbent clayey soil* may occasionally be prevented from being *barren* by the influence of a substratum of *rubble* or *shivery* rock, of gravel or sand. In the present case the terms *good, bad*, and *tolerable* have been employed as the sub-soils seemed respectively adapted for promoting the fertility and improvement of the surface.

The *exposure* has also been added as being of material consequence in estimating the value and capability of lands.

In column nineteenth the improvements in *fencing* and the *state* of *draining* and *tillage* are briefly noticed. Perhaps there are comparatively few instances in which the *epithet good* in its strictest meaning would be correctly applicable, and therefore the terms *good, bad*, and *tolerable* as here applied are to be understood as only applying comparatively to the *present state* of improvement; as it is considered but *ill*-calculated to convey a useful and satisfactory idea of the actual state thereof to compare it with what exists in countries in which the mode of occupancy is different and where *rural* management has attained so high a degree of perfection as to bear little analogy where it is still as it were in its infancy.

In column twentieth is shown the quantity of land *planted* in p. 11 *orchard*, the number of trees and the years planted. As the lands from their retentive *subsoil* etc., are in general not *well* adapted to ensure productive orchards, they are therefore not numerous and any notice relating to them might perhaps have been omitted but from the *clauses* inserted in *former* leases on the estate they seem to have been considered important. Such as still remain or have been subsequently attempted are inserted.

In column twenty-first are inserted the *forest trees* planted by tenants and whether they are registered, because considerable and successful attempts have been made in this branch of improvement by some of the tenants.

In column twenty-second the number and description of *buildings*, the kind of covering (whether slates or thatch), and their state of repair are given as fully as the limits would admit, as an elucidation of these, although thus far imperfect, may lead to a variety of important conclusions as to the industry and merits of the occupiers.

In column twenty-third the number of *looms* occupied and unoccupied are given, because when the loom is occupied in aid of the plough and so frequently to make up its deficiencies, these become important and in many cases their *number* and state of occupation may be taken as a criterion of the opulence and industry of the owners.

In column twenty-fourth the *livestock* is given under the head of cows, other cattle, horses, sheep, and pigs. Although the management of live stock does not form a very prominent feature in the rural economy of the district under consideration, yet it is too important to be omitted as without their *aid* it is impossible to occupy lands, particularly those of an inferior description, with advantage.

In column twenty-fifth the *religion* of the tenants whether Protestant or Catholic is given, not with any view to perpetuate any invidious distinctions but because the subject is interesting from so frequently being taken into account in political calculations and reasoning. Perhaps there are few situations in which there is less difference to be remarked between the industry of the two persuasions when placed in similar circumstances than in this country. Very many instances occur of Catholic occupiers being industrious and consequently comfortable, and there are many instances of Protestant occupiers even with all the advantage of old leases held at very low rents, from their sloth and improvidence very truly disgraceful.

In column twenty-sixth is inserted the trade or employment of the tenants beside farming which it is also of importance to notice.

In column twenty-seventh the *apparent character* of the tenant of each farm as to *industry* etc., is hazarded; in estimating which it must be kept in view that many causes of a more or less temporary nature may tend to retard or promote this. Yet in the generality of cases the condition of farms and families may be taken as a tolerably certain indication of the degree of industry which may be ascribed to the occupiers.

In column twenty-eighth the population of each farm is given in considerable detail because it is considered *most* important that this should be particularly attended to for the reasons urged in the General Remarks (page 262). The *age* of husband and wife are stated, also the total number of children: the number which are males and females with the extreme ages of each sex, that is the youngest and oldest. If these are mostly in childhood they are to be considered as a serious drawback on their parents, but if otherwise they may be considered as aids in assisting their industry and labour. And in order to show in how far these appear to be rendered available, the number who have been learned or who are learning trades and what trade are also inserted. Where the holdings are sufficiently large or otherwise circumstanced so as to require hired servants these are also given, with the *total* population on *each farm*.

In column twenty-ninth the number of cottagers or cottiers is inserted, their occupation and description of holding and rent charged, which is exclusively applicable to such cottiers as hold under occupying tenants. And although they are not immediately connected with the proprietor, yet are not unworthy of attention as a source of emolument and convenience to the tenants or as to the *burthen* which they entail on estates during periods of scarcity and disease.

In column thirtieth reference is given to additional remarks at the end of the tables as some farms and circumstances require a more particular detail than could be included in the brief notices in the columns, particularly as relates to *proposed arrangements* and alterations in their boundaries—particulars of *leases* etc.

The General Observations on the present circumstances of p. 12 the lands and tenantry, which have been considered necessary, refer to the modes of *occupancy* and *tillage*, size of *farms*, population, etc., and a particular inquiry into the effects of recent occurrences as *scarcity*, *contagion*, etc. And from the whole of this extensive review to deduce the practicable means of improvement, which are farther illustrated by an examination of the subject of *rents*, of the arguments for and against an *abatement*, with remarks on relative subjects such as *arrear rent*, *leases*, *encouragements*, *premiums*, etc. With a view to render the foregoing more explicit several of the subjects noticed are more particularly discussed in the Appendix which contains remarks on the *linen* and *cotton manufactures*, *flax mills*, *plantations of forest trees*, *bog-earth composts*, etc., *premiums*, *tabular view of the increase of population*, *designs* for *cottages and farm buildings*, *outlines and sections illustrative of the mineral formation*, *soil*, *drainage*, comparative *elevation* etc., of the lands.

Annexed to the Reporter's observations a blank space has been left in each page in which *additional notices* or future changes may be inserted. In discussing an investigation so

widely extended some degree of complexity was perhaps
unavoidable, particularly amidst the hurried routine of professional labours but this is obviated as much as possible by a
general index, *marginal* notes and frequent reference to the
different pages. And although with the same intention this
Preface has been thus extended to a considerable length,
farther indulgence is solicited in offering additional remarks
which may be more properly introduced here than in any
subsequent part.

In offering a form of *report* etc., in many respects so entirely
new, and of course likely to objections or at least to be received
with diffidence, it may be necessary to state that no arrangements or means of improvement have been recommended
which are not the result of much reflection, at the time carefully
taking into account the *peculiar* circumstances of the *country*
and *tenantry*, both *temporary* and what are to be considered
more permanent, nor of the practicability and utility of which
the Reporter is not decidedly convinced, from much observations and considerable practical knowledge. When he has otherwise hazarded to suggest, it has been with a peradventure, which
should always be attached to whatever has not been submitted
to the convincing test of experiment. Convinced of the vast
distance which often exists between *theory* and *practice* and
knowing how often unforeseen accidents occur to retard or
defeat even well-concerted measures, he has not considered
himself warranted in offering any specious calculations, or the
hopes of any instantaneous advantage. None such can be
effected without considerable risk, and generally with much
temporary embarrassment: such would unavoidably be the
result in Ireland. To ensure and undertake extensive rural
improvements requires much judgment in considering the
subject and choosing the means, where a choice is afforded,
and how they are to be pursued to best advantage in the end;
zeal, patience, and perseverance to prosecute the endeavours,
resolution to wrestle with and despise trouble and difficulty;
temper to bear disappointments, from *man* and *things*. It is
certainly rare to find all these qualities united but they are more
or less indispensable to ensure ultimate success.

It is confidently hoped that recommending attempts without
any or only very inconsiderable outlay and sacrifice of income
will not be found the least safe and practicable method, nor the
least recommendation which the opinions offered may be
found to merit. Should the circumstances of the country be
less desperate than has been represented no inconvenience or
loss can possibly be occasioned by adopting the means recom-

mended, as they are considered necessary and calculated to promote improvement, how prosperous soever the country may be.

In such an investigation as the present it has been considered p. 13 the business of the Reporter and his imperative duty to state facts and circumstances as they are really found to exist, without attempting to conceal what may be painful to know or difficult to remedy. To view evils in their true colours is the best method to ascertain their extent and to devise a remedy. But in painting these in the most impressive manner no exaggeration has been used with a view to confer meretricious importance to the proposals for their removal. To have viewed and reported things otherwise than as they are, he could not have so accurately and forcibly submitted what occurs to him, in reflecting how they ought or may be.

Instead of endeavouring to devise a slow and partial improvement of the present circumstance as the surest road to the greatest ultimate advantages in future, it would have been comparatively easy in the manner of some *reporters* on the improvement of *estates* in *Ireland*, to have enlarged on systems of rural management as pursued in the highly improved districts in Britain and adapted to the *soil* etc. of the Gosford estates, if under a different mode of occupancy. But however plausible and entertaining such an exhibition might be it would have been of trifling utility. His object if more difficult has been made with a different intention and which he trusts will not be altogether unavailing. A wish to avoid being unnecessarily minute and tedious may have induced him to discuss some topics too briefly, and to render his ideas and opinions in some other particulars sufficiently explicit, may have betrayed him into the opposite extreme of prolixity. Those who do not view the important subjects discussed with equal interest might prefer a more superficial investigation. Without a desire to exaggerate the merits of his labours it may not be improper to offer some observations on the superior utility of the documents he has submitted to consideration, and some of the advantages to which it is presumed they may be rendered subservient to promote.

A little reflection will suffice to render it sufficiently obvious that the *ground work of improvement* on which practice may be founded with safety and full effect, in addition to an accurate and minute delineation of the existing state and distribution of the lands with a faithful *estimate* of their *quality* and *value*, ought to consist in a similar detail of such of their circumstances and of the tenantry as do not admit of graphic delineation etc.,

the whole forming a comprehensive and useful subject of study
to the practical improver. Being to him what the *map* of a
country is to a traveller, or a sea *chart* to a navigator—enabling
him in a few hours to set out with advantages respecting the
connections and dependences of the whole estate and its
several parts and occupiers, without which as many days,
weeks, or months could not furnish him with such scientific
assistance. Without some such guide how often do we see
persons of the best intentions engage in arduous undertakings
and embark on the wide ocean of improvement, as it were
without rudder, compass or chart to direct them, depending
on casual or, what is worse, prejudiced or interested information, having no facts or *data* as a standard of practice to rally at.
[They] are liable to be led astray by the plausible schemes of
theorists who know not the difficulties of practice, who, under
the fair semblance of the good office of friendship, or the sometimes more imposing speeches of professional projectors and
speculators, hide or garnish with specious colouring their
own sanguine, selfish, or ignorant opinions. It were perhaps
in most cases better that no change should be attempted than
that they should prove unsuccessful. Agriculture has been not
unfrequently retarded rather than promoted by anticipating
improvements for which the circumstances and ideas of the
tenantry and country were not ripe. And as all rural operations
must be more or less public, observers will not fail to criticise.
If experiments and proposed improvement prove abortive the
ardour of the improver will be liable to be damped and his
tenants discontented. But by pursuing a more cautious though
plainer and less attractive line of conduct he will gain confidence
in himself and that of his people and thus the pleasure as well
as the advantages of improvement will be secured, embarrassment, loss and discomfiture avoided.

p. 14   It is not merely in arranging an estate previous to the granting
of new leases etc., that the form of details here produced are
necessary and may be useful. But they will be found important
at all times as an accurate and interesting *register* of incidents
and occurrences respecting the estate, and of each farm and
occupier, which may require to be remembered; and with
reference to the other books and documents which may pertain
to the several particulars, thus forming at *one view* a complete
abstract of the history and present state of every farm, together
with the particulars of attention which each may require to
promote, enforce and ascertain this improvement.

The trouble and expense of procuring details or reports of
this kind or of renewing them is inconsiderable compared with

their many uses and advantages which cannot be more obvious in theory than they have and will be found fully established in practice. On returning to an estate after an absence of one or more years it will be generally found that by consulting a register of this sort and through its means making systematic enquiries respecting changes and incidents which have in the meantime occurred on the several farms, a proprietor or agent will in this summary way become better acquainted not only with the general interests but with the more ordinary business of the estate than an active manager who has been constantly resident upon it without such a remembrancer.

To the proprietor or his confidential friend or man of business who may go over his estate occasionally such an intelligent companion will be found essentially serviceable. He cannot so profitably direct nor so safely suggest advice as by consulting so distinct and useful an oracle.

The utility of such a report etc., while a proprietor is absent from his estate—if he can in one sense be said to be so with such a faithful mirror in his possession—must be too obvious to require illustrations.

There is no other method by which the progress of an estate and of the individual farms can be so readily and accurately ascertained at any time. For otherwise it must be difficult to know whether they be advancing or be retrograde when under lease or when other circumstances of the country tend to the progressive increase of the value of lands. If that value is in any degree stationary the rental will be an inadequate criterion. And when the rapid increase of the price of produce ensures a proportional rise in the rent at the end of the term of agreement, the property may be notwithstanding becoming gradually less valuable from the injury which such rise may occasion, in order for a time to meet excessive rents or to make up for the necessities or indolence of the tenants, which is a case not merely conjectural but proved in numerous instances in Ireland. But by having a correct and accurate register of their circumstances a comparison with these at any future period will at once show in the most satisfactory manner any difference which may exist and for this purpose alone would be most important. Few documents would better merit a place in the archives of a family: none of which would be of greater assistance to a future historian in tracing the progress of domestic and rural improvements, or afford more accurate data for the local, fiscal or statistical reasonings and calculations of political economists and legislators.

In attempting to develop what may be termed the good government of an estate, the utility of such reviews and of their stated recurrences must be further evident. To view and record the state of cultivation, the stock, the condition of buildings, fences and drainage, and the growing timber and other circumstances belonging to each farm, and hence to ascertain the degree of merit of their respective occupiers in order that each may be dealt with according to his deserts. For the tenant who is found improving his lands, keeping his buildings and fences in substantial repair, and nursing up or protecting valuable timber on his farm, is surely deserving of praise, if not of reward: while he who perseveres to do the contrary ought to be admonished, discountenanced, punished, or removed.

In short after much reflection, the observations of many years and favourable means of experience, the Reporter has been led to consider investigations of this kind or somewhat p. 15 similar to be a *sine qua non* to ensure the certain improvement and consequently the stable or increased value of estates, to the full extent of which their situation and circumstances may render practicable. But he is not so weak or so vain as to suppose that any arguments he can urge will be sufficient to lead to its general adoption or to convince those of its importance who either have not bestowed the same degree of attention on this subject or have not enjoyed the same opportunities of knowing and appreciating its many advantages, aware how frequently rural affairs and the improvement and management of landed estates are undervalued and neglected; attention and money being too often bestowed in preference on pursuits infinitely less important but to some more attractive and engaging. Many are losing hundreds (perhaps thousands) annually by neglect, mistaken frugality, or considering the management and improvement of their estates as a matter of little difficulty or of secondary importance. Such will consider the details and executive arrangements here recommended as unavailing, extravagant or unnecessary troublesome, it never having sufficiently occurred to their reflection that by incurring inconsiderable expense in the first instance, and a moderate portion of attention in future, they may not only secure or add to their own income but promote the comfort of their tenantry. And it is presumed that there are scarce any instances in which the advantages to be derived will not ultimately if not immediately be amply returned. In the present instance in addition to the benefits and return which it is most anxiously hoped will accrue, the investigation has already led to the discovery or appropriation of as much to the rental from the mere article of spent or cut-out bog alone, as will more than repay any expense incurred in this respect.

While the effects of the *war* and other circumstances of the empire at large tended to the rapid increase in the value of lands a sedulous attention to their improvement, as being less urgent, might have been considered less necessary and the neglect more pardonable. But should a like concurrence of events as presently exist continue to operate in the same manner and when in fact a remarkable change has already taken place, increased attention must be bestowed to obviate any defalcation, much more to ensure an augmentation in future. And it is gratifying to hail the dawn of a more general attention and better system of estate management than what in most cases existing heretofore, a circumstance which will be productive of permanent and essential benefits to landlords and tenants.

Landed proprietors may be said to have above most other classes a two-fold motive to induce them to attend to the improvement of their estates: namely, to augment their personal income, to promote the happiness of their tenantry and to increase the prosperity of their country. Hence beside the profits issuing to a landed proprietor there are other considerations which he ought not and cannot overlook without loss to himself and in so far he differs essentially from the possessor of ordinary property, being not merely in possession of the lands but as it were of their inhabitants also. For where an estate is under lease, tenants are, as it were, firmly rooted like the trees which grow upon it. And even where tenants are at will (particularly in Ireland), in general so great is their attachment to their wonted residence and connections that it is considered little less than banishment to be forced from them, a prejudice engendered in the human heart which ought and may be cherished with advantage. The owner of an extent of territory has infinitely more control over its inhabitants than the government itself: he may not only banish or render the inhabitants uncomfortable, depopulate the country; or, he may increase the number and happiness of its population as to his pleasure may seem meet by changing the inhabitants, or forwarding a change in their morals and manners, as from vice to virtue, from sloth and despondence to industry, or the reverse; thus having it in his power to render the little world of which he is the centre, as well as himself. miserable or happy according to the principles of management pursued. Than which there can be no more powerful inducements for men of fortune to bend their minds cheerfully to their territorial concerns con- p. 16 vinced that, having power and authority over persons as well as

things, the elevated situation they occupy has therefore a
dignity and a peculiar set of duties which cannot be neglected
or contemned without moral responsibility and a natural loss of
emolument and respectability. He is one of society's most
valuable members provided he attends to the judicious conduct
of his affairs. But if on the contrary he is regardless of this
dignity and the duties incident to his station, living but to spend
or squander the income derived from estates and their tenantry,
unconcerned in their welfare or inattentive to the character of
those to whose oversight they are entrusted, he sinks proportionately low in moral worth and public advantage, becoming
at once an enemy to himself, his family, tenantry, and to the
community.

But although it is an essential part of the duty of a man of
fortune to be sufficiently acquainted with his affairs, it does not
follow that he should be absorbed in them to the neglect of his
other important duties as a superior member of society. It
would be unpardonable in the commanding officer of a regiment
to be ignorant of the discipline and number of his men but he
does not act as drill serjeant or call the muster: he has subordinate officers to convey his commands and others to execute
them, but he ought at the same time to be well acquainted with
military affairs. The facility with which a man of fortune may
become acquainted with so much of the nature of business and
the facts and circumstances of his property as are requisite to
the direction of his own affairs will be comparatively less than
the attention and fatigue which are necessary to qualify him to
command a regiment. A month given up in the first instance
to the drill, and afterwards a parade once a week, and at length
a review once a year, make up the quantum of time and attention
that are requisite and due from the proprietor of a tenanted
estate to his own interest, his family's welfare and the public
good.

The ignorance and obstinacy of tenants are frequently
powerful discouragements to attentions of this kind. But a
judicious and encouraging line of conduct steadily pursued will
always gain the attention and regard of members, for motives
of self interest will generally sooner or later induce the more
obdurate to adopt and acquiesce in arrangements which from
experience tend to promote their comfort or advantage.

Could a large proportion of human pursuits and enjoyments
be fairly suspended in the impartial balance of common sense
or of their own genuine interest, which are never perhaps at
variance, many would be grievously mortified to find the
objects of their most ardent wishes and ambition of so unsub-

stantial a kind. If the arguments urged tend to prove that the
attention of proprietors to their estates is no less an object of
duty and of advantage to themselves, families, tenantry, and
their country, and that a moderate share of time and attention
is sufficient to achieve the end and to overcome difficulties and
discouragements it is equally certain that scarce any other
pursuit can be named which holds out the same inducements,
as affording such a rational and permanent source of pleasure
and gratification, as may be reasonably looked for in any
station or employment on earth: exercise to the most valuable
faculties of the mind, devising and anticipating, health in the
execution, self-approbation in the retrospect, and tending to
extend the sum of human felicity through so many channels of
whose extent no limits can be assigned, as that of encouragement and employment for the proper improvement and
embellishment of their hereditary patrimony, of which others
as well as himself are to reap the pleasure and benefit. A source
of pleasure is afforded in this truly noble though too much
neglected field of pleasure, of usefulness, influence and future
profit such as very few ever fully avail themselves of. It has been
wisely said that he who plants a single oak confers a favour on
generations not yet in existence. But how much more valuable
and meritorious are the efforts of that individual who bestows
such lasting obligations on the present as well as on future
generations, promotes the education, morals and consequently
industry and improvements of his lands and tenantry! His p. 17
feelings must be truly enviable, who in the possession of the
means has also the desire and resolution and perseverance to
bestow such lasting obligations on the present and the future.
It is impossible to imagine an earthly paradise in which the
heart can so rationally luxuriate for this application of wealth
and influence will above all others afford the greatest recom-
pense on the pillow of reflection.

   Nor let it be supposed that the exertion and endeavour of an
individual proprietor is inadequate to effect not merely the
improvement of his own estate but even of the general agriculture of the country, for many instances to the contrary are on
record. Take the following which merits particular attention
from the incidents connected with it bearing so strict an analogy
to the present circumstances and situation of Ireland: in Scotland towards the close of the seventeenth century the direful
calamities which preceded the domestic wars which the memor-
able Revolution (in 1688) occasioned. A succession of bad
seasons and the mortal contagion which followed heightened
their calamities. The facts rest on undoubted evidence that at

that time innumerable farms remained unoccupied, so extensive and dreadful had been the mortality and destruction, proprietors having to search after tenants who were able to stock and cultivate the ground, with almost the same assiduity that has been since displayed by tenants who are out of possession. Indeed the condition of Scotland at that time called for the utmost exertion of all its proprietors: agriculture was in the most languid and feeble state, occupiers of ground were generally destitute of capital stock for carrying on improvement, and few of them were qualified for introducing these with success even had the means been within their reach. Trade and manufactures were then in their infancy and money was such a scarce article that the circulating medium of the two Edinburgh banks, whose capital was below £200,000, was quite sufficient for every useful purpose. Under these circumstances the situation of Scottish agriculture at the period here adverted to, may be easily ascertained. In short the rents were low and the people poor and imperfectly fed, badly clothed and often without employment. If the picture is brought forward and made to include the present period, it will at once be discovered that a complete alteration has taken place in all their circumstances. Though the Low Country districts of Scotland are at this day equally improved and as well cultivated as any of the English counties, yet their state was formerly very different. Lord Kames, an adept in the history of mankind and a sound and practical agriculturist, declares in the most pointed terms that the tenantry in Scotland at the end of the seventeenth and beginning of the eighteenth century were so benumbed with oppression or poverty that the most able instructor in husbandry would have made nothing of them. The celebrated Fletcher of Saltoun, a contemporary historian, describes their situation as truly deplorable. In fact many farms remained unoccupied. Even tenants rarely accepted of leases: at least they were shy and unwilling to accept them for any considerable number of years. Hence improvement of every kind was totally neglected and the general poverty of the tenantry necessarily occasioned landed property to be of little value because while rents were trifling they were also ill paid which of course placed many proprietors in something like a state of mendicity.

The spirit and extent of improvement which subsequently followed this depressed state of the country has been with propriety in the first instance chiefly ascribed to the encouragement and attention of a few individual proprietors, among whom John Cockburn Esqr, heritable proprietor of the lands of Orniston in the county of Haddington, appears to have been the first mover. He was a person of considerable fortune and influence, representing that county in parliament from 1707 till 1741 and for many years a Lord of the Admiralty. He succeeded to the estate of Orniston in 1714 when, as has been remarked, the state of agriculture was so imperfectly understood and the condition of the tenantry so reduced that improvements could not be expected from them unless the strongest encouragement was previously held out. This was done by p. 18 Mr. Cockburn even in his father's lifetime. One Robert Wright, a tenant on Orniston, had early shown an uncommon spirit to enter into Mr. Cockburn's views, being supposed to be among the first farmers in Scotland who enclosed by ditches and hedges and planted hedgerow trees on his own proper charge. He was wisely singled out for favours and in 1718 received a lease of a farm (still well known) on very favourable terms. The original deed is still extant, witnessed by two gentlemen invited on this occasion by Mr. Cockburn in order that his example might animate them with the like liberal and patriotic desire to improve the agriculture of their respective properties, and we accordingly find that in 1723 a society was formed for the improvement of agriculture, and joined by many of the principal nobility and gentlemen of Scotland, not merely as a matter of course, but for useful and active purposes. And for more than twenty years they continued their unwearied labours, greatly to their own credit and to the public benefit, and proofs exist that they were of immense furtherance to the improvement of the country. Beside Mr. Cockburn, Mr. Maxwell of Arkland, Mr. Hope of Rankeiller, the Dukes of Hamilton and Athole, Lords Stair, Hopeton and Islay, were the most indefatigable. In fact the seed was at that time sown and though the soil in which it was deposited was of an unpromising and sterile nature, yet an abundant crop was in due time reaped and in this way the foundation of Scottish improvement was laid. Let it be also remembered that both knowledge and capital were the undoubted result of the ameliorated system then introduced: Mr. Cockburn laid the first stone, his brethren in different quarters assisted in raising the fabric, though perhaps their aid was not in any instance so munificent.

The success which accompanied it served, however, to convince almost all the landholders of Scotland that the surest way of extending improvements was to give the tenantry an interest in their accomplishments. Hence the bond of connection between proprietors and tenants in Scotland is founded upon more liberal principles than perhaps prevail in almost any other country, and the results are manifest.

In corroboration of the above, a briefer notice may be added of the case of Mr. Coke of Holkburn in the County of Suffolk whose long and honourable career, unwearied perseverance and princely countenance he confers on agriculture with an ample fortune which his own efforts in promoting the improvements of his estate has tended to augment and secure, are too well known to require further mention in this place. With a soil far inferior to many other parts of England, the system of tillage very imperfect and inconsiderable, rents paid with difficulty, by his encouragement has raised its value to an almost incredible degree above what it formerly was, from the remarkable improvements in the system of tillage which has also had an extensive effect in promoting the improvement of other districts. And such was the persevering merit of this illustrious agriculturist that for the period of eleven years he could not induce so much as one of his tenants to adopt the alteration he proposed and the advantage of which he so clearly exhibited.

The catalogue might be easily extended in noticing the numbers whose individual exertions and example have been productive of incalculable benefit. Mr. Dawson of Roxburgh-shire, the bold innovator in the more recent improvements of tillage in Scotland which have been introduced within the last fifty years, still lives to enjoy the gratification and profits of his labours. The very remarkable and almost instantaneous change effected in the remote and until within the last twenty years barren and unprofitable country of Caithness, has been brought about chiefly through the instrumentality of Sir John Sinclair who, if the same public honours and rewards were bestowed upon those who excel in the arts of preserving life equal to what is on those who pursue the arts of destruction, would have trophies raised to his memory and territories p. 19 conferred on his posterity. But it is to be hoped he will have less perishable monuments in the veneration, respect and gratitude of his country.

It may no doubt be urged against this that the circumstances of the country and subsequent events powerfully promoted improvements and doubtless this is true. But there are many more circumstances in the present condition of Ireland to encourage than discourage similar efforts.

It is at the same time gratifying to remark that many proofs still remain that at a former period a Sir Archibald Acheson was the means of effecting considerable improvements on the Gosford estates, considering the circumstances of the period in which his laudable and patriotic attentions were bestowed.

The attention and encouragement he then afforded is still gratefully remembered by many of the old tenants, their descendants and successors; and the trees and plantation throughout the property which are now ripe for the hatchet were planted by him or under his directions and influence.

It is not only now become necessary to replant and replace those which shall be now cut down but it is confidently asserted that at no former period was attention to estates in Ireland more imperatively called for than at present. This is not given as a hasty conclusion, although to be fully convinced of it may require an attentive study of the domestic history of Ireland, more particularly for the last twenty or ten years, with an intimate knowledge of the circumstances of the country and its inhabitants during that time.

To recite all the proofs which might be adduced in support of this fact would much exceed the limits and intention of the present discussion: so much as more immediately regards it will appear in the sequel. Those who have attentively traced the progress of improvement in Ireland compared with the same in the sister kingdoms, cannot have failed to remark that while in the latter the systems of agriculture have been advancing with astonishing rapidity from one step of perfection to another, *rents* have *risen* in proportion, and the means, comforts and opulence of the occupying tenants have been increasing in nearly the same ratio, in Ireland although much improvement has in several respects taken place, with some increase of industry and a prodigious rise in the value of land, the systems of agriculture among the mere occupying tenants (for the improvements in demesnes and gentlemen farming generally but erroneously brought forward, ought not to be taken into account in this case) are almost too inconsiderable to be traced. Their comforts and opulence have not augmented in any considerable degree. On the contrary, it is most certain that in a great proportion of instances they are much lessened, even before the late calamitous events occurred; the increase of rents having been often made up from increased privations and from excessive cropping, and other expedients which have only served to entail and produce future loss and inconvenience. It is no less grievous than dangerous to insist on disagreeable facts of this kind. Those who do not feel or who have not opportunities of knowing them, those who have an interest in concealing them, and many more who because they wish it were otherwise are not only slow to give credit but often ready to deny their existence and almost to charge those who have the hardihood to assert them with ignorance, unnecessary fears, discontent, if not dissatisfaction with the present order of things. But if each state and stage of society has its advantages and blessings, it has also always at the same time evils incident to it which require to be guarded against and remedied. Those which are beyond human control may be safely and contentedly left to the settled order of moral causes in the wise arrangements of providence, but those which originated in the faults or neglect and are within the scope of man's efforts, demand and ought to receive attention.

It may appear to involve a contradiction of terms to further assert that amidst the progress of Ireland's prosperity evils have originated which, unless timely and judiciously checked and obviated, will ultimately, and some of them ere long, tend to much personal loss and inconvenience and to public calamities. Among other subjects which will be noticed hereafter, the rapid progress of population and the consequent minute sub-division of farms with all the necessary results of superabundant labour are in alarming progress and have in numerous instances advanced so far as almost to deprive the proprietor of the soil p. 20 [of] any or at least an inconsiderable and precarious return, and to the occupiers' misery and distress which beggars description. And although this solitary evil in addition to others may not yet have advanced so far in many districts as to excite just alarm it would be difficult to point out an extensive estate at least in Ulster where the same causes are not operating with the same tendency (see table in Appendix page 313*). Many seem to consider the fertility and valuable natural qualities of Ireland as sufficient to ensure and secure prosperity. That it is possessed of these in a remarkable degree is most certain and, but for this, under the same system of management it would long since have ceased to reward the imperfect labour of the occupiers. But although goodness of soil and climate will do much, they have been proved to be quite inadequate of themselves to effect much. Labour judiciously applied and steadily pursued will render an inferior soil far more productive than a much richer soil neglected or imperfectly managed: part of Flanders and Scotland are proofs in point. Many others, reflecting the progress which Ireland has made under a fortunate concurrence of circumstances, take it for granted that the same effects will continue although the former causes are removed or altered, and either consider innovations or attempts to encourage and promote improvement unnecessary or dangerous.

It is said that great as well as little minds are too apt to complain of the miseries of the present but we also learn from

*Page 220 of this book.

experience that prosperity often leads on to adversity, as the highest health is often the forerunner of the worst diseases, the chills of ague, or the flames of calenture. Nations and branches of labour like individuals are liable to meet with reversions: history tells they have often occurred and that when least expected. What has happened may take place again. That a sad reverse has taken place in these countries is no longer matter of dispute: whether temporary or otherwise time must tell. Provision should be made for the worst and if a favourable change again takes place no great loss can be incurred, but if it should be delayed temporary expedients and patience will not avail. Numbers have at length been convinced who not long since derided the idea that any remedies were necessary to relieve the embarrassed state of the agricultural interest, and every day makes converts of those who have been still more slow to believe facts which personal experience at length press to conviction, or to doubts which ultimately tend to the same.

That something is requisite to be done is now generally admitted but a great variety of opinions is abroad not only as to the extent and nature of the evil but of the remedies which ought to be applied. Medicines of efficacy are seldom palatable and therefore rejected. Cordials in the shape of palliatives are more agreeable and it is much to be feared that they are too frequently resorted to, without operating to remove if not to confirm the disorder. The surest line of conduct is to probe to the bottom, to declare the truth however distressing or disagreeable, for it is only by so doing that any effectual good or rational cure can be discovered.

Our well-intending fathers taught us to believe that one source of national riches consisted in a numerous population, almost without limit. Bitter experience has made us reluctantly see that the relations of society are now widely different. A superabundant population now, however, assail the stability of personal security and national peace and prosperity in Great Britain, and have long been injurious to the genuine interest of landed proprietors in Ireland but less adverted to because this same cause for a time tended to increase the demand for land, and consequently an increase of rent. And the effect is still evident, having now nearly attained its ultimate effect in this respect and already begun to seriously occasion its* falling beyond the fair and equitable value, at least in the actual receipts. Nominal rentals will be long kept up but time will bring it also into its true estimation. Reason and common

---

*Referring to rent.

sense might have always shown that any provision made for
p. 21   such redundant population would be of very partial effect, and
has in fact proved to increase the evil. But to treat more particularly of the means which have hitherto been generally
employed and considered sufficient to promote improvement
in Ireland—which is in fact the only feasible prospect now to
ensure stationary or increased rents punctually paid [but] will
be long indeed in producing the anticipated results—societies
and demesne farms are here more particularly alluded to.

In some districts where the tenantry are more than commonly
opulent and intelligent, farming societies have been instituted
with very essential advantage nor can any be found without
some beneficial tendency. But it must be evident that when
none but proprietors and gentlemen farmers can afford to
avail themselves of this aid millions may be expended and a
century elapse before it can have any material tendency to
better the condition or improve the tillage of the indigent and
ignorant. And there are hundreds of demesne farms managed
under the best systems by skilful persons from Britain and have
been so for half a century without in the smallest tending to
improve the tenants surrounding them and that not from any
obstinacy on their part but a total inability from want of means,
and the too remarkable difference between *rude* and first rate
fashionable system of management.

Farming has much to recommend it as a rational amusement
as it occupies time agreeably, leads to the study and acquisition
of various arts and sciences, gives to a country life a social
interest in the seasons as well as in the general prosperity of
neighbours and dependants, and on reflection furnishes a
heartfelt satisfaction of which field sports of any description
are certainly not susceptible. For they not only often fail to
afford the promised enjoyment, are generally more or less
dangerous, and often lead to serious accidents, and to the
reflecting mind leave behind them a recollection which if not
stifled would lead to self-reproach of cruelty to unoffending
creatures. Besides, these pursuits are often the bane of social
intercourse, giving rise to inveterate jealousies and animosities
which descend a malediction to future generations. On the
contrary, farming pursuits tend to very different results in a
desire to emulate successful attempts which hold out to the
exertions of friends and competitors substantial rewards.

When a nobleman or gentleman chooses to prefer the
laudable expenditures of his income or endeavours to improve
his residence, he at least deserves merit for his intentions, and

in rendering the expenditure contributory to the comforts and prosperity of his dependants. When the tame or impressive features of nature are corrected or set off by the well-directed and superb embellishments of art, the eye and the mind are gratified by the union, and the gratification will be extended where the neatness of cottages afford evidence of the comforts diffused by such costly efforts. But unless this is further extended to the country all around, the pleasure must cease. But rural improvements are seductive and alluring whether applied to permanent or temporary improvement, and unless steadily pursued with rigid persevering economy, the consequence as well as the example may be injurious. If vanity be not the chief promoter it may supply a reward to the proprietor from the admiration which his fortune, taste and industry may command. But his own tenants will look to more substantial profits, for neither will the influence of fashionable theoretical agriculturist nor the admiration of competent judges be sufficient to induce experiments of an expensive kind to be adopted until they are justified by repeated trials on a contracted scale and found to be practically useful. It would perhaps be difficult to adduce one instance in Ireland where the improvements and system of tillage carried on by a proprietor on the demesne lands have been followed by his tenants solely dependent on farming.

The system of estate management as pursued in Scotland and England so far as relate to the promoting improvements among the tenantry, is inapplicable to Ireland from the remarkable difference in the circumstances which exist in the respective countries. In the former, lands have become more valuable by p. 22 enlarging the size of farms, from the investment of large capitals, and from agriculture being pursued on scientific principles, under the direction of intelligent persons, whose education entitles them to think and whose confidence in well-tried experiments teaches them to act for themselves. In Ireland the subdivision of lands and other causes have tended to a temporary increase in their value, which increased privations have hitherto in most cases enabled them to pay, but from the want of capital and skill, agriculture has undergone little improvement; bigoted to the errors of their predecessors and from ignorance and prejudice fearful and disinclined to abandon the ever-beaten path of mismanagement. Immense sums are frequently embarked in the improvement of estates by their proprietors in Britain, but it would be little less than ruinous to venture on such attempts in Ireland. A country must be far advanced in rural science before this can be done safely and with effect, because skill is essential to derive due advantage from such expenditure. Nor is the sudden consolidation of small farms either practicable or advisable for were the lands to be thrown into profitable large farms independent of the capital requisite to be in the possession of the occupier, a great expenditure on the part of the proprietor would necessarily be incurred in building etc., to the manifest reduction of his income in the first instance. And indeed, on many of the inferior description of lands the same rents as are at present paid or at least any rise could not be expected from such a change of occupancy, not to mention the distressing calamities which would attend families dispossessed of their homes and holdings, pangs that could not be assuaged by any prospective benefit capable of being shown to the present occupiers or future promise of advantage to their posterity. In fact, to attempt a change of this kind, such a scene of distress if not rebellion which Ireland, notwithstanding the manifold commotions it has experienced, never before endured.

The formidable nature of all these obstacles have induced many to consider the task of removing or of even retarding them too Herculean to invite an attempt, and sit down in hopeless despondence in which they sometimes find consolation, from the injudicious attempts which have been made therefor proving abortive and often injurious. It may be many of the evils are already too long in operation to admit of an entire, at least of a speedy removal, but they may be retarded. The obstacles being all of a moral nature may be therefore difficult and as such they certainly admit of removal or remedy. Difficulties are said only to stimulate great minds to overcome them but the steady and patient perseverance of common minds are adequate and it is the business of true science to work wonders with the materials which the given situation affords. The ignorance and sloth of the Irish character in common life are commonly urged as insurmountable obstacles. These certainly present obstacles but there is also much in the composition of this singular character which may furnish apt materials to bring into profitable action. The longer the remedy is of being applied, the greater will be the difficulty, and the rapidity with which the evil is increasing is nearly in due proportion to the increase of population, and everyone knows the astonishing rapidity of its advances in Ireland. It is not perhaps asserting too much to say that had unremitting assiduity been directed for the same length of time to promote the substantial and permanent improvement of estates and the melioration of the tenantry which has been bestowed to acquire parliamentary influences, the advantages would have been long ere now incalculable.

Partial and gradual improvement on the existing systems pursued in the country as meeting the ideas and means of the occupiers will be found the only and certainly the safest means of obtaining any ultimate change for the better. How encouragement may be afforded to effect this is a principal intention in many of the observations which are afforded in the present p. 23 volume, and meant to point out the necessity and importance of which has occasioned the above remarks to be this far extended. For it is far from being intended to insinuate that the distinguished personage for whose use and information the present labours have been prosecuted is not fully impressed and influenced by the sentiments here attempted to be enforced. But amidst the diversified avocation and pursuits of life, not a few of the most important are liable to be overlooked and subjects which have been long peculiar to the mind may occasionally lose much of their importance from that familiarity, and may therefore require to be placed in a new and feasible light. And besides, friends real and pretended will both advise and criticise. It is therefore necessary that the subject should be treated off in all its extended bearings as fully as the limits will admit. The *arrangements* and *means of improvement* proposed, will, it is presumed, be found very generally applicable, but in many respects they are only fully adapted to the present peculiar circumstances of the districts to which they are intended to apply, and before pronouncing any hasty opinion of their merits and practicability it is further hoped those circumstances will be attentively considered.

Indeed, had the Reporter not been firmly persuaded that both the proprietor of the estates now under consideration, and his present active and intelligent agent were most anxious to avail themselves of the facts collected and detailed, and of such hints as have been suggested so far as may appear to them worthy of being adopted in practice, he would have spared himself much thought and labour. The confidence which has been already reposed in him and the readiness with which such of his opinions as have been already submitted to their consideration, have been adopted, while it merits and has received his unfeigned gratitude, has been a powerful stimulus to his subsequent exertions and anxiety to promote the best interests of so attentive employers. If this anxiety may have in some instances in these pages insensibly led to the adoption of a style apparently too dictatorial for the cautious reserve with which it may be supposed properly belongs to him to advise, or if in departing from the usual commonplace details of business he may have evinced an excess of familiarity or officiousness, being done with the best intentions, he begs it may be received and pardoned in the spirit of indulgence. He trusts he has too sacred a regard for the interest of his employers and too much respect to his own professional credit to hazard any recommendation of the utility of which he is not fully satisfied in his own mind, and where arguments are not supported by facts he does not expect or require approval. It must also be sufficiently obvious that he can have no sinister object in their being adopted and any mortification he might feel in their rejection would be more than counterbalanced in what he considers as being the conscientious discharge of a paramount duty. Could he flatter himself that his labour would in any wise contribute to promote the advancement of arts which have long formed the study and business of his life, and which he is warranted in considering amongst the most important which can occupy attention, and to have had it in his power to suggest any thing which in practice might be found calculated to augment the value of the Gosford estates would be considered among the most gratifying incidents of his life.

The idea that we are co-operating in forwarding so important an object is the most satisfactory and honourable we can entertain of our employments. And it is a still more gratifying consideration when we can discern the tendency and efficacy of our occupation and endeavours; when they lead to important and beneficial results, how inconsiderable soever the share of reward and applause conferred on us may be, compared with what is derived from other avocations far less important, but more generally noticed because directed to please instead of instruct and benefit (and this even when we are destined like the subordinate labourers in the erection of a complicated building to the most obscure situation and the meanest drudgery), it must confer some degree of elevation or at least of consolation that we are even in the humblest station and the most trifling degree contributing to the completion of so splendid an edifice, as that of promoting individual happiness, and national prosperity on a permanent basis.

It has been well observed that advice ought not to be contemned on account of the situation of those by whom it is given. p. 24 The roughest fisherman is a useful pilot when a gallant vessel is near the breakers, the meanest shepherd may be a sure guide over a pathless heath, and the admonition which is given in well-meant kindness should not be despised, even were it tendered with a frankness which may resemble a want of courtesy.

Sensible of the defects which remain after the best endeavours, but not without a considerable degree of confidence in the correctness of the facts and of the utility of the means of improvement, and arrangements recommended and suggested in the following report, it is humbly and respectfully submitted to the EARL OF GOSFORD.

*   *   *   *

Opinion of Sir John Sinclair, Bart., on the importance and utility of detailed reports etc.

Since writing the foregoing, William Greig has met with the following remarks in a work by Sir John Sinclair, recently published, which he considers worth extracting into this place as a further confirmation by so competent a judge of the utility of such reports as he has the honour at this time of drawing up on the Gosford estates:

'On estates of great extent it has in general been found expedient by the proprietors to nominate proper persons to assist them in their management etc. It is necessary that such should be thoroughly acquainted with all the affairs of the estate or estates by means of proper documents such as *reports* of the boundaries, state and number of the farms, nature of the leases and covenants in them, number of *livestock* etc., the state of *culture, rotations* adopted etc., with such plans of improvement as alterations in the *size* of *farms*, and the boundaries; also *detailed information* in proper documents, regarding the state of the *woods, drainage, roads, bridges*, etc.

'Those *reports* properly arranged and inserted in books accompanied by sufficient references, would give a view of an estate capable of bringing every important particular under the eye of the proprietor or of his agents at a *single glance*, whilst at the same time a curious and interesting account of a great portion of a country might be preserved for future information.

'In conducting the business of such a property every legal question, and every demand of a *tenant*, or of a *neighbour*, every question about roads, bridges, etc. will be thus brought under the consideration of intelligent men, capable of deciding and judging impartially on the points that come before them.

'Under the superintendence of such the affairs of a great property would be as well conducted as on the best-managed small moderate sized estates, while the duties of the proprietor

would principally be to carry those exercises of true benevol-
p. 25 ence into effect, and would consist in granting those marks of
approbation and reward which when bestowed by the proprietor
himself, are the most likely to produce the most beneficial
consequences.' (*Code of Agriculture*, page 59).

[*Pages 26 to 231 contain the Tabular Reports on the Manors
of Baleek and Coolmalish with the townlands of Hamilton's
Bawn and Ardgonnell, to each of which is appended a section
entitled Additional Remarks. Specimen pages of these Tabular
Reports and the Additional Remarks for the townland of Carrickgallogly are reproduced following the text of the Report. The map
of the townland drawn by William Greig and John Hill for this
survey has been included.*]

II GENERAL OBSERVATIONS

p. 232 Having in the preceding pages detailed the particular circumstances of the individual farms and their occupiers, it becomes
necessary in the next place to offer such additional observations
as relate to those circumstances and the means of improvement
in general.

Circumstances   The Gosford estates in this county, from being spread over a
affecting the soil considerable extent of country differing considerably in point
and climate   of elevation and other circumstances affecting the *soil* and
climate, contain lands very dissimilar in *quality* and *value*,
Mineral   notwithstanding the great uniformity of the mineral formation
formation   on which they rest, viz. an argillaceous schist etc., forming an
irregular and hilly surface which extends with little interruption
across the whole island from the Atlantic to the Irish Channel,
through the counties of Leitrim, Cavan, Monaghan, Armagh
and Down. This extensive tract is bounded on the north by
newer formations of limestone, freestone, etc., forming fertile
valleys from Belturbet at the head of Lough Erne to Lough
Neagh, including the vicinities of Clones, Monaghan, Armagh,
Middletown, etc., the lands of Argonnell being situated near
the latter on a *limestone strata*.

Basalt   The great *basalt formation* of the North of Ireland which
occupies so considerable a portion of the counties of Londonderry and Antrim, extends into the county of Armagh, by
Lurgan etc., and its most southern extremity appears to be the
valley of the river passing Mowhan and separating the manors
of Coolmalish and Baleek. The whole of the lower part of the
former is, therefore, more or less connected with the basalt

formation and the public road leading from Mullaghbrack church through Markethill to Mowhan, from where it enters this manor may be taken as the boundary betwixt the *basalt* and *schist* formations as its deviations do not extend far on either side of that road. Indeed, the line of separation is obvious and the junction of *two formations*, so dissimilar in some respects, occasions some peculiarities of soil and substratum. The remainder or *upper* part of Coolmalish manor above the road just mentioned, with the whole of Baleek manor and lands of Hamilton's Bawn is solely connected with the *argillaceous schist formation*, all which is more particularly detailed in the sections etc., already noticed in the Prefatory Remarks (page 8) and need not be repeated here. Argillaceous schist

Although the soil *incumbent* on *basalt* and *argillaceous* rocks, particularly those on the latter, are *naturally deficient in calcareous matter* and the *subsoil* in general *cold and retentive*, yet the lands so circumstanced in other respects possess considerable *capabilities* and *local* accommodations and facilities for improvement.

Of the climate it may be remarked any difference or peculiarities which exist are owing to the difference in elevation etc.; a considerable ridge of country ascends from the near vicinity of the city of Armagh towards the *mountain group* of which *Slieve Gullion* is the summit. The manors of Baleek and Coolmalish occupy the *lower skirt* of the east and north-east declivities of this ridge and the lands of Hamilton's Bawn are situated still lower, the whole being thereby in a great measure protected from the violent western storms, and this is more particularly the case from the great hang or slope with which the general surface *declines* towards those points of the horizon. Difference of climate

The elevation and variety of sloped surface most happily tends in a considerable degree to *counteract* the retentive nature of the soil and subsoil by allowing *free escape* for the surface water and facilitates the drainage of the subsoil.

The whole of the townland of Baleek, unless a small portion of the lower division, and the upper and middle divisions of Corromannon possess a climature incredibly inferior to other parts of the estate immediately adjoining. The soil over this tract is in general wet and boggy and the subsoil retentive and cold from the vicinity to Slieve Gullion and the great extent of wet bog and unreclaimed land which intervenes, occasioning *early* and long continued *frosts*, frequent *fogs* during spring and autumn, excessive moisture and of course such a degree of *chillness* as is unfavourable to the regular and certain ripening Of Baleek p. 233 Effects of the climate of corn or to the production of sweet and nutritious herbage. More effectual *drainage* would essentially tend to *improve* both *soil* and *climate*.

Turf bog

The abundance of turf bog, however, immediately at hand gives a preference in this particular above lands of a superior soil and better situation where this article of prime necessity is daily becoming scarcer.

Second gradation of soil and climate

Thus Corromannon, Carrickollogly, Carrickananey, and Drumhoney may be considered as the next gradation of *soil* and *situation* possessing a *climate* greatly *preferable* to the townlands of Baleek and upper and middle Corromannon, in a much greater degree than the mere difference in point of elevation would indicate, probably owing to the general rockiness of the soil in this quarter, which may retard the operations of tillage but, as there is in general scarce any *retentive clay substratum* but only rubble or an *under-layer of rock* on which the surface soil immediately rests, is thereby rendered kindly, though light, producing good herbage, to which the degree of moisture which prevails is rather a favourable circumstance in this respect than otherwise.

Third gradation of soil and climate

The entire remainder of the lands except part of Upper Brackly in Coolmalish Manor, which is high and moory, *improve in quality*, *etc*., nearly in proportion as they are found to *occupy* the *higher* or *lower* parts of the *general hang* of the country in which they are situated and are interspersed with partial tracts of *alluvial* and gravelly lands such as at Mowhan, which are or may be rendered highly productive.

Surface hilly, which facilitates draining, irrigation, etc

The entire surface consists of *ridges* and *hills* of greater or lesser extent which give rise to numerous springs or are separated and interspersed by hollows branching off into narrow lateral *glens* or *vales* through most of which streams and rivulets pass, furnishing a supply of excellent water for domestic purposes, driving mills, steeping flax, etc., and might in many cases be employed for the purposes of *irrigation* for which the general slope of the country would afford additional facility, as well as for the *drainage* which ought to be a precursory improvement in all cases *on retentive soils*, in order to check the growth of coarse *aquatic plants* which would otherwise luxuriate in place of *better herbage*.

Crops, etc

Unless part of the uplands already noticed where *inferior* crops of *oats* and *potatoes* are chiefly produced, the entire lands are *well adapted* for the production of *oats*, excellent *flax*, etc., and a very considerable portion, if properly improved, for the production of *wheat*, *barley* and *clover*, the two former of which are pretty successfully cultivated by some of the more substantial and industrious of the tenants.

Soils formed from *argillaceous strata* are, in general, more favourable to vegetation than those from any other of the same *class* of *rocks*. The *disadvantages* which clay *soils* labour under, are being precarious and difficult to work, requiring great industry and care as well as a considerable portion of knowledge and experience in the mode of managing them, so as to keep them in good condition. But they are *susceptible* of essential *improvement* when their natural toughness and other defects are got the better of: they always yield the heaviest and most abundant crops and are therefore usually termed *strong* in opposition to sandy soils which from retaining manure for a shorter time are called *hungry*. *Clay soils* to be productive must, however, be kept as *full* of *manure* as possible, for a poor worn out and exhausted clay is the most ungrateful of all soils, being in that state hardly capable of repaying the expense of labour and of all others the most difficult to renew. Hence they cannot be so easily occupied by the poor class of tenants when in this state, as lands which although they may not be ultimately so productive, if improved are laboured with less difficulty. But clay soils from containing (as it is thought) a greater quantity and variety of materials capable of being rendered *sources of fertility* when properly *mixed* with the addition of a due portion of *lime* and other manures, and from the usual *depth* of a *substratum* of similar materials the depth of the *vegetable soil* may be increased and at the same time renewed by bringing up a part of this *substratum* to be acted upon by the weather or mixed in composts and so fitted for the purpose of a *fresh* vegetable mould.

Argillaceous soils, their disadvantages

advantages and

management

p. 234

Clay soils may be deepened and renewed

Under common cultivation they are better adapted for the production of *oats* than any *other grain* and wherever moderately improved they are calculated to produce excellent *flax*, sometimes even where inferior crops of oats could only be obtained, the retentive subsoil being supposed more effectually to resist the drought of *June and July* than an absorbent subsoil. When not too elevated and sufficiently improved, lands of a clayey nature are better adapted for *wheat* than for *barley:* the latter being a more tender grain, requires land of a warmer quality. In proportion as clay land is improved it approaches the nature of *loam*, to which all clay soils are more or less all capable of being changed by *manure* and *tillage* and are thereby better adapted for *barley* and *green crops* to which as already remarked, nothing more powerfully contributes than the liberal and judicious application of lime.

Particularly fit for flax

May be changed to loam

8

Importance of draining before applying lime, etc

But in order to allow *lime* to operate with full effects, or indeed in most cases to render it of any avail and even to *prevent* its being *injurious*, sufficient *draining* is most indispensable. While water is allowed to remain on the surface or stagnate in the *substratum*, fermentation will be prevented or retarded and the *lime* be apt to *cake* the land, instead of rendering the land more *friable*. When *clay soils* are flat as in many parts of Britain and Flanders, the expense of rendering them dry is frequently enormous viz. from £4 to £8 per English acre, but from the general inequality of the surface on the Gosford estates, already remarked, such great expenditure is not necessary, for with the exception of the flat *alluvial* lands at Mowhan, etc., which possess a *gravelly substratum*, there is scarce an acre throughout the whole which does not enjoy a sufficient fall for drainage.

Difficulty of draining flat clay soils

Gravelly clay

From the lands being in general hilly and the *soil* in consequence *shallow* over a large extent, from the *shivery* nature of the *rock*, in many places at no great distance underneath, and by the constant attrition of the plough etc., fragments are thereby detached which become so intimately mixed with the surface soil as to render *gravelly clay* an *appropriate* designation, the heavier descriptions of clay being restricted to the hollows and lower declivities etc.

Peculiar soil at the junction of the basaltic and schist strata

It was before observed (in page 232) that the lower part of Coolmalish Manor was more or less connected with the *basaltic formation. Basalt* containing a *less* portion of *alumine* but more of *oxide* of *iron*, lime, etc., naturally forms a more *friable* soil than *schist* and from the less compact arrangement of the rock the *substratum* is also less retentive. Yet in the present case, whether from the near vicinity of the *schist formation* or some peculiar effect of their junction, some considerable portions are found having their surface spread over with a clay, excessively tough and tenacious, much more so than any which occurs on the *schist*. They are interspersed among the more fertile tracts, differing from the latter in having fragments of flint and the soil being of a darker *chocolate blue colour*; perhaps *lime* alone applied to this kind of soil is less efficacious in rendering it more friable than when employed in composts, in particular with *peat* or *bog mould*, as further noticed (in page 283).

The local circumstances which have a powerful tendency to *increase the value* of lands and facilitate improvement are *good roads* leading to *markets*, a supply of *fuel, lime*, etc. With regard to roads and markets the Gosford estates are favourably circumstanced.

An inspection of the general maps will show how well the lands are intersected and accommodated by leading lines of road which in general are in tolerable repair. The by-roads or lanes are also numerous and although some of them are in bad repair this defect may be remedied as suggested (in page 261). In arranging the farms due attention has been paid to provide lanes or for the trespass to and from the farms more remote from the existing roads and lanes.

Roads

p. 235

Lanes and trespass

The markets are good and numerous. In looking over the column of the Tabular Report in which are inserted the names and distances to the three principal markets nearest to the individual farms, it will be seen that none of them are to be considered as very remote. Newry is one of the best corn and butter markets in Ulster, Armagh one of the best linen markets, and Tanderagee has also a good linen and butter market and flax purchased in it is reckoned the best from Ireland when exported to Britain. Markethill and Newtownhamilton are good yarn and meal markets, etc. Argonnell has Monaghan (besides Armagh), a good general inland market, and Middleton immediately adjoining has a yarn market, etc.

Good markets

Fuel is a most important article, particularly where so considerable an additional supply is wanted beyond the usual consumption for mere domestic purposes, viz. for burning of lime and carrying on the linen manufacture. The abundance and vicinity of excellent turf bog in the upper part of Baleek Manor in some degree makes up for the deficiency of *soil* and *situation*, rendering the lands there proportionally valuable and although the turbaries in the lower parts of this manor are few and nearly exhausted, the tenantry obtain a supply from Sir Walter Synnot's mountains and although those are at a considerable distance, yet afford a material convenience.

A supply of fuel important

Abundant in the upper part of Baleek Manor

In Coolmalish Manor and lands of Hamilton's Bawn the turbaries are almost entirely exhausted (unless a few portions bound in old leases) and a very serious inconvenience is now sustained therein for the want of fuel, more particularly since they have been refused turf bog in the bogs belonging to the Earl of Charlemont which is said now to be the case. If any arrangement could be made to obtain a supply elsewhere, or if by *opening a new road or roads* as would bring a supply within such a distance as would be of utility in this respect, it would be of most essential advantage in extending the *burning of lime* and the consequent improvements, which are now from the *want of fuel* almost totally suspended by most of the tenants on this part of the property although they are much nearer lime quarries than the tenants on Baleek manor, but the latter

Become scarce in Coolmalish, etc

Fuel wanted for burning lime

burn considerable quantities from having a better supply of fuel. The Reporter regrets that he has not been able to ascertain any feasible means of remedying the defect here alluded to; the subject is introduced in order to excite further enquiry.

Scarcity of food occasioning the injury of meadows The scarcity of fuel is, however, in the meantime the occasion of *material injury of a permanent* kind to valuable tracts of *meadow ground* formed on *boggy subsoils* which are cut up in the most wasteful and ruinous manner for the purpose of obtaining a scanty supply of *mud or baked turf* which ought speedily to be put a stop to, more particularly as this depredation is chiefly committed on lands held under old leases at a cheap rate. The individual cases have been already noticed in the additional remarks to the tables; see farm no.   page   , no.   , page   .*

CIRCUMSTANCES OF THE TENANTRY ETC.

Importance of attending to the tenantry In devising the most judicious and practicable means of improvement of which the lands are susceptible, it is not only necessary to advert to their *natural* and *local* circumstance but also to the *present* circumstances of the *tenantry*. The *latter* is perhaps of *primary* importance as being most difficult to change or amend and on their *industry, skill, and capital* the success of any attempt to promote improvements will chiefly depend, and according to the facilities or obstacles which they afford such attempts ought to be regulated.

Effects of the introduction of colonists into Ulster From the county of Armagh having been *colonised* at the *plantation of Ulster* from *Scotland* and *England* (it is said chiefly from the latter) a spirit and neatness of improvement was then introduced which has continued to give a decided preference to this county in the respect of superior industry etc., above many other parts of this province.

p. 236
Probable origin of the prevailing characteristics of the tenantry Perhaps it is not altogether fanciful to observe that the great body of the tenantry in this country seem to possess a portion of the different *characteristics* of the *three* several *lineages* from which they have originated, or from the influence of their miscellaneous residence and intercourse, circumstances which have had greater effect on the domestic affairs of the people than those who have only taken superficial views have imagined. Thus the tenantry in this county may be said to partake of the *vivacity* of the *Celt* and a portion of the *sloth* and the *cunning*

*Greig did not fill in the blanks.

which a deficiency of industry generally renders necessary, with much of the *sullen reserve* but at the same time of the persevering *industry* of the *Scoto-Saxon* and evidently some degree of the attention to *neatness* and *comfort* in houses and gardens etc., so congenial to the mongrel Anglo. From this curious moral amalgamation of materials so dissimilar but most of them in a degree excellent or at least useful, a subject is the result, more aptly fitted for industry and capable of being more readily and effectually encouraged and excited to profitable exertion and progressive improvement than the generality of the tenantry in most of the other districts in this country. From *infancy* accustomed to engage in the *linen manufacture*, they are   Early industry through life less habitually slothful than where the former period is spent in herding cattle or in vicious idleness, and from being early accustomed to marketing and traffic they acquire a habit of discerning and jealously watching their own real or imagined interests and of pursuing them with considerable activity and ardour. There must obviously be numerous *partial* exceptions to this general *character* but it is   Beneficial results only from the operation of such causes that we can satisfactorily account for the fact that with all the disadvantages of *small farms*, the *division* of attention and means which *manufacture* requires where carried on in connection with *agriculture*, the mode of tillage in this county is in some respects superior to that which is followed in many of the more agricultural counties possessing a superior soil. Hence *higher rents* have been *better paid* in the county of *Armagh*, soil etc. considered, than almost any other part of Ireland and the tenantry at the same time infinitely better *educated*, *clothed*, *fed* and *lodged*. Indeed the rents in many cases may be said to have hitherto been in a great measure paid for accommodation, the proceeds of manufacture enabling them to do so, and the *pressure of population* stimulating to great exertions in order to provide food, circumstances which, if not allowed to operate so far as to produce a very opposite effect (which, however, is much to be feared and guarded against), may be taken due advantage of by affording *further scope* and encouragement to this spirit of *industry*, so valuable but so difficult to *excite* and *preserve* in many parts of Ireland.

When *cheapness of living* and *domestic economy* are accom-   Cheap-living panied with *industry*, these operate favourably for enabling tenants to pay higher rents, than where *mere cheapness of living* exists. It is the difference in the expense of feeding farm servants, as well as the superior management, in many parts of Scotland, which enable the tenants there to pay more than *treble* the rents paid for similar lands in England (poor rates considered). While men are *contented with potatoes* and a scanty supply of the commonest clothing, it is impossible that improvements can be forwarded. Fortunately, in the county of Armagh along with plain living there is much to admire in the

Economy *domestic management* of the tenantry, viz. by the use of *rosin for light*, the household manufacture of *coloured* and *stamped linens* etc. etc. they are enabled to enlarge their means and comforts greatly and a desire to appear as well dressed as possible, especially on Sundays, at markets, etc., is a powerful excitement of the industry of *both sexes*.

General industry   Although too many instances of sloth and want of industry are to be found, yet the *tenantry* on the Gosford estates (compared with many others) are *generally industrious*. Many of them are so in an eminent degree and *making such improvements* as can be reasonably expected from their *skill* and *capital*: both of which, particularly the *former*, will, it is hoped, admit of essential amendment and to which the *latter* would,

Present   in due time, follow, as a necessary consequence. But it ought to
circumstances be kept in view that the present situation of the tenantry is not
different from to be taken as a *correct criterion* of what it *lately was* and may
the former in some measure again be.

It would much exceed the limited nature of this report to take an extensive retrospect of the *causes* which *influenced* the

p. 237   *former* remarkable degree of *agricultural prosperity* and all of
Former prosperity those which have occasioned the present depression. The leading facts are well known, viz. the remarkable degree of prosperity which Ireland enjoyed for some ten, twenty, or thirty years, notwithstanding the distractions of civil commotions which must have interrupted industry for a time and were attended with a waste of *georgical property*. This prosperity may be *dated* from the close of the colonial war in 1782. During this disastrous conflict Ireland had participated in the embarrassment and obstructed commerce of Britain and suffered much from a stop being put to the *demand for linen* etc., in America. It was not until a few years after the peace which happily followed, that the restoration of public credit and augmented circulation occasioned a *rise* on the purchase and *rent of lands* from the great depression they had experienced. To the beginning of the war with France in 1793 Ireland seems to have enjoyed considerable prosperity, during which the *linen trade* perhaps attained its *acme*: at least the *gains* of the *weavers* have seldom been subsequently exceeded.

Effects of the   During the long period of warfare in which Britain was
late war engaged until the final overthrow of Bonaparte, the *brisker*

demands for *provisions* etc., and a variety of concurrent events tending to produce the same beneficial effects, Ireland experienced an unequalled prosperity. Although this was progressive it was more remarkably obvious from the effects of the *blockade* which the *Berlin decree* (in 1807) occasioned, for in consequence of her peculiar situation she derived important benefits from this unprecedented measure although it was certainly injurious to other members of the empire. In ordinary times her *agricultural* produce and *manufactures* were more or less exposed to the *competition* of *rival* articles imported into the British markets, but through the operations of the *blockade*, Ireland exchanged *competition* for *monopoly*, for by contracting the *usual supply* of that market, both the *exports* and *imports* of the *poorer* country were increased and *raised* the value of *Irish produce*, both of which effects took place in a remarkable degree.

Particularly from the blockade

Competition exchanged for monopoly

An attentive examination of the official documents connected with the trade of Ireland which cannot *mislead*, develops many singular and at the same time highly important *facts* which lead to deductions intimately connected with the present investigation, viz. that although the Irish had increased their imports at least as rapidly as their exports, the commercial balance in their favour was before the conclusion of the late war *eight times* greater than it was twenty years before. From 1802 to 1806 the exports of Ireland increased only by *one* million and from 1808 to 1810 by *three* millions so that the rate of increase appears then from the effects of the *blockade* etc., to have been *six times* more *rapid*, an acceleration which can only be supposed to have taken place from the concurring influence of a *temporary monopoly*.

Proofs and illustrations

About the year 1800 the value of one cwt. of *flax* was exactly equal to the value of one cwt. of *sugar*: in 1810 the price of the former had *doubled* whilst that of the latter had diminished by *one-half*, so that the Irish farmer had it in his power to consume a *quadruple quantity* of this sort of colonial produce without increasing his own exertions. And it was further notorious that in many other striking instances the state of the English market had been after the general interruption of commerce particularly propitious to Irish industry, for the *rise* of *value* on the total amount of *exports* from *Ireland* during 1807 and 1808 was no less than nineteen per cent, and that the whole sum of *exports* from *Great Britain* during the same interval, experienced a *depression* of price about three per cent, *facts* which are quite decisive and the inference obvious, viz. that while tenants in Ireland were enabled to pay an *increase* of *rent*

Remarkable facts

Occurrences which were peculiarly favourable to Irish industry

proportionate to the augumented *price* of *produce*, they were
at the same time enabled, from the reduced price of British
manufactures etc., to *increase* their *comforts* and consumption
of *imported necessaries*. And this is further proved from the
official details of the enormous increase which accordingly
took place in the amount of imported articles, chiefly consumed
by the *poor* and *middle classes* of society in Ireland. And whilst
the importation of this kind of manufactures from Great
Britain far exceeded all former experience, it would be easy from
p. 238 the same *authentic documents* to enumerate various instances
in which there was a simultaneous increase took place in the
import of *raw materials* for the purpose of being employed in
fabrics of a coarse texture. All of which show that the comforts
of the people improved greatly, accompanied with increased
industry, but still not in the same proportion which some
persons had supposed from an examination of the same
documents just mentioned.

Difference between those holding old leases and those paying modern rents

For numerous tenants enjoyed old and favourable leases:
the exorbitant price of produce enabled such to *extend* their
comforts or to realise considerable *sums* of *money*. But the
tenants who *paid* the *war price* of *lands* required the *war price*
of *produce* to pay rents. The latter had not this kind of expenditure or accumulation so much in their power and any extra
indulgence in articles of dress etc., or any sums they were able
to realise, were frequently owing to voluntary privations in
other respects, for it is a fact that at no time were bacon
and butter, etc., chief articles of luxury not merely to the

Importance of attending to this

poor but to the great body of the occupiers of the soil, *less*
sparingly *used* than when they were *most abundant* and could
obtain excessive prices in the market. This may at first view
appear a trivial circumstance but it is worth attending to,
since an erroneous estimate has been often entertained of
the former clear gains of tenants in general, without taking
into account how differently those who held *old leases* and
those who paid *modern rents* [were circumstanced], or have
given rise to equally *erroneous* opinions of their *present ability*
to *pay high rents* by foregoing their former indulgences. But
were this opinion correct the ultimate good policy of such
conduct is very questionable, since man will not toil cheerfully
for bread alone; he must enjoy some portion of comfort
because without the desire to gratify some fresh *real* or
imaginary want he will cease to be industrious in an eminent
degree for mere subsistence. The fact is that, although there
was evidently an improvement in the comforts of every class
of the tenantry, especially in articles of dress etc., long before

the commencement of the *present depression*, the *subsistence* of the generality had been and still is *progressively getting poorer. Buttermilk* has actually become a *luxury* to thousands, for as industry and *improvements* in *tillage*, particularly the *latter*, did not *keep pace* with the progressive *rise* of *rent* and taxes, privations therefore became necessary to make up the deficiency, and with the constant *sub-division* of *farms* among the younger branches of families (even where held under cheap leases) and the wants of their increasing numbers, the effect of augmented wealth was in such cases less obvious. It is only those who enjoy favourable opportunities of knowing the domestic affairs of the rural population in Ireland, who can correctly ascertain and appreciate their real situations: that pride of which perhaps fortunately the generality of tenants in Ulster are more or less possessed, leads to considerable *outside show*, not always so much to gratify vanity as to appear as *substantial* as *possible*.

Improvements have not been progressive with the rise of rents

It has been matter of wonder to many intelligent persons on *both sides* of the Irish Channel that the *products* of *tillage* in *Ireland* increased with such *rapidity* while the *exports* of her pasture products remained undiminished and when at the same time from the rapid increase of population, growing opulence of the towns, residence of so many troops etc., daily tended to augment the internal consumption, and all this without any remarkable improvement in the *systems* of *tillage* and occupation; but it admits of easy solution.

but the export of produce increased

For while no extraordinary inducements existed to produce an *extra* quantity of *grain* etc., the natural *fertility* of the *soil* was adequate without any or much artificial stimulus, but when the *rapid advance* of *prices* was attended with a proportional *advance* of *rent* more exertion on the part of the tenantry became necessary. Lands long under pasture were broken up and *limings* etc., were called in aid to *assist the fertility* of those long under the plough, and immense *tracts* of *unreclaimed* lands were in the same way brought into productive cultivation. But it seems to have *escaped notice* that although the effects of all this was beneficial in the *first instance*, yet from being unaccompanied with *any improved system of tillage* or adequate *rotations* of *crops*, the effects *are now* become infinitely *less* beneficial and in addition to other occurrences tend to render the occupiers of *uplands* or what are provincially termed *mountain lands*, unable to pay rents as formerly.

Causes which enabled this to be done

and were

needless of tillage

beneficial in the first instance

p. 239

For it is a well known *effect* of *liming*, burning, etc., to bring into action and to render the natural materials of the given

Effects of liming etc

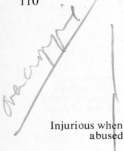

soil more productive. The *ruinous systems*, so generally pursued in Ireland, of *excessive cropping* while the land will yield anything worth reaping, and the *extra* means employed only served to extend the same system of *exhausting* without end. The value put upon such modes of enriching was chiefly estimated in proportion to the additional number of successive crops of corn which they enabled the occupiers to obtain, the consequence of which has been that the natural *staple fertility* of the soil in numerous instances has been materially injured. Hence those farmers who cannot clearly discern the true cause are surprised to find that on repeating the same process of *liming* etc., the effects are in some cases not perceptible as before, in most infinitely *less considerable*, and this opinion is still more consonant to facts when applied to the present state of most arable lands in *upland situations*. Many of them before the inducement to reclaim them or produce effects of this kind, were considered too barren for tillage, possessing a thin and infertile soil, but from being covered with a sward composed of the decayed vegetable growth of ages, when this coarse organised matter was decomposed and otherwise rendered fertile by the application of *lime, ashes, etc.*, a succession of good or tolerable crops was the result. But as this *fresh* excitement tended to bring *every* particle of fertility into action the process of exhaustion was continued while the lands afforded any; and when again thrown into pasture, the herbage has been after many years rest inferior to its former natural state, and in many cases from being brought by such an injudicious system to an *inert state*, scanty arable crops can only now be obtained.

Hence the *abuse* of *lime* has originated and occasioned the prepossessions which have become prevalent against its importance in some districts. From a conviction of the importance of adverting to this circumstance, the Reporter has been induced to notice thus at large, and of the correctness of which he flatters himself few have had better or more extensive opportunity on this property as on others, not only with a view to point out this *one effect* of the *war prices* but also the necessity of endeavouring to *introduce* a *better system* of management, calculated to ensure the full benefits which the judicious application of *lime* on *clayey* soils is capable of affording, instead of the *injurious results* from its *abuse*.

While circumstances *occasioned* a continued *rise* of *rents* almost beyond the most sanguine expectation of proprietors, much attention or control over the conduct of tenants as to the mode of their occupation etc., as being apparently less urgent,

Injurious when abused

and

in what manner

Importance of attending to this

and of introducing a better system

Former neglect of this accounted for

seems to have been too generally neglected. It is not therefore surprising, that in the course of *temporary* or extraordinary prosperity, *evils* of a *permanent* nature should have in the meantime originated or been overlooked, such as the effects of the increasing population occasioning the ruinous sub-division of lands etc., as will be adverted in the course of this discussion.

Having noticed the effects of *war prices*, a more painful although no less necessary task remains, to describe the situation of the tenantry under the gloomy and adverse periods which subsequently clouded the sunshine of *peace*.

Enquiry into the effects of the peace

Up to the moment of the remarkable and almost instantaneous change in the political relations of Europe, all, particularly the agricultural classes, seem to have been as it were intoxicated with prosperity. Although the *temporary causes* which occasioned this prosperity were then as obvious as now, yet it was hazardous to hint that any change was likely to occur which might retard so rapid a progress, that when the *causes* which *shut* the *continental ports against* Britain were removed Ireland could no longer enjoy the *peculiar* advantage of *monopoly*: when the sister country could again obtain the usual supplies, then the prices of agricultural produce must necessarily fall to their former average rates.

What is wished is easy and insensibly believed, and the same dislike to inquiry when of an unpleasant nature, has been and is still too generally indulged, and to which much of the present embarrassment of the *agricultural interest* is attributable. It is an injurious weakness in so important a concern as the means of income and comfort of the tenantry, not to view matters in their real colours, however dark and disagreeable the picture: a temper of self delusion, or of palliation, is the worst possible to remedy any evil which may exist or to effect any real permanent good. The Reporter has, therefore, at the risk of being thought tedious or querulous, endeavoured to represent the whole truth according to the best of his judgement, convinced that, should his opinion be more despondent than others may be willing to admit, yet no injurious results can follow from adopting the remedies he has suggested. On the contrary, in any case they will be found calculated, he humbly trusts, to produce much real permanent advantage. Under this impression and a conviction of the candour of his present distinguished employer, he does so with a considerable degree of confidence that his labours will not be altogether unavailing.

ought to be candidly examined

p. 240

As the rent of lands in Ireland, from the pressure of population and other causes in many instances, increased in a more rapid progression than the industry or at least the improved

Arrears began to accumulate before the conclusion of the war

tillage of the tenantry, considerable arrears of rent had begun
to accumulate *even before the conclusion of the war*. That they
have since accumulated beyond all precedent is not surprising,
considering the variety and magnitude of the occurrences
which have taken place. Perhaps the state of payments in rentals,
where the rents are not exorbitant, may be taken as a criterion
of a country's prosperity or the contrary. Their present state
in Ireland is sufficient to contradict all that is urged against the
real situation of the agricultural classes.

First shock to agricultural prosperity

The extensive and long continued warfare on the continent
had laid waste some of the fairest portions of the globe and so
deranged industry that the most luxuriant soils no longer
furnished the necessary supplies for the numerous armies. A
very considerable portion of the produce of Ireland was sent
direct for our armies in the Peninsula etc., and the *first shock*
which affected the *agricultural prosperity* of this country was a
stop being put to this demand after Bonaparte's removal to
Elba and the consequent restoration of commercial intercourse.

The importation of foreign grain increased the embarrassment

Grain from other parts of the continent (from France etc.,
where agriculture had also flourished, as being seldom the
immediate seat of the war she was engaged in) was poured
from thence to the British ports, the effects of which were most
ruinous to Ireland from this glut of the market. The difficulty
of procuring an adequate supply for Britain and her depend-
encies had rendered all former restrictions on the importation
of corn nugatory and in the midst of rejoicings and pacific
arrangements it was forgotten to provide against the importation of foreign grain; and from an abundant crop and lower
rent and taxes, the continental farmers were able to undersell
those of our country where the cost of farming is much greater
and where the crop during the same season was rather deficient.
When the loud complaints of the *agricultural interest* at length
engaged the attention of the legislature, a bill was passed with
a view to protect this interest but during the interval and
pending the discussion immense quantities were assiduously
collected which for a long time after kept the price of home
produce very low.

which the renewal of war tended to prolong

A long continued tempest seldom subsides at once into a
steady calm and a state of war so singular and extended could
not be expected to be at once finally ended. The state of France
etc., and other circumstances occasioned anticipations of a
further continuance of the conflict which were justified by the
re-appearance of the ex-emperor at the head of his former
legions. It was but reasonable to expect that the *renewal of war*
would be followed by the *former high price* of produce. War,

however, did not continue so long as to affect the latter in any remarkable degree but on the contrary, was productive of much embarrassment, for had there been *no further expectation* or renewal of the war a more equitable understanding would most likely have sooner taken place betwixt *landlords* and *tenants* to the mutual benefit of both. But landlords were of course afraid to reduce the nominal rate of rents without being more fully assured that in so doing they ran no risk of for- p. 241
feiting any future advantage than they could be from the and to increase
unsettled state of affairs; and with the recollection of the arrears
remarkable and unlooked-for changes they had so lately witnessed, and which were calculated to put all prior calcula- tions at defiance, and from the influence of an habitual associa- tion of ideas, few imagined that peace, come when it would, could not fail to be big with blessings to all. During this period of uncertainty and distrust *heavy arrears* accumulated unless where the tenants had saved and were induced to disburse any of their former gains or where their stock etc., was immediately brought to sale, and although many cruel instances of this occurred the advantages have been seldom adequate to the subsequent loss from the *ruin of the tenants* or, where they were removed, the indigence of those placed in their stead. Fortun- ately no such conduct has injured the Gosford Estates; timely abatement of rents, where necessary, has proved the most beneficial method by encouraging the tenants to persevere, [and] has more generally enabled them to pay rents, while those who have been treated otherwise have been dispirited from making improvements or exerting themselves to liquidate rent for arrears.

Thus after enjoying remarkable advantages from the *war* of Further augmented
unequalled high prices for produce, the tenantry in Ireland by adverse seasons
have not merely had to sustain the effects of a great and rapid and contagion
fall in those prices but also when struggling under the dis- advantages this change occasioned, the inflictions of providence were superadded to much previous adversity by the *failure of crops from two adverse seasons*, attended by *contagion* and calamities unparalleled in the memory of any person alive.

The summer of 1816 proved remarkably wet and the crops 1816
were found so deficient in quantity and quality as to be quite unequal for the support of the tenantry in all the *upland* Ruinous effect of
situation and over a considerable portion of all retentive soils. wet summer
The scarcity of wholesome provender and the want of human subsistence obliged many to slaughter or sell the whole or greater part of their *livestock*, and the numbers disposed of in this way for very trifling sums—frequently for little more than

the price of the hides—were quite incredible, being little better than carrion, the wetness of this season having prevented their thriving: the *flesh was quite unfit* to be cured for *winter use* but afforded a temporary assistance. Winter came on without the usual *supply of fuel* which the *wet season* also prevented being saved or drawn out of the bogs. Nor were these ruinous and distressing effects confined to the year 1816 for the spring of 1817 found many who had struggled through the preceding year, with their supply of food quite exhausted and obliged to dispose of the remainder of their livestock and other articles in order to purchase *seed-corn and potatoes* for subsistence for the summer. The *delay* which attended the *importation* of *seed-corn* into Ireland occasioned considerable inconvenience as the season was far advanced before it came, and what reached Newry was said to be so *coarse*, and of so *damaged a quality*, that little of this was purchased for sowing. The humane and laudable grant of *seed-corn and potatoes* by the Earl of Gosford was highly seasonable, as very little of the crop of 1816 could be spared or was fit for seed, or indeed fit *for food* unless of an unhealthy quality. On the *upper part* of the estates the potatoes were so bad and infertile as to be actually without buds, from the defective quality of the seed and from the effects of the preceding *wet season* on grounds even of a good quality and well-improved, and more particularly on boggy and inferior soils. The crop of 1817 was in many situations little better than that of 1816: *much in Baleek was never cut* and if cut never carried from the land being unfit for almost any purpose; and the want of food during the summer of 1817 prevented the poorer classes from cutting or saving turf for the winter of 1817-18. Those *two melancholy winters* fortunately proved open for the want of fuel would have been more dreadful. As it was the distress was very great and led to the destruction of *hedges*, *trees* and even household articles. In short the distress was truly enormous in extent and degree and it would be endless to detail the sufferings sustained and the miserable and even disgusting substitutes for food to which many were driven, sufficient to produce horror as well as pity were they recited. *Pollard or fine bran*, purchased at the flour mills in the County of Louth at 1s. per stone and this even often obtained with difficulty, both from the want of money and a limited supply of this article, furnished a large share of the food, for subsistence it could scarce be called, of say eight families out of ten for nearly two years over a large extent of country, either mixed with meal or potatoes (at that time generally wet and sour) boiled with milk, even eaten alone, or with the leaves of

Calamities of the winter

continued, in 1817

Want of seed corn etc

Winter of 1817-18

p. 242

Great distress, substitutes for food

nettles, wild mustard and other common *weeds* which could in any degree be made palatable. Many were found possessed of several cows, who, rather than part with them, submitted to this kind of subsistence. But it is unnecessary to continue the shocking minutiae of this subject.

The want of proper clothing, joined to the want of fuel already mentioned, was an evil of first rate magnitude for from the termination of the war the difficulty of paying rent etc., had tended to lessen the usual stock and the difficulty of obtaining food was too pressing to spare much for raiment, particularly while an unprecedented *stagnation* of every branch of *trade and manufacture* also marked the gloomy years of 1816 and 1817; the *prices of yarn and linen* were then exceeding low. The hand of benevolence was certainly interposed to alleviate the distress but where so many required aid, contributions could avail little and very many possessed of an honest pride could not stoop to receive any assistance in the shape of alms. Starvation was by such persons considered preferable, a prevailing spirit in this part of the country which speaks much in their favour.

Want of clothes and other aggravations of calamity

Thus persons who in ordinary times had been able to maintain themselves and families in tolerable comfort, were abandoned not only to hunger and cold and their results, debility, etc., but to that heart-breaking depression of spirits which is doubtless more *deleterious* to the health and the functions of the human frame than *inclement* seasons or any ordinary morbid causes of a mere physical description, [and] rendered wretchedness scarcely susceptible of additional aggravation. It is not then at all wonderful that a *variety of diseases* were engendered and should spread rapidly in such a *mass of apt materials* or that, when fanned by the sigh of *despair* on the one hand and of *hunger and cold* on the other, they should have been blown up into one of the most *raging and mortal epidemics* that has appeared for many generations. The blood being impoverished and the solids deprived, swellings and dropsical disorders appeared to be first prevalent towards the end of the summer of 1817 and after the *new potatoes* were voraciously devoured, long before they had ripened to a due degree of consistence and nutriment, the disorders seemed to increase with alarming violence until the *typhus fever* broke out with such rapidity and virulence as induced some to suppose that it must have been a species of plague, imported, as was said, with some goods from the Levant; forgetting that in every area of the world such epidemics have always committed their *chief* ravages at those distressing junctures when *war or scarcity* have been extending the dominion of evil beyond its

Origin of contagion from

predisposing causes etc

Virulent typhus-fever

and its

ordinary limits. Whether from the peculiar virulence of the disorder, its various modifications, or the continuance of *pre-disposing* causes, it appeared to baffle the skill of most general and medical practitioners and scarce a family escapted a visitation destructive ravages and comparatively few who did not in its first progress sustain a loss of some of the members, too often of one of their heads. And its unhappy prevalence was at length not confined to the destitute but was extended amongst the classes placed above the causes generally supposed to occasion an attack. Indeed numbers of the latter fell victims from a too unguarded assiduity in the kind offices of administering to the wants of their poorer neighbours. Its extension to Britain and other p. 243 countries will long be known in the annals of medicine, as it certainly will in the domestic history of Ireland.

Perhaps little less   It has been very properly questioned whether in the present calamitous than state of society the epidemical visitations of such a contagious those of war disease are not productive of more real misery than war itself, fertile, as it unquestionably is, in every species of calamity. Certain it is that no previous effect of civil war, at least for the last fifty years, was so injurious to the province of Ulster or attended with so great a destruction of *georgical property and capital*. The appearance of some places, from waste fields and ruinous dwellings, bore no faint resemblance to the devastations which mark the route of a ravaging army.

Have occasioned a   In the course of two years (1816-17) the gains which had great waste of been saved during the years of prosperity were almost entirely capital and exhausted in the payment of rent without an adequate return georgical property of produce, or perhaps more generally in the purchase of food. The want of demand for live *cattle* and scarcity of provender and human food occasioned the destruction of perhaps *half* the cattle which existed in the spring of 1816 in this province. which Many farms were left to *widows and orphans*, impoverished and destitute. Almost every tenant, unless those who were in some degree substantial, was more or less in *arrear* or otherwise in prevented and *debt*. From so long suffering under privations and incon- discouraged improvements veniences and the diseases which they brought on and pro- longed, not only soured the tempers of many but rendered all more or less gloomy or desponding which, joined to their lessened ability, for a time put a stop to almost every kind of improvement or even the desire of making any.

Favourable results   The return of better seasons and the supply of food and from the return of better seasons and renovation of health which they have ensured (although very encouragement many of the tenants on the Gosford estates are much reduced held out to the tenantry in their *stock and capital* and of course still in considerable arrears) has again encouraged their industry, to which perhaps nothing has more powerfully contributed than the expectations they have entertained from the indulgence of the proprietor who, being superior to the cruel and suicidal avarice by which many honest tenants have been ruined on some estates, has already afforded proofs of his liberal intentions toward them. And it is hoped that the present details will aid his laudable endeavours and while the latter must gratify his own reflections, will by their *immediate and remote* effects be ultimately found the most advantageous, even in a pecuniary point of view. It has been considered unnecessary to excite feelings of this kind by any exaggerated description of calamities which his properties have sustained in common with others. The picture of those distresses just given was originally sketched *surrounded by the scenes* which have been portrayed, and now *twelve months after*, on reviewing the whole, the colouring is not considered *too strong* for describing the *realities* of individual suffering and of public distress which by swallowing up so considerable a portion of *stock and capital* has *put* the country *far back* in the *progress of improvement*, and in order to discover the *means* of again promoting its *acceleration* it was proper to recur to the original causes.

Different from the ruinous conduct pursued on some estates and will be productive of present and future benefits

It was during the years 1816-7 that the Reporter was employed in his first inspection of the Gosford estates and as a considerable and beneficial change has taken place in the meantime, while he has been employed in preparing the materials then collected, he has again recurred to the ground for the purpose of finally ascertaining their true situation and circumstances, so that the opinions given in this report are from an attentive consideration of the past and the present; with such a look into futurity as can be reasonably indulged from analogy in the common course of human affairs, and also discriminating betwixt the temporary and more permanent effects of the occurrences and calamities which have so recently taken place. Had the same degree of scarcity and contagion been continued for a third year (viz. for 1818) there is no doubt that the result would have formed a *piteous set-off* against any afflicting occurrence of the same kind recorded in history; most providentially this has not been the case and a less difficult task now remains to remedy what has occurred. In further pursuing the *present investigation* which is specially directed to this object, it may be proper in the next place to notice what effect the return of more genial seasons etc., have had on the circumstances of the tenantry.

Intention of the foregoing details

p. 244

The crop of 1817 proved considerably *better* than that of 1816 on the superior descriptions of soil and was the means of

The circumstances of the tenantry

9

assisting many of the tenants in the *lower* and more fertile parts of the estates, but on the *upper parts* the difference was scarcely perceptible. Indeed many were worse for, beside the sacrifices to subsist through the winter of 1816, many had disposed of the remainder of their effects to purchase seed-corn and potatoes at a high price (the lowest being from 2s. 6d. to 3s. per stone, an enormous price considering the scarcity of money) which did not produce much return, in many instances not even the seed. Hence, in the spring of 1818 many were unable to purchase any or a very inconsiderable quantity of *seed*. Some in the upper part of Baleek, etc. were discouraged from the *bad success* of the *two* preceding *years*, to sow any corn, from a conviction that the seasons had so altered as to render such attempts fruitless. Much of the crop of 1817 was also unfit for sowing but the difficulty of procuring good seed at the current prices induced numbers to sow what they had or could procure. Notwithstanding the reduced state of the generality a considerable breadth of *corn and potatoes* were got in and most fortunate it was so, for the summer of 1818 proved remarkably propitious and whilst it served effectually to *dry up* and counteract the *excessive moisture* which the *soil had imbibed* during the *rains* which prevailed in 1816 and 1817, it so injured the growth of *grass* and *oats* in England as proved most beneficial to Ireland, by furnishing a greater demand for *two of her chief articles of export, viz. oats and butter*, than would probably have been the case that season. From this circumstance and the limited supply of Irish butter the price approached the former *war rates* but comparatively few of the tenants were able fully to avail themselves of this as scarce any had the usual number of cows: some had not one-half their usual number and many none at all. The crop of oats of 1818 was also productive; the *price* of this *grain* from the same cause and no old stock remaining, was also considerable and both enabled the tenantry, unless those most reduced, to make *liberal payments*, which they endeavoured to do, by disposing of almost the *entire of their corn* (beside keeping seed for 1819) contenting themselves with the *potato crop* only for their own consumption, which also proved productive and of a good quality. But so small a consumption of *oaten food* in this part of the country was quite unprecedented for in ordinary years the quantity of this kind of food formerly consumed was considerable and they certainly deserve credit for this sacrifice.

Flax was a tolerable crop in 1818 but the quantity sown was less than usual from the difficulty of purchasing seed. The linen manufacture, however, in consequence enjoyed some

Margin notes:

have again progressively improved

Beneficial effects of the dry summer of 1818

Cause of the high price of oats and butter

Want of cows

More corn disposed of by the tenants than usual

Flax

advance of prices but the gains of this branch of labour were not on the whole very considerable.

Pork bore a high price in 1818 from its scarcity. Formerly   Pork
pigs formed not only a valuable article of food or luxury to the Irish tenant but during the war a most considerable source of wealth. During 1816 and 1817 they became exceeding scarce as food of any kind was too precious to be bestowed on them but when a sufficient supply of potatoes was obtained (by the crop of 1818) *lean stock* of this kind *bore* extravagant prices, which was great drawback on the profits of feeding them and which few but the more substantial farmers attempted. And this will account for the small number entered in the tabular report of an animal which formerly was so numerous everywhere in Ireland.

The great *destruction of cattle during the bad seasons* has raised their price so high that it will not be until some three or   p. 245
four years hence, when they again get cheap from their number   Want of live-stock
of increase, that many of the tenants will be able to obtain a sufficient number. And this will tend to prevent their getting forward with improvements and rent equal to those who do possess some stock as the produce from butter forms a considerable item of their gains, and the manure which can only be produced by aid of livestock is indispensable to ensure productive crops. The too general want of horses also, from the same causes, is a material obstacle to improvement from drawing lime etc. Many of the more provident tenants looking forward to the value of livestock and the difficulty there would be of purchasing them after so great a destruction, endured great privation rather than part with them and they now find the reward. Many had endeavoured to bring on part of their livestock to the spring, which from the want of provender or its unhealthy quality they were not able to effect as the death of cattle from disease was common, particularly during the spring of 1817. And many who were so fortunate as to preserve their cow or cows to this period, did not derive much benefit from them until they regained strength, which was not until far in the season.

Several tenants left their farms during 1816, having been   Some farms given
reduced to beggary from the total failure of crops etc., and a   up but again
few fled in the spring of 1817 even after they had tilled and   tenanted
partly cropped their farms; and there is no doubt, but for the timely encouragement afforded by an expected reduction of rent etc., many more would have followed, for at that time there was a temper of dispirited carelessness prevailing, which seemed to deaden all exertion. Happily this has passed away

in a great degree on this property and all the farms so vacated have been re-let to tenants as solvent as circumstances afforded, and several who could no longer retain the possession have relinquished in favour of others who have either paid or come under some part of the arrears.

Buildings again repaired

The buildings on the farms which were vacated were of course very ruinous, and indeed a large proportion of those throughout the estates had been allowed to fall into very bad repair. The seasonable grant of timber for repair by the Earl of Gosford and increased activity and attention on the part of the occupiers have, however, well-nigh restored them to their former state, unless where indigence or sloth still exist.

Tenantry patient under the late distresses

The patience with which the tenantry bore the late severe visitations of providence has been only equalled by the desire which the generality has evinced to pay rents since their improved circumstances enabled them, to which the altered state of the rental will, it is presumed, bear testimony. And while it gratifies the Reporter to make this remark, he considers it but right at the same time to mention that, had no arrangement been made to meet the necessities and expectation of the tenantry in respect of some abatement, the same anxiety to pay rents in all likelihood would not have been so evident (for the tenants were informed of the intended abatement in the spring of 1818). On the contrary, there is little doubt but that the number of tenants who would have thrown up their farms, would have been far more numerous and when the difficulty and risk of getting solvent ones in their stead under such circumstances is taken into account, the wisdom and advantage of the measure which has been adopted becomes more evident; and that the gross amount of the payments would have been far less considerable, as is unquestionably proved from the present comparative state of those properties where no such compromise and attention have been bestowed. For the Reporter in the course of his professional labours has not met with one instance of lands let at what is appropriately termed *war prices*, on which no abatement has been made, where the tenants are not dissatisfied and getting farther in arrear, or so dispirited and reduced as to be incapable or careless of paying rents and making any improvements; and it will always be so while the common principles which ought to regulate every transaction between man and man are not attended to. In some cases temporary palliatives have been adopted but with little better success.

Benefits from the abatement of rent

Essential to encourage tenants

Only applicable to the lands out of lease

Many of the remarks which have been made, as well as those which follow so far as relates to the subject of rents, arrears,

etc., are only applicable to the lands at present out of lease and
hitherto held in this way at high rates. A very considerable
portion of the best lands on the estates is held under old leases,
generally at low rates, and the tenants who hold the latter,
where industrious, are comfortable and even substantial;
but many from indolence or misfortune or both, are poor and
pay their rents with difficulty. But many of the remarks on the
means of improvement are also intended to apply in some
measure to the lands at present under lease, as specified in the
course of the discussion.

p. 246

Best lands under
old leases

Before taking leave of this part of the subject it may be
noticed that, in addition to the desire of paying rents, which
warrants the hope of their being, as far as circumstances will
permit, punctually paid in future, and is so different from the
present disinclination to pay rents and force necessary in some
parts of the country, the Reporter has to remark a very prevalent feeling of shame in having cattle etc., seized or drove
for non-payment thereof throughout the estates, which he
considers a most valuable trait in their character, which ought
to be respected and cherished, for while it is a very satisfactory
truth of the degree of industry which exists, it affords a gratifying prospect of their future perseverance and also a powerful
motive to countenance, aid and encourage their industrious
endeavours.

Favourable
character of
the tenantry

After the lengthened detail which has already been given of
the present circumstances of the estates and tenantry, it is now
proper to proceed with the application in devising and suggesting

THE MEANS OF IMPROVEMENT

It has appeared very evident to the Reporter that the *first* and
chief step in attempting to remedy the present situation of the
tenantry, or to promote improvement, must be a *fair* and
equitable *abatement* of the former *rents* where they are found
to be *too high*. Although this has not been a hastily formed
opinion on his part but after much reflection and considerable
observations throughout many districts and is, he supposes,
equally obvious to many others, yet from a desire to urge the
indispensable utility of this measure and to satisfy his present
distinguished employer, who, although he readily honoured
the Reporter's recommendation by adopting it before all the
details (now produced) on which it was founded could be

An abatement of
rent a
primary step

submitted to his consideration, may wish to hear further arguments and proofs adduced that in so doing he has not only consulted the comfort of his tenantry, but also his *own* pecuniary interest. The Reporter will, therefore, in the next place offer a more comprehensive view of his reasons for considering it so urgent and also take notice of some objections commonly urged against the advantages he has ventured to assert will result from its adoption, and further mention the principles and views under which he made a new valuation of the Gosford estates.

Truisms and postulations connected with the subject of rents

In considering the subject of rents there are some *truisms* which ought to be kept in mind and many more *postulations* which require to be received with caution. That every proprietor is entitled to a fair income for his lands, especially where he parts with a control over his estate by granting leases, is evident and that the progressive rise of rents is in most cases a spur to industry in cultivation as well as economy of management, is a common and, to a certain extent, a just maxim; but *any* sum beyond what will have the effect of exciting tenants to exertion, will become oppressive and have an opposite tendency for the addition of rent may be pushed too far. There are some individual tenants who by superior means and industry, may be able to pay exorbitant rents which would ruin thousands, and there are many who, if they had land for nothing, would be wretched from their indolence. The more common case, however, is that when tenants find that all their exertions will not do they become dispirited and desperate and allow themselves to be carried along by the stream which they cannot stem; the land and landlord suffer, arrears accumulate, and a certain *loss* is sustained. Improvements, or at least the ability to bear them, ought therefore to precede a great increase of rent. It is much to be apprehended that the *cause* in this case is too often mistaken for the *effect:* indeed they may be said to change places and become alternately one and the other just as the state of the country is more or less propitious for improvement.

p. 247

That rents have often preceded improvement in Ireland is a fact too evident to be a matter of doubt, since the rise of rents has not been attended with any proportionate increase either in the comforts of the tenants, or melioration of the lands, as in the sister kingdoms. Abundant proofs everywhere abound to show that in many cases lands given at very low rents are not productive of either improvement or comfort, but nineteen cases out of twenty prove that where the rent is beyond the means of the tenant none can possibly take place. There are parts of Ireland in which no species of improvement can be said to be at present taking place under almost any circumstance but the case is otherwise in the county of Armagh.

To fix a fair and equitable rent on lands in this country is a most difficult matter. In countries where the tenants are substantial and skilful, lands will more easily find their true level as to what they can yield in rent, but in a country where the great body of the tenantry are only in part dependent on agriculture (manufacture furnishing a part) and are possessed of means and industry almost as various in degree as their numbers and situations, it is a most difficult task. It seems, however, to have been reckoned a very easy one and so that the rents were increased it mattered little what ultimate consequences might be involved. Hence those valuators who ventured fartherest in this respect were often most in repute and best rewarded. It can be no matter of wonder then, that under this fallacious system the *nominal* rents have so generally, even in good times, differed from the *actual* receipts after deducting arrears and losses from impoverished or ruined tenants. If it had not been for the remarkable and continued rise in the price of produce and the immense additional issues of a *paper currency*, which served to enhance the value and rents of land for so many years, the evil would, long ere now, have in some degree worked its own remedy by the more general ruin of tenants and inconvenience of proprietors, and if longer persevered in, the consequences must be mischievous.

Why it is difficult to fix equitable rent in Ireland

Nominal different from real rents

In a state of society when, from the irresistible pressure of population, existence may often be said in a great measure to depend on obtaining the occupation of a portion of land, high rents will not be so often objected to by tenants, as they will be found unable to pay them punctually afterwards. Much cunning and every species of out-bidding when allowed, will be excited with jealousy and heartburnings without end; he who has least to lose will often be the most forward to offer and will make the least hesitation in bargaining at a higher rate than he considers himself able to pay rather than lose the possession, for anything is preferable to be thrown destitute on the world, or in such cases he will easily flatter himself on his ability or take chance of indulgence. Frequently envy or an extreme solicitude to extend limited portions of ground will likewise induce tenants of greater substance to lose sight of the true value, to offer exorbitant rents which a proprietor or an agent is tempted to accept. Indeed the latter cannot always refuse, what [ever] may be his own opinion or suspicions, to which either may be more easily reconciled from the erroneous opinions generally abroad of the extraordinary profits of

The pressure of population

and

anxiety to obtain land

induce tenants to offer exorbitant rents which are frequently accepted from an erroneous opinion of the profits of farming

farming, deduced from partial instances which it requires a
thorough experimental acquaintance with risks and casualties
of husbandry (but which theoretical speculators seldom think
of) to undeceive. Most of the farmers in Ireland toil hard, live
poorly, and in common times for one who has a trifle for his
pains perhaps two or three give their pains for nothing. The
generality are satisfied if they can contrive, with a large share
of privation, not to fall into arrear with the rent, and too many,
if indulged or spared, will from thoughtlessness or necessity
Proposals of rent
to be received
with caution let this accumulate beyond their power to liquidate. The want
of care and inadequate means with which farms are rented in
Ireland and the results, ought to serve as a caution to receive
proposals with diffidence, or in forming hasty estimates of the
p. 248 value of lands from offers of rent by such adventurers.

Injurious to
landlords and
tenants Excessive rents are merely *nominal*. They look on a rent roll
very flattering and imposing while they have a right to stand
there but if the arrears be received through the distress and ruin
of the tenants, the injury done to the estate (not to mention its
loss of character) ought surely to be deducted from the nominal
rent.

Were the loss from arrears etc., on many properties fairly
deducted in this way, it would be found that the *real* rent did
not much exceed (if it would equal) a rent which beside being
cheerfully paid would have forwarded improvements, or at
least not been any bar to them. It would be rare to find a considerable property, as before remarked, on which some individuals from extraneous means, superior industry, etc.,
would be able to pay excessive rents, and at the same time
many who are poor at low rents, but it is what the great body
of the occupiers are able to pay which ought to regulate the
opinion of such ability. *Nominal* rents while they harass,
dishearten and impoverish the tenantry, often induce the proprietors to launch into an expenditure which might not otherwise have been the case and, where the expected finances are
not forthcoming, much unpleasant embarrassment in the
consequence. The injury which *fictitious* rentals have done to
agriculture and landlords is incalculable.

The foregoing remarks have been recited in order to show
that they have not been lost sight of. Many will be ready to
Application of
the term
excessive rents admit their general correctness, who do not adopt them in
practice, because the great difficulty exists in the application
of the term *high* or *excessive rents*. The definition for the present
purpose is not perhaps very difficult if it is so in any case. If
rents rose from the influence of peculiar causes, such as those
which occurred during the last war, and if when those causes

ceased to operate the prices immediately fell towards their former rates, it would be a waste of time to attempt proving that when such rents are continued longer than the prices which occasioned their rise and enabled their being paid without distress and the greatest difficulty, they must be too high and indeed facts prove this to have been the case for they have not since been otherwise paid. They may be retained on the rent roll and some individuals may continue to pay them still, from some peculiar circumstance by which they are enabled to do so, but the great body of the tenantry who rented lands at the rates which the *war prices* occasioned, have not been able to pay the former high rents without those prices, as the rental of every considerable estate, so let, will testify; or if obtained, it must be by the impoverishment of the tenantry, and by which they will not only be incapacitated but disheartened from making any improvements, and in such case the lands must be getting worse. It is presumed the fact is not doubted, whatever opinions may exist with regard to the probable duration of the causes which have occasioned a reduction of the prices, for surely few persons of moderate inclination can long continue to think that the profits of husbandry are equal to meet *any* rents, or that the privations and extra industry of the tenantry can at once make up the deficiency.

War rents not paid during peace

A consideration of the effects of what is commonly the *appreciation of money*, resulting from the remarkable change which has taken place, may also serve to point out the propriety of making a reasonable abatement of rent, where necessary, which may be explained as follows. One of the many remarkable occurrences of modern times is the wonderful operation of a *paper currency*, which seems to have the all-powerful force of steam. The immense amount of this, which was issued by the numerous banks, augmented circulation even to an overflow. *Money* was accordingly said to be *plenty*, and in this happy state of things, owing to the facilities which it afforded, the *value of money* fell or became *depreciated* and had perhaps as powerful an effect as any other in promoting industry and improvement from the artificial capitals it furnished. It was this fullness of circulation which lubricated the movements of domestic industry, the wheels of state, and the gigantic efforts of war, and which enhanced the value of lands, because increased rents and taxes were easily paid. When Britain could no longer boast of possessing the trade of the world, or when it was overdriven by an excess of capital together with the changes which took place on the return of peace and the freer commercial intercourse of nations, the

The depreciation and appreciation of money materially affect rents

p. 249

Further
illustrations

quantity of *paper currency* was found to be too abundant for the diminished trade of the country, and as numbers had issued notes beyond their capital or credit, many banks failed and the national and more cautious private bankers withdrew their usual credits, so that circulation very suddenly became obstructed, which never fails to create every evil which can afflict an industrious people. In other words *money* became *scarce*, rents and taxes paid with difficulty, manufactures unpurchased and the consequent want of employment and fall in the price of labour and of produce, the value of lands and rents actually paid sustaining a proportionate defalcation, mischiefs which will always distress individuals and embarrass the community while circulation is impeded. The effects of the *depreciation* of money from a circulation constantly augmenting, as they are subtle and silent, cannot easily be foreseen or wholly prevented. Annuitants and those having stationary incomes suffered during this progress, which is so beneficial to others whose incomes rise with the times, because as money becomes less valuable or *depreciated* it requires more to command the necessaries and superfluities of life. To the landed proprietor and his tenant it is quite different. Their means increase but when a change comes the annuitant has again the advantage because he can purchase more for his money, while the person who pays rent or the interest of money settled for a particular rate during the *depreciation*, finds his means in-

Effect of the
relative value of
money at two
different periods

adequate or greatly circumscribed when an appreciation takes place. Some idea may be learned of the affect of this on the relative value of money at two periods: thus in 1760 £1 was equal to £1 12s. 10d. in 1800. These are not theoretical reasonings but familiar facts confirmed by daily experience and would alone be sufficient to prove the necessity of altering rents, taken at rates which no longer bear a due proportion to the

Intended to prove
that an abatement
of rent
only lessens the
nominal and not the
real value of an
estate

depreciated value of produce. And the particular object in view from thus reciting the principles on which it depends, was to show that a proprietor in making an *abatement of rent*, only lowered the *nominal* value: he still receives a sum equal in command over the necessaries of life and the labour of others, as when his rental was *nominally* higher—that is if the reduction is fairly made; indeed if he has interest or annuities to pay he will find a disadvantage. When the national banks find it necessary to return to metallic payments (which in all probability will not be many years) the preparations for, and consequence will be to still further circumscribe their issues of paper, which will in the meantime tend to narrow the circulation still more. And although the capitals employed in trade etc., may be of a more safe and steady kind, their number and amount will be less unless some powerful causes occasion a series of concurring events to again excite a constantly augmenting circulation, which is not very likely to take place for a considerable time, seeing that although an abundant paper currency tends in the first instance to promote trade and improvement, yet from not being of a stable nature and liable to abuse, it carries in it the seed of many evils which at length operate to bring about ruin if not timely remedied; the latter of which is now perhaps fortunately, though disagreeably and incommodiously in process.

Amongst the arguments brought forward against the necessity of *abatement* of *rent*, or at least of considerable allowance of this kind being necessary, some appear so plausible as to bias many persons who are willing to grant such abatement to their tenants as they can be convinced the circumstance of the case may demand. It is urged that the price of produce is not so very low as to require a considerable abatement. The sudden fall of prices on the close of the war, which the importation of foreign grain increased and prolonged, has been already noticed (in page 240). That the prices would have advanced when that glut was expended and the corn laws came into operation, even had the adversity of seasons not interposed, is pretty certain but if the latter had not occurred there is nothing to prove that they would have advanced to their late and present rates. England will long, perhaps always, continue to require more corn than she can produce and laws will no doubt be enacted to ensure much of that additional supply from Ireland, but while so many jarring interests are to be reconciled this limitation can only be to a certain extent, and although corn laws may prevent the markets getting to a very low rate or to an exorbitant height, yet they cannot increase the price beyond the demand. The former great importation from Ireland during the war of *oats* was chiefly for the purpose of supplying the numerous bodies of cavalry etc., which ceased with the war, and the number of horses for business and pleasure are also greatly diminished; and when no deficiency of crops exists the price of oats in future cannot be suppose to exceed from 10d. to 1s. 3d. per stone, a great difference from 1s. 6d. to 2s. during the war. Butter will perhaps seldom fall below 10d. per lb. as England will always require a considerable supply of this article, if the butter of Holland etc., is not allowed to reduce the price. Wheat will in all probability be an article of pretty steady demand at similar prices; it must, however, be kept in view that the late high prices have been entirely

Arguments against an abatement of rents

p. 250
Arguments relative to an abatement of rent, continued

Probable price of produce in future

owing to the limited supply, whereas the former high prices
during the war existed with an abundant supply and it is from
not attending to this evident and important distinction that
erroneous opinions are formed of the profits of the farmer at
present. That this must have been very different under the two
circumstances, is proved from the immense *exportation* from
Ireland under the former or abundant supply, compared with
the *importation* into Ireland in 1816 or very lessened export in
1817. The present (1818) prices of butter and oats have been
already accounted for (in page 244) and must doubtless sustain
a fall, when the same accidental causes no longer remain.
Cattle were exceeding cheap before the great destruction in
1816, 1817 and their high prices at present will also diminish
Price of   as they again become more numerous and their future price in
Irish produce Ireland will, in a great measure, like other articles of her produce
dependent on   depend on the degree of prosperity which the trade and manu-
England   facture of England will enable the numerous classes dependent
on them to spend, which, in all probability, cannot now be so
extensive as when they served the world. Other nations will
stretch every nerve to equal and rival her in what they consider
has been the source of her wealth at their expense but the
capital, machinery and intelligence of Britain will long ensure
a decided preference for our empire; in this respect more
particularly when our superabundant artisans will be contented
to labour on the lowest terms. It is also necessary to observe
that although a few particular articles of produce of prime
necessity have been high from the limited supply, yet during the
war every article was of a simultaneous value. The want of the
usual supplies of tallow, hides, etc., from the Baltic raised the
value of these articles in the home markets when our own
supply was inadequate to the demand. In the same manner
when the flax of Holland and Riga no longer found its way
into the British ports the prices in Ireland rose to an enormous
height. From the same inattention to a comparison of the
supply with the prices, or the abundance of money for purchasing, many have been unwilling to allow the extent and
extraordinary nature of the late scarcity from a comparison
of the prices during the last and those which occurred during
the scarcity of 1801 and 1802. Various articles of subsistence
were then much higher than in that of 1816 and 1817 because
the circulation was full or money plenty. The middle classes
had it more in their power to assist the indigent and work was
plenty and liberally paid for. In Ulster oatmeal was nearly
double the price in 1801 and 1802 that it was in 1816 and 1817:
although double the quantity was consumed during the former

scarcity, the people were better fed, none died of famine and no remarkable contagion resulted. In 1816-17 the price was nominally lower, yet in fact it was far more exorbitant than in 1801 and 1802; during the last scarcity, viz. in 1816 and 1817, money was exceeding scarce; the prices of flax, linen, etc., were not above one-third what they were during the former period, and to aggravate the evil further, labour of all kinds was scarce; thousands could not obtain half subsistence for their labour, and the embarrassment of the middle classes prevented the same aid from them as formerly.

p. 251

While we are told by some that the prices which the scarcity evidently occasioned, are to be considered as an argument against abatement of rent, we are told by others that the loss and embarrassment arising out of this scarcity can only be of a *temporary* nature, and of the latter, to a certain extent, can be little doubt. It is truly astonishing how soon good seasons and industry on good soils will repair the waste of war and famine. The province of Flanders, so often the seat of the most destructive wars, after a respite of a few years has always appeared as rich and populous as ever. Of the great scarcity which ended in 1699 Swift remarked that 'there have been terrible years, dearths of corn and every place strewed with beggars, but dearths are common in better climates and our evils lie much deeper'. The same is applicable to the present period. The effects of scarcity are not to be taken into account so much as the probable situation of the country hereafter from other causes. At the same time it must be acknowledged that there is no greater evil can easily happen to a country than the ruin of tenants from .the loss of agricultural stock and capital. The great scarcity in Scotland from the adverse seasons of 1782 and 1783 were in some places evident in their effects for more than ten years after from the continued poverty of the people, although the subsequent situation of that kingdom was propitious to improvement and the acquisition of wealth.

Effects of the late scarcity

From the effects of the late adverse seasons in Ireland, beside the number of tenants ruined beyond recovery, it will require many years even of tolerable prosperity to enable others to recover their former situation and ability. And this will very generally be the case in the *uplands* and on the poorer soils where the losses sustained were the greatest and the means of remedying them the least. Indeed throughout Ulster it will be very good management if, at the final winding-up, no more than from one to one and a half year's rent be lost, even with tolerable times for some years to come, and if they should happen to prove otherwise the loss may unavoidably be greater.

A portion of rent will perhaps be lost

Times of scarcity and contagion from the effects of cold, debility, etc., engender diseases which continue for many years and the vice and crimes which increased indigence generally entails, are far from unimportant since whatever tends to immorality and want of self-respect is injurious to industry.

Further review of arguments on abatement of rents

Another argument urged against the abatement of rent in Ulster is that the great body of the tenantry are only partly dependent on agriculture, paying for accommodation and making up the deficiency from manufacture. That this is the case need not be told but like most general opinions may be found incorrect when applied in detail. Formerly the prices of the staple or linen manufacture, as to labour, were very ample: for a long time about double and even treble the gains which it has brought for many years; and no wonder when the export from Ireland of this manufacture has decreased about $1\frac{1}{2}$ million. There is no doubt that without its aid they could not pay the same rents so easily, perhaps not at all, when the farms are so small and the produce in many cases little more than sufficient to support the families who occupy them. But in general throughout Ulster the tenants must now in a much greater degree depend on the produce of their farms to pay rents. In the uplands situations butter forms the chief article they have to spare; in others butter, oats, barley, etc., and in many parts of Armagh the produce of the wheat crop sown after potatoes is a great source of rent. That the linen manu-

p. 252

Linen trade less beneficial than formerly

facture has been long on the decline, in point of profit to the individuals engaged in it, is very evident and not very flattering hopes can be entertained of its ever, in any considerable degree, again attaining its former importance. The coarser article never can, since the steam and water machinery of Britain can be employed on them so as to keep the manual labour low in this country; cotton articles have supplanted the use of linen to an enormous extent. We originally borrowed the linen manufacture from the continent where they, from the abundance of the raw materials and of labour at low rates and by their late efforts, will prove hurtful rivals in foreign markets, so that instead of any additional reliance being placed on the aid of this manufacture, it appears on the whole more likely that the tenantry in Ulster will become more and more dependent on agriculture, as has certainly been the case for some years, and therefore the means of enabling it to be so becomes more important.

An inquiry into the probable restoration of trade

It remains to take notice of another argument against the propriety of abating rents, the most plausible of any although perhaps not the most difficult to answer, viz. that matters, after the effects of a transition from war to peace and of adverse seasons are passed away—which they suppose must be ere long—trade etc., will then again flow in their former currents, and that to make any abatement under the present circumstances especially if confirmed by lease, would be to forego a considerable income in future.

It is true that in taking a retrospective view of the commerce of the British empire, it is easy to discern a power of resuscitation which occasionally interposed to save the state as well as to restore traffic, an impeded circulation often distressing flourishing manufactures and foreign wars sometimes deranging oversea trade. Even the first return of peace, in one or more instances, [was] obscured by public embarrassment and private distress, yet patient industry and ingenious enterprise never failed to restore both to their former vigour and usual success to their gainful intercourse and their accustomed reduplications. And as the circumstances of the peace of 1782, at the close of the American or Colonial war, are best remembered and recorded, they are brought forward as a subject of consolation and argument against the real state and continuance of the present embarrassments. A striking analogy is certainly very obvious between the circumstances of the country at that time and as at present, but there are other particulars, no less striking, which are quite dissimilar. Let us briefly compare them for it is presumed attention to the facts connected with this subject is of great importance if any advantage is to be derived from past experience. The *Colonial* war was both different in its object and results from the late contest. The seventy years which had preceded the American revolt had been to Britain years of secure and dignified peace or of successful war. But the aspect of her affairs changed; her arms were unfortunate; she was pressed by a combination of the most powerful nations of Europe; her councils appeared to have lost their wonted skill; public distress was great; the funds had fallen in a few years 27 per cent, the purchase of lands from 33 to 23 [years], the price of all products from 30 to 100 per cent, wheat from 7s. to 3s. per bushel, other grain in proportion; hence rents were not paid. Ireland suffered also: the exports of linen sustained a severe decline and an embargo **had** been laid on the exportation of provisions from this country in 1776; the price of internal products fell and the usual rents and taxes could not be paid. But notwithstanding, the circumstances of Ireland improved before the arrival of peace as it proved, from an augmented trade and exchange in her favour owing to a superlucration of wealth arising to her in some way, although

Present peace compared with the peace in 1782

State of the country at the close of the American war in 1782-3 the complaints of distress were continued for political purposes until the termination of the war, which for a time only served to increase the embarrassment of Britain. The latter had been greatly debilitated by the war. When the vast national debts which had been contracted were exposed to the world in exaggerated figures, a panic seized the stock-holders; there was a great run upon the Bank of England, which drained its cash of vast sums; the price of public funds and of lands fell still lower, and it was almost impossible for individuals to borrow money on any security for any premium. The scarcity of 1782 and 1783 particularly in Scotland served to augment the distress which had previously existed but before 1786 the commercial embarrassments were removed. The value of the public funds rose although the stipulated interest on them had been reduced. The natural interest of money fell and in the mean time lands rose again to 26 and 27 years purchase. Ireland also participated in the increasing prosperity. The Colonial war was productive of many evils but like other evils

p. 253   brought with them a happy portion of good, and subsequent events proved that Great Britain actually derived many benefits from the independence of the American states. They had deducted from her naval strength and required a great annual expense of military and civil establishments without which, experience proved, she could still derive the same commercial profits for extensive demands were created for her manufactures and Ireland derived great advantage from the increased demand for her linens. The restrictions on her trade were in a great measure removed and the establishment of the Bank of Ireland in 1783 on a capital of £600,000, and since imitated by numerous banks throughout the country, promoted circulation and all its benefits. It is obvious then that the circumstances of Great Britain and Ireland were in many important respects very different from what they are at this time and therefore we cannot expect that precisely the same results will follow. In the late war Britain was opposed to the combined force of Europe and obliged to rely on her own supplies and resources during a long and arduous struggle, and the remarkable and increasing prosperity of the empire, particularly of Ireland, during the whole of this eventful period is well known and has been noticed (in page 237).

The present situation of affairs different from the effects of the peace of 1782   But a transition from this state of prosperous warfare to an embarrassed peace has reversed the picture and the results need not be repeated. It requires but slight consideration, however, to discover that the commercial and political relations of the British Empire as well as the domestic situation of affairs are diametrically opposite to what they were at the peace of 1783. There was then an extensive field for enterprise, of which ample advantage has been taken, even to excess; every branch of industry has been pushed to the uttermost. The continental nations certainly suffered much more from the blockade resulting from the Berlin decree than Britain but they were urged to depend more on their own industry and resources than at any time before and they have learned to prize them, for the spirit of the anti-commercial system of the ex-emperor has been adopted by his successors. Hence the difficulty of finding a market for our manufactures. In 1810 cotton was selling in Britain at 2s. per lb., in France for 8s. per lb.; the principal articles of our export to the continent at that time brought from 50 to 200 and even 300 per cent higher than they brought at home. The produce of Asia and America is now at their disposal as well as ours, an advantage which must be proportionally injurious to our manufactures. The Bank of Ireland was not established till the peace in 1783; the Bank of England in 1797 was restrained from paying in cash and the other banks willingly followed the same course; the amazing issues of paper which subsequently took place were great to excess, as is shown on the return of peace and how brittle and insecure the foundation on which our imposing prosperity had been raised. The sudden rise in the price of stock about 1785 which occasioned a rise in the price of lands and complete restoration of public and private credit, was said to be, in a great measure, owing to the financial measures of Mr. Pitt in imposing a million of *new* taxes (which the nation was found able to bear) and the consequent operation of the sinking fund, whereas at present the existing taxes are paid with difficulty and are found to depress industry and trade. The admirable speech of that able statesman on the peace of 1783 also shows how different our commercial prospects and relations were then, and how just and liberal were his views for promoting them. There is a third remarkable difference, viz. our population at the close of the American war in 1783 was not equal to the numerous departments of industry which soon opened and it is well known how rapidly it has since increased, that of Ireland having *doubled*. And this augmented number instead of promoting is found to retard prosperity and instead of being a strength is, in fact, become a source of weakness and even terror. It appears then, that at the peace of 1783, there was an ample field for the progress of trade, population and a *paper* currency, all of which have been already extended to excess, at least under the present state of things. If the nations

Temporary nature of the embarrassment of 1782

of Europe were sufficiently aware of their own individual interests, it might be difficult to set bounds to the progress of industry and improvement, but while commercial systems, which have long since been shown to be absurd and proved to be injurious, are generally enforced, if possible with double rigour, and when the nations are impoverished by so considerable a portion of their capitals having been expended in the unproductive pursuit of war, to expect any remarkable or p. 254 instantaneous change in trade etc., would be chimerical. At least we have no prior facts from which to deduce the probability of such results speedily taking place.

But even if Britain should in a few years extend her trade as formerly, Ireland from the want of capital and commercial correspondence cannot expect to participate to an equal extent in it. She enjoyed superior advantages during the late war; the trade and prosperity of Britain toward the close was rather on the decline but up to the last moment Ireland prospered and will always prosper most when her provisions etc., are in demand for war and it would only be from a war of the same nature that Ireland could derive the same peculiar advantages, that is until Britain should be prevented from receiving the usual supplies from the continent. This can only take place through the powerful influence of another dominator like Bonaparte and while the nations are galling from the effects of his yoke, it is not likely that anything of this kind can take place for a very long period. And their present poverty is a surer guarantee than treaties that the general repose of Europe will not be again soon interrupted.

High price of the public funds It is scarcely necessary to advert to the present high price of the public funds, notwithstanding the great and general embarrassment of the commercial and agricultural interests, because they have not been as usual accompanied by any proportionate rise in the purchase of lands and none in the rise of rent and price of labour: an unprecedented circumstance accounted for from the great portion of capital being withdrawn from unsuccessful or hazardous employments etc., and invested in public securities, until they can be more advantageously disposed of, and hence the great abundance of disposable capital in what is called the money market.

An abatement of rent farther considered The Reporter in the conscientious discharge of his professional duty has considered it incumbent to recommend an *abatement of rent* where requisite, under the present circumstances of the country but finding this kind of advice in some cases to give offence, in others to be misrepresented, he has been induced in the present instance to take the foregoing review of the arguments usually urged against such abatement. He has also endeavoured to account for the late rapid increase of rents, the cause of their decline, and the circumstances which may tend to influence their present and probable value in future, and he hopes that he has not trespassed in so doing. More facts might have been adduced in support of his opinions. If considered wanting, he refers to views of the same subject in the *Irish Farmer's Journal* under the signature of 'a Caledonian', which he drew up in 1816 and 1817.

The propriety and necessity of an *abatement of rent* is every day becoming more evident and there are now comparatively few proprietors who have not granted it. Some who are convinced of this necessity still withhold any declaration to their tenantry, supposing that they may still obtain as much actually paid as if they made an abatement at once—an arrear accumulating at the same time which they may never regain—but in case [of] any favourable change taking place they will then have it in their power to enforce it, or at least the former annual rent, forgetting that, as their tenantry are fully aware of this reasoning against them, [they] will not attempt making any improvement under such circumstances or indeed of striving to make ample payments. The proportion of arrear will be found in most cases annually to increase, for say they: 'Will we strive for a landlord who treats us so unlike others who have joined their tenants in a share of the losses which have originated out of circumstances which no human foresight could prevent or control, and will we expend labour or money on improvements p. 255 which may be transferred to another to reap the benefit?' These are not imaginary apprehensions but are founded upon real and solid principles and will operate less or more upon every farmer according to his situation and circumstances. Should any very favourable change take place it is not likely that much of this arrear could be recovered, for in some ten years hence an estate and tenantry, who now have received a fair abatement and of course [are] going on improving, must present a very different aspect from one where none has taken place, but impoverished and disheartened; nor will they entertain that confidence in their landlord which is ever indispensable to ensure improvement in any case.

It is frequently urged that because [they lie] under the disheartening influence of excessive rents tenants have fallen into great arrear. It is not the payments of those rents which have injured them but when a tenant finds it impossible to pay the whole he generally uses little exertion to pay any considerable part thereof and such will always be the ruinous effects of rents which are too high.

It has been further urged that it is often impossible to satisfy tenants for that when a fair abatement is made they rise in their demands. If the abatement at first has not been judiciously made this may be the case and if the tenantry have been previously ruined or mismanaged its effects will certainly be less obvious. Tenants, even of the better description, will often use much artifice to obtain as low terms as possible, but because some difficulty may exist, or in some partial instance not be always productive of the expected benefit, it would be absurd on this account to withhold it where beneficial and the case must be very peculiar where it would not be so sooner or later. If abatement is withheld too long until the tenantry are impoverished, or until they see that it has been granted when there was no alternative, it will not be so highly prized as if done sooner with more appearance of liberality, and when they have it in their power to avail themselves of it. The propriety of this measure appears at first view so reasonable that did not existing facts prove its being questioned and resisted, such a long disquisition would have been quite unnecessary.

Some observations on the inutility of granting temporary abatement otherwise than secured by lease will be noticed under the head of leases (see page 259) or of granting allowances and premiums in lieu of abatement, will in like manner be noticed under the head of premiums (see page 277).

On the business of valuation   The observations which have been given on the present situation of the country and of the political relations which must affect its agricultural interest may appear too gloomy and exaggerated. But although the Reporter firmly believes they will be found strictly correct he can see no cause for despondence. It has been now proved that all sudden changes in the situation of a country are evils in themselves or in their consequences, and unless a determination to resist any remedy or to effect it by too forced and expeditious means, the changes which have occurred may serve to lay the foundation of a more steady and durable although a less splendid progressive prosperity. It is unnecessary and would be endless to recite the multiplicity of circumstances which require consideration in the business of valuation, one of the most difficult duties which can engage the attention of a professional person, and in the present situation of affairs it is peculiarly so, and also unpleasant, for while he finds difficulty in fully satisfying his own mind his labours cannot be so satisfactory to tenants and landlords as when additional rents could be imposed with a firmer hope of being paid than moderate reduction can be at present. To make a reduction in rent is one of the most unpleasant that can occupy attention and ought not to be resorted to or recommended unless very powerful reasons render it indispensably necessary to avoid a much greater evil. In so strenuously recommending this, the Reporter can have no sinister object in view; he cannot expect much credit and his percentage on the reduced valuations must be less. But as this must form the *groundwork*, it would be useless without it to devise or attempt any other *mode of improvement*. He has used his best endeavours to value the lands according to their peculiar quality, situation and circumstance, but will be found in some cases to differ widely from the former valuations, for while some are estimated at nearly from one quarter to one third less others are only a few per cent lower and some equal, if not somewhat higher. It does not belong to him to enquire how so great a difference in the relative value of many farms previously existed. He has valued every field etc., separately and taken the average on each farm, but where so much is to consider and tends to mislead, some partial oversights may remain after using the most careful scrutiny. The valuation of some of the upper parts of Baleek etc., may appear very trifling compared with the good lands, well circumstanced, but perhaps the former are actually higher than the latter. The *soil* is of the very worst kind for reclaiming with profit, viz. a wet boggy soil on a cold retentive bottom, and would not, in fact, repay the money necessary to improve it thoroughly and under the present mode of occupation is, on an average of years, *scarce* worth the cultivation. The grass they afford and the great accommodation as to the vicinity and abundance of excellent turf bog are the chief circumstances which render them of value.

p. 256

New valuation in some cases very different from the former

It is here necessary to notice that, of the farms *out of lease*, the few which have been more highly improved by the occupying tenants than those around them of similar soil and circumstance, have not been valued higher from a *firm* and experimental conviction that to do so would form a very material *bar* to improvement in future. Although a proprietor is certainly fully entitled to derive any advantage out of improvements, which may have in the meantime taken place, yet when an individual, by superior industry, builds himself a better and more comfortable house, *encloses*, *drains*, or cultivates his farm better than his neighbours who occupy the same quality of soil, to augment his rent in proportion would be to discourage him from further exertions and his neighbours from following his industrious example.

The more improved farms are so valued

as not to retard further improvement

A criterion
suggested in
estimating rents   The Reporter has before alluded to the extreme difficulty of valuing lands in Ireland (see page 247) not with an intention to exaggerate his labours but from a conviction of the fact, and after many years experience in observation he has fixed on a criterion which may assist very much in ascertaining with some degree of certainty whether lands are too high or too low, namely the amount of purchase for the goodwill or tenant right which could be obtained. Formerly when lands were constantly rising in value and money abundant this was often very high even for farms by no means cheap, viz. from five to ten and even fifteen pounds per acre, but taking the present circumstances of the country into account it will very generally be found to hold good that where a tenant cannot obtain the amount of one year's rent of his holding for his goodwill, it is too high rented to ensure punctual payment or to encourage improvement. If the occupier can obtain two years' rent for his goodwill the bargain is to be considered a fair one and if more can be obtained it is either very favourable or the purchaser has more than a common command of money or anxiety to obtain land, and some partial instances of this will take place.

Considerations in
valuing the
Gosford estates   The Reporter found the Gosford estates as *high rented* (unless such parts as are held by lease) as almost any around them and as now reduced they will be found proportionately high still. He has valued the whole under the expectation that the *prices of produce and linen manufacture* will continue to bring what p. 257 may be considered tolerably fair prices (see page 250). Although the late period of scarcity and distress has been minutely Further
considerations on
the valuation detailed (see page 241) he has divested himself of any undue attention to circumstances of so *temporary* a kind. It would be arrogant in the extreme to pretend to dive *too* far into the future condition of the country as affecting the ability of tenants to pay rents; he has given the reasoning which he conceives may be taken as the most likely and *safest* guide. If prices should fall below his estimate a still greater deficiency in rent may be expected and it is presumed that they cannot reasonably be expected in the common course of human affairs to become much higher or at least to become so speedily. Indeed he would not have considered himself justified in making so small a reduction, considering the former high rents in many cases, if he were not satisfied that, in a country like Ireland where the state of society generally tends to encourage indolence, what may be called a *smart rent*, when not too high, may more generally prove a spur to industry than any bar to improvement; and that the proprietor would be willing to give such *aid* and *encouragement* as would powerfully stimulate to

exertion, viz. to grant the abatement at least from May or November 1816; to grant leases at least for 21 years and *one life*; and to promote and encourage improvement in other respects in such a way as not to require any sacrifice of capital or income nor interfere too much with the occupation and rural management of the tenantry.

After the *deductions* are allowed a considerable *arrear* will still remain against numbers on the estates and when it is taken into account that during the two years 1816 and 1817 many of those not only derived little or *no produce* from their lands but actually consumed the whole or greater part of their substance in procuring subsistence; that from this want of means and even where they do exist, it will require their utmost exertions to pay the *current rent* punctually, which still remains, it cannot reasonably be expected that the *by-past arrears* can be liquidated by *cash payments* by many. No occasion of arrear ought to be allowed to remain on the part of the proprietor and none ought to be allowed to accumulate in future, if it can be possibly avoided, since it is not only so much lost from the rental but tends to dishearten and incapacitate a tenant from exertion, when every year brings demands with it fully equal to its ability. The profits of farming are steady and therefore seldom admit of easily making up by-past deficiencies. A firm conviction that rents must be punctually paid is frequently one of the greatest motives to industry and exertion that can influence tenants, and indulgence should therefore never be granted unless in peculiar cases, even should the withholding of it sometimes appear harsh. But it is not here insinuated that rents in Ulster can always be obtained in any particular week or month as, where so many articles of produce, manufacture and labour assist in paying rent, they cannot always be promptly sold or disposed of with due advantage. But after the most vigilant *enforcement* of rent some of the more indigent and improvident tenants will unavoidably fall into arrear and perhaps in some cases require to be speedily but *cautiously* replaced by more substantial or industrious tenants (see page 275).

From the late peculiar circumstances of the country, the accumulation of arrear was unavoidable (and in every recurrence of a great scarcity it will be so: see page 241) and it now becomes a difficult though an *important* consideration how to dispose of this *arrear*, not so much to prevent its being lost entirely, as to clear it off without injury to the tenants (if it is not considered advisable to discharge it at once, as many have done from the little probability of the generality ever being able

Marginal notes:

Arrears will remain after deductions

The injurious consequences of arrears

Late arrears unavoidable

p. 258

Observations relative to arrears

to pay it up or clear it off without injury to their future exertions) or [without giving] any encouragement to allow any to accumulate in future under more favourable circumstances. For indulgence in allowing *rent* to remain unpaid, beyond such a period as circumstances may point out, is a most mistaken feeling which generally ends in much greater perplexity or ruin.

Part may be recovered

Some of the more substantial tenants may be able to liquidate a portion of their *arrears* as their circumstances improve with the times, and many of the *new* tenants (see page [276]) who enter such farms as are relinquished by their present indigent

and occupiers, may by way of *purchase* be induced to pay a *part* of the *arrears* on the holdings they enter into, but in so doing care ought to be taken that in their anxiety to obtain possession they may not either injure their future ability or come under greater obligations than what they may be able to fulfil, as they are often ready to trust too far to indulgence.

part may be expended on general improvements

The inutility and risk of proprietors expending *capital* on rural improvements beyond the precincts of their own demesnes is obvious in a country where the tenantry are not generally possessed of sufficient skill to avail themselves of such, and where they are in most cases inclined to take the greatest immediate advantages without regard to future consequences. At the same time it would be absurd to say that there are none

but whatever on which proprietors may not judiciously expend moderate sums with a prospect of a suitable return of profit and advantage. The improvements of this kind which appear to be advisable on the Gosford estates are explained in page

ought to be done with caution

[316] and in executing them part of the arrears may be cleared off but, as every day withdrawn from the cultivation of their farms or the gains of their looms thereby lessens their ability to pay rent in cash, great caution and consideration will be necessary in taking such portions of labour and at such times and seasons as will best suit the conveniences and circumstances of the particular individuals; because otherwise a greater loss might be incurred for while they were thus employed in clearing arrears, they might be prevented from punctually making *cash payments* of the current rent, and an attempt to recover the past arrear only tends to increase more in future.

Part of arrear may be expended on the different farms

The Reporter therefore is of opinion that with regard to the *greater* part of the *arrear* of the generality, it will be found most advisable to allow them for certain improvement of a more permanent kind on their own farms as has been more fully pointed out in the details of the different farms in the preceding pages and are further considered in a general point of view in page [22]. As many have to *purchase cattle* etc., to supply the place of those which were lost or disposed during 1816 and 1817 they cannot be expected to pay much arrear in cash in addition to the current rents and the same necessity will prevent their giving a large portion of labour at *once*, as it is only at particular seasons that they could spare subsistence while so employed. A considerable part of the arrear due on the lower part of the estates may perhaps be cleared off by labour and *cartage* required for the erection of the *new castle* at Gosford, if part of their earnings are given for support, to purchase carts etc. The propriety of granting *leases at reduced rents* is a subject little less important than those already discussed and it is necessary to point out the utility of granting leases at present, the arguments urged against this, the arrangements under which those should be granted, etc.

Utility of granting leases

A proprietor cannot be expected to give up the control over his lands by granting leases without an adequate remuneration. Although improvements are not carried on in Ireland on the same scale as in Britain yet in the County of Armagh an industrious tenant can afford to pay from twenty to thirty per cent more rent under lease than if held at will. The conduct of the indigent and indolent is not very different whether they hold their lands under lease or at will but this is no sufficient argument against them being granted where the generality of the tenants are industrious and, as the precise distinction between the *two* classes cannot be easily defined, no exceptions can be easily made. Under the presumption that leases are intended to be granted, the new valuations have been made.

p. 259

Permanence and security of tenure will always form the greatest incitement to improvement and without it, none which are material on the part of the tenant can be expected. Although tenants in Ireland seldom fear being turned out yet they fear what is equivalent: that after having made improvements on lands held at will they will be raised before they can derive any adequate return. There may be a few instances of improving tenants on lands held at will but it can only generally take place where great *faith* and good understanding has been established for a great length of time. It is therefore extremely ill-judged of a landlord to neglect his immediate interests and to prevent the future improvement of his estate by withholding leases, which is proved by taking a view of *two* districts where leases have been granted and where they have not, and the difference will be manifest unless some very peculiar circumstance of rent etc., exists to prevent it. Leases at fair rents are therefore the *first*, the *greatest*, most *rational* and *cheapest* encouragement

Leases a principal means of improvement

that can be given to improvement, without which every other will be fruitless.

If tenants refuse to take leases, as is very generally the case in Ireland at present, there can be little doubt but that the lands are too high to ensure any improvement and ought to be reduced. Individuals may sometimes resist taking leases when they find the proprietor has any political or other pressing intention in granting them, with a view to extract a further concession of rent, but where the tenantry of a whole estate refuse taking leases at existing rents, there is a strong presumption of such rents being too high. Because the desire to acquire possession is too strong to be generally resisted, they will rather be inclined to take them even above what they are satisfied is a fair rent. An estate let under lease to industrious tenants will present a very different appearance and become of a different value, in the course of fifteen or twenty years, from one held at will, even at somewhat lower rents. While circumstances tended to improve the condition and means of tenants the want of leases might be less severely felt but now, when this is no longer the case and capital from its scarceness [has] become more and more rare and valuable, little will be expended without a certainty of advantage.

Review of arguments urged against granting leases

Evident as the utility of granting leases is here asserted to be, arguments are sometimes urged against them, viz. that in Ireland they only bind the landlord as tenants consider themselves no longer bound than what it can serve them. But it should be remembered that [that] will certainly be while they can pay the rent or in any way retain them, for the pressure of population and the avidity to procure land is such that any farm (more particularly any one under lease) which would not be retained must be too high. This argument, however, is perhaps seldom urged in good earnest but at the present many are reluctant to grant leases at such rents as the tenants can think of taking them at, from an apprehension of *foregoing* a portion of *income* in future (as already mentioned in page 252). Under such circumstances little improvement will take place and even reduced rents will seldom be punctually paid because tenants are fully aware that to make any improvement under a temporary abatement may tend to their future disadvantage: and this conduct differs little in its nature or tendency from making no abatement at all, but merely taking what can be got

p. 260 and allowing arrears to accumulate.

Leases for 21 years and one life

In Ireland leases cannot be granted with advantage for less than 21 years, and if a vigorous system of improvement prevailed, requiring a great outlay of capital, that period would be too short to return an expenditure in building, fences, roads, etc., of from £5 to £15 per acre solely on the part of the tenant. But as this is seldom thought of or could be enforced, 21 years and one life is to be considered as a fair lease. With a view to point out, reward and encourage a few of the most improving tenants, the addition of another life or some years would perhaps be highly advisable and might be productive of tenfold advantage, ultimately, from the encouragement it would hold forth to any pecuniary loss which this sacrifice might cost in the first instance.

An additional tenure to a few of the most improving tenants

Considerable advantage may result from leaving some choice of the life to the tenants. If a miscellaneous choice is not considered advisable a few *suitable lives* may be named for them to select out of. Perhaps the lives ought to be known to them and persons of some rank or notoriety in life, that their demise may be speedily known and easily ascertained. And it is not desirable to have too large a portion of an estate under lease dependent on one life. Sudden additions to the rental may not be so advantageous as a more gradual increase. Large portions of estates falling out of lease together have been often attended with difficulties and disadvantages in Ireland, viz. the tenants entering into compact to resist an equitable rise of rent or the discouraging panic which may be excited by a rise of rent over a large portion of country feeling a simultaneous interest. And perhaps the proprietor will find it most advantageous on the whole, to have the lands gradually falling out, for they may chance to come into his power either at a time unfavourable to his future interest to re-let them, or to induce their being let at a higher rent than the subsequent circumstances of the country may enable to be paid.

The tenants to have some choice of the life

There is certainly one advantage may result from a large portion of an estate falling out of lease together: that the proprietor has it more in his power to make such alterations and arrangements as the improved circumstances of the country and tenantry may render advisable, than if falling out in detached portions. But this may be easily obviated and secured in another way, viz. the ancient and fiscal division of the counties into townlands and similar denominations cannot be done away without an entire change in the police arrangements of the country, and as they are besides very natural divisions, that is marked out by rivers, streams and other permanent boundaries, there is no apparent or probable change of estate arrangement that would be prevented or incommoded by such existing divisions.

Reasons for
granting
each townland
under one life   Therefore it is *strongly recommended* to grant all the leases in *each townland* under *one life* (the partial occurrence of an additional life being granted as a motive of encouragement, as just mentioned above, would not much interfere with this intention), either the life which shall be first chosen by any tenant in the townland or such life as the majority in that townland shall fix on. By this mode each townland can be remodelled or arranged at the expiration of their respective leases for, were it otherwise, much obstruction might arise to better arrangements in future, particularly from the detached portions of meadow ground which occurs in most townlands.

In the present state of the country such portions are *too essential* a convenience to be taken away from the farms and if held at will might occasion much trouble. But should the *use of artificial grasses for hay* happen to be introduced into general use before the expiration of the leases now about to be
p. 261 granted (and of which the Reporter does not despair), the detached meadows may be then perhaps better arranged so as to occasion less trespass and intermixture of the holding, a source of many disputes and of considerable trouble, which cannot at present be altogether prevented, the advantage of procuring even a scanty supply of natural hay and pasture counter-balancing almost any trouble in procuring it.

On granting leases
of town parks   For lands to be held as town-parks etc., at Markethill, a lease for *ten years* without any life may be sufficient (unless their importance as freeholders may form an inducement to add an *old* life) but some tenure of the town fields ought to be granted, as less improvement will be made on them if held at will.

On covenants
inserted in
leases   The covenants inserted in the leases should be as few, as simple, and as easily understood as possible, and none should be inserted which cannot and are not intended to be strictly enforced. Skill and capital are not yet in sufficient abundance in Ireland to enforce particular systems of management, however advantageous they might be to the tenants, but of the utility of which they are not convinced and if they were, have not the means of adopting them. Some clauses such as *white-washing* houses etc., at certain periods, which are not expensive and so essentially tend to the health and comfort of the occupiers may be introduced, if not with much advantage, at least without injury; one day of a man and horse *once or twice* in the year, to draw for the proprietor, cannot be a great hardship on the tenant to give; but beyond this it may become so, particularly if called for at a precarious and important season when the loss of a day in putting in or saving a crop might prove a great loss.

Compulsory labour for the immediate accommodation of the tenant, in repairing lanes, etc., may be of great advantage to him (as stated in page 234) but the obligation should be strictly confined to this, and account taken to works in which he has not an intimate advantage; or perhaps the latter may be sufficiently enforced by being signed in the form of an estate regulation at the same time with the lease.

It is not recommended to grant any turf bog in lease unless in the upland parts where it is abundant and lies within the bounds of the farms (see page 233). Those having turf bog within their farms to be bound not to cut or dispose of any unless for their own use.

Turf bog not to be leased

The obligation to grind at particular mills is a practice of long standing but now frequently discontinued and perhaps it ought to be so for numerous disputes arise between millers and the tenants bound to grind at their mills, and the good policy of obliging them to grind where it is often worst done and at a much higher rate than elsewhere is very questionable. This is one of those feudal practices which will gradually give way to a more liberal system. If any part is bound in the existing leases of the mills, if no moderate compromise could be made with the lessees, the tenants need only be bound during the existence of such leases. Rents should be wholly payable in money and all bondages and prestations avoided; nor will the additional rents obtained for mills having lands bound to them, often equal the disadvantages in other respects.

On being bound to grind at particular mills

It is scarcely necessary to mentioned the trouble and mischief which generally results from granting joint leases as the industrious have often to suffer for the indolence of poverty of those joined with them: it has often formed a great discouragement to improvement. No lease ought to be granted to more than one individual and the boundaries of the lands so leased ought to be distinctly defined as to lanes, streets, etc.

No joint leases ought to be granted

It is now become imperative to insert and strictly to enforce a clause or clauses against alienating, assigning, or in any way underletting the whole or any part of the premises, under whatsoever size or arrangement they may be leased, and the same ought to extend to prevent sub-letting to cottiers of any kind without written permission; the farms, however, being allowed to pass to a wife, child, or grandchild, but in such cases to come into the occupation of no more than one person, for the reasons urged (in page [271]).

Importance of inserting clauses against alienation, etc

p. 262

Observations have already been given in the Additional Remarks to the *Tabular Report* on each farm, of such changes as are recommended in their boundaries and general remarks on the size of farms etc., are given (in pages 266, 273).

In order to illustrate the two preceding subjects, viz. clauses against alienation and the size of farms, it is necessary in the next place to examine the ruinous effects

OF THE RAPID INCREASE OF POPULATION
and the consequent evils resulting from
THE MINUTE SUB-DIVISION OF LANDS

Both are in many respects so obvious and a theme so often dwelt upon, that its notice in a report of this kind may appear trite or unnecessary, or at least to offer little so interesting as to excite attention. It is however of *vast* importance and if the following views have little pretention to novelty, they cannot be wholly overlooked without real loss to a proprietor, especially in granting leases which may be beneficial or otherwise in the course of their duration and operation as they shall happen to be adapted to correct the evils arising out of the present peculiar state of the rural population in this country.

The Reporter solicits a particular share of attention to the investigation of the ruinous effects and frequent losses which have been occasioned and are constantly augmenting from the pressure of population tending to promote a too minute subdivision of the lands, as there is no part of his professional labours which he conceives more important than stating this evil fully in its operation and consequences. And he should consider himself as performing a very meritorious part if he could flatter himself with the hope of being instrumental in directing sufficient attention to it, as there is no part of estate management in Ireland which in general demands a more thorough change than in respect of vigilant and increased attention to check and prevent so great an evil and to which the frequent recurrence of arrears is chiefly owing. For nearly ten years his attention has been almost exclusively devoted to rural affairs in Ireland, during which the experience and observations of every day have more and more convinced him of the tremendous evils which have been long occasioned by allowing the unrestrained sub-division of lands, the many distressing calamities it is now occasioning, the immense loss to proprietors and above all the future consequences with which it is amply fraught. His pursuits may have given him superior opportunities of more fully discerning the manifold modifications of the evil but he freely confesses that he is not so much astonished at that happy ignorance (if so it may be called) which removes from the view of the ignorant and wretched victims and the indigence to which it inevitably tends, as at the neglect of proprietors in not adopting a preventive or remedy. And it is not without concern that he sees well-intended persons either give up the attempt as hopeless or trying such as he knows must ever prove unavailing, which is to be the more lamented as every day augments the general calamity and night comes on without hearing any plausible suggestion of the means of its prevention. The difficulties are great and many but let their number and magnitude be what they may, to-morrow they will be still greater.

It is melancholy to dilate on the effects of so ruinous a system and it would be still more so to witness its operations if no practical means could be suggested for its being remedied or checked. A view of the present misery and the sad assurance of its daily increase, unless a suitable remedy is adopted and vigorously enforced, damps the hope and pleasurable prospects which might otherwise be confidently anticipated from the improvement of this fine country. The sub-division of lands has not in every instance advanced so far on the Gosford estates as in many other parts of this country but it is already too far and in rapid progress unless retarded. Every year this is delayed the consequences will become more extended and permanent and of course more and more difficult to overcome. And there are several reasons which will be stated in the sequel why it is more imperative to prevent its further extension on them than even on others. It may here occur to inquire why so great an evil as is here urged, has not already excited a greater degree of attention. The answer is that it has hitherto been often pro-ductive of temporary advantage or at least been attended with such consequences as render the evils, which were in progress and are now begun to operate with increasing and destructive rapidity, less obvious and unimpressive. It may therefore be useful to notice some of the causes which have tended to the progressive sub-division of lands; proofs of its extent, parti-cularly on the Gosford estates; the evils resulting therefrom to the tenantry and ultimately to the proprietor; why it is particularly important to prevent the further continuance of this practice on these estates; difficulties and objections to such an attempt examined and answered; means by which it may be checked and prevented without inconvenience or loss to the tenants or proprietor.

p. 263

Importance of the subject

The impolitic conduct of England towards Ireland not only during a barbarous age but at a period not very remote, by

Causes of the rapid increase

O['s work overtyped]

preventing the introduction of manufacture and the extension
of trade when they might have been successfully pursued,
prevented the increase of a numerous respectable middle class,
on the number, education, and wealth of which the great prosperity of every country must chiefly consist. Hence the principal infelicity of so populous a country as Ireland undoubtedly
is, representing an unnatural state of society, without a just
gradation of ranks having the several classes properly assorted
of rich, poor, middling and many. This misfortune together
with the unhappy prevalence of religious dissensions with their
numerous train of consequences inimical to national aggran-
dizement, have occasioned a state of things which proves of
how little avail the most advantageous physical circumstances
of a country are without a suitable degree of industry and
improvement. Trade and manufacture would have introduced
profitable labour, many comforts and more artificial wants and
indulgences which are necessary to overcome the natural
propensity of man to inactivity: they create exertions and if
properly regulated by a moral education, inspire a disposition
to provident care. But if no such inducements exist the greater
proportion of the people will be glad to drag on, merely to exist
in the lowest state. And this want of desire and inability to
attain a greatly improved condition by persevering efforts has
been the bane of Ireland's prosperity and will in all probability
occasion much future distress. While the capital and enterprise
of Britain is more than sufficient for the existing demand, their
p. 264   introduction into this country so extensively as to produce a
radical change in society is hopeless. But the present purpose
is to enquire into the effect of the existing state of the rural
population on the past, present and future interests of landed
proprietors.

p. 264

Causes attributable   The sub-division of lands in Ireland is considered as a matter
to tenants   of course. Few proprietors think of preventing or restraining it.
Some even injudiciously encourage it from an erroneous belief
that it is the best mode of advancing their incomes, or the
surest way of obtaining political consequence. And tenants are
very ready to question the right of preventive interference.
And it is generally reckoned a hardship when enforced, for
almost every tenant shares his portion of land amongst two
or more of his children and so on *ad infinitum*, and this is still
further extended, for whenever he becomes indigent or improvident he disposes of a part to strangers. Hence many families
become resident on one lease, and of course the increase of
population is proportionably accelerated. It is, in general, the
interest of middlemen to apportion the lands which they hold

into small-holdings. This ruinous system is now almost entirely given up in Ulster. About fifty or sixty years ago it seems to have been difficult to find tenants to occupy large tracts, particularly of unreclaimed or partially improved uplands, and they were frequently leased to opulent individuals who procured sub-tenants for them (Doctor Robinson's and Bell's leases in Glassdrumond, Brackley, etc., are instances of this kind on the Gosford estates). And from the former general abundance of turf bog on such places they have become filled with crowds of poor and indigent sub-tenants and cottiers, leaving to the proprietors at the expiration of the tenures, occupiers who have rarely had much in their power and are in many cases but ill-qualified to pay rent punctually, and must be afterwards either ejected with much unpleasant feelings or retained with the hazard, trouble and loss.

But although the circumstances of the tenantry have tended to this sub-division of land, it would never have so generally extended without the direct concurrence or oversight of the proprietors and managers of estates, and both have operated most powerfully to encourage this. The desire to acquire political influence or the apparent necessity to follow the same procedure, has encouraged the sub-division of lands as the number of freeholders has too often been considered paramount to any other interest or consideration. It is incorrect in principle to attach the right of voting to any specified amount of profit rent, unless it can be made to answer the depreciation of money: forty shillings would probably be now found to equal from ten to twenty pounds (see page 249) and much good would have accrued to Ireland if it had been made so progressive. Yet after all, the same restriction as to a right of voting has not been productive of the same injurious results to the landed interest in England, and the share which the proprietors have in erecting farm buildings etc., leads to a more intimate knowledge and superintendance than in Ireland. The more general neglect of estates in this country, provided the stipulated rents were paid, has been the chief cause of the sub-division of lands together with the temporary advantages it has conferred, the state of society and the country admitting of little accumulation of capital or acquirement of agricultural skill. The pressure of population has hitherto served in a considerable degree to make up for the defective system of husbandry by inducing the tenantry to offer the highest possible rent which could be paid from their system of management, with a mere subsistence to themselves and a large portion of privation. Hence there is no part of Europe where so large a share of produce falls to the

Causes attributable to proprietors

p. 265

landlord as in Ireland, but then that produce is inferior to what it might be under different management. And from the great competition for land, rents advance beyond what the occupiers can pay and live with a sufficient degree of comfort, the landlord's due too often furnishing the tenant's capital.

Causes   It would be almost endless to enumerate the many causes which have tended to promote the sub-division of lands in Ireland and the consequence. The latent fertility of the soil and Turf bog   in many cases the abundance of turf bog for fuel have extended the evil beyond what it could have otherwise taken place. The former increasing high price of produce and the demand for people to supply the army etc., during the late war has served to increase the evil and at the same time to conceal it. But when this no longer operates it is exposed to a less deceptive view. Linen trade The linen manufacture has also served to extend the practice by affording employment for hands beyond what the farms could require. The long and numerous emigrations from Ulster, if they have not promoted the practice, they have in some degree retarded its effects and have been so far a source of blessing, perhaps more than any drain of capital which has attended them, although they have often been jealously dis-
War and peace couraged. If the *war* served to conceal the former tendency to the sub-division of lands, the return of *peace* has only served to increase the evil. The return of many from the army either with the command of some money to purchase portions of land, or from having no occupation or residence, have received a share from their relations or connections, the fall of prices and occurrence of adverse seasons, have also tended to promote
Adverse seasons sub-divisions. From the failure of many who occupied con-
and want of capital siderable portions of land, they have been obliged to part with or dispose of a portion in order to enable them to retain the remainder, and indeed from the want of capital or of persons able to occupy many of the lands relinquished by the ruin of the former tenants, landlords and agents have been induced to allow *sub-divisions* with a view to recover arrear-rents or to meet the reduced circumstances of such tenants as they could most readily procure.

In those parts of the country where the lands have been lately reclaimed or taken from pasture, where fuel is exceedingly scarce, and where such a degree of opulence has been acquired as to create a desire for a considerable degree of comfort, the farms are still found tolerably large compared with the common mode of occupation. But in other places the population has become so exceeding dense and over every estate many instances occur of holdings having become sub-divided to a ruinous degree and throughout the whole the same process is more or less obviously in rapid progression. Scarce a lease of ten or twenty years standing which is not already more or less sub-divided, many of no considerable extent, amongst an astonishing number of occupiers, and what must the result be when they shall again be sub-divided. In the Appendix to this report (page 313) some examples of this process on the Gosford estates are given and should they fail in conveying full conviction that the most ruinous consequences will result, if not checked, anything else which can be added here will be of little avail.

It ought to be kept in view that population increases in a geometrical ratio and the sub-division of lands in an inverse ratio. Thus for instance one farm on the estate was formerly held by one person and now by his three sons holding about eleven acres. Now suppose they each leave three children (on an average which would be very few considering the usual   p. 266 number from each marriage), in the second generation there will   Illustrations be 9 persons, each holding 1 acre and 35 perches; in the third generation 27 persons each holding 1 rood and 25 perches; and in the fourth generation 81 persons each holding 21 perches merely. Now when it is taken into account how very early and prolific the generality of marriages are (numbers see their grandchildren), that they divide their holdings with their children at an early period and during their own lives, and that this sub-division is still further promoted by the sale and disposal of portions to others who again sub-divide theirs in the same manner, the general increase and rate of division is not only wonderfully rapid but truly alarming. There are numerous instances where these results are in the most rapid progression, and scarce a single instance where they are not more or less so, as there are few leases or holdings granted ten, fifteen or thirty years ago which are not at this time occupied by two or more families.

Some who have acquired a desire and the means to appear above indigence have educated their children for professional pursuits or forwarded their emigration to America, from a conviction that to sub-divide their farms would be to beggar their descendants, but the check from an increased taste for comforts and conveniences is very limited in their number and affects. It more generally happens that if part of the children have been so disposed of, the farm is divided among *two*: the eldest son who marries first and the youngest who remains at home to assist in supporting the old age of his parents, and who gets this inheritance for his pains. In this way the process is

slower but tends to the same results for, as every sub-division
lowers the occupier in the scale of ability, notwithstanding
their increased industry, the lower they become the less is the
desire or the opportunity of providing for their children otherwise than by sharing the farm with them. If the farm happens
to be held under an old lease and at a cheap rate they may
still contrive to live with tolerable comfort, even after the sub-
division, but when the lease expires and higher rents must be
paid, misery and privation begin. From being able to keep a
Consequences   pair of horses the division reduces them to one for each or for
illustrated   the use of several holdings and even that from the want of
pasture or fodder retained with difficulty or little profit. At
last even this must be given up and a cow forms the chief
treasure, the butter paying a large portion of rent; the owner
being happy in retaining the buttermilk and potatoes with the
whole or part of the grain crop. If he again sub-divides or
loses his cow he must then be satisfied with the potato crop
alone, the grain and flax crops being barely sufficient to pay
his rent; and as from the want of animal manure they are
yearly becoming worse and at length from the exhausted state
of the lands prove inadequate to pay rents, particularly in
bad seasons, beyond this stage misery and ruin are rarely
avoidable. A large arrear is accumulated, which after long indulgence cannot be paid, and the holding given up not only
with so much loss to the rental but the lands and buildings in
bad order. Where the *linen* and *cotton* manufacture is vigorously followed, the evils may be a little longer averted while
the family can be maintained from the whole or greater part
of the lands, the tenant depending on the spinning wheel and
the loom to pay his rent. But when the farm is again divided,
as it generally is, among his children, who when they obtain
families of their own, their diminished portion of land cannot
produce sufficient for their support, and they must of course
labour for it, and when provisions get high or the price of
cloth and yarn falls their whole labour is barely adequate, if
equal, to purchase food for increased numbers. To pay rent
in such case is totally beyond their power and when the lands
happen to be re-let to persons of somewhat better means the
same process again goes on. If it happens to be let to a tenant
occupying another portion, such addition is generally only so
much thrown into a common stock to be again portioned out,
and in this way is almost every property frittering down into
holdings which can only be occupied with increasing misery
to the tenants and ultimate loss to the proprietor. Where the
p. 267 increase of opulence from superior industry etc., has afforded

some temporary check, less of this is to be seen but there are now large tracts in the last stages of the progress; at least any punctual payment of rent is hopeless and the occurrence of arrears unavoidable.

This progressive declension of the great body of the tenantry is not imaginary: every single townland, almost every single farm or lease, furnishes illustrations or proofs. Hence in going over estates one is constantly assailed by the many who bring to mind the late substantial condition of their predecessors, even by individuals who were brought up in comparative opulence being in one short generation reduced to great poverty. The very prevalence of such melancholy feeling must alone operate very disadvantageously to industry, as its best support is a cheerful contentment arising from the enjoyment of bettering their condition; brooding over distresses which they are ever ready to exaggerate and to ascribe the cause to anything in preference to their own conduct, for the persons who reason thus are following the same course with their own children, frequently from the want of reflection on the consequences, perhaps as often from a hopeless, careless inability to do otherwise. The increasing poverty of each succeeding generation has therefore a most injurious effect on morals. Poverty generally operates to depress and consequently to degrade and when no wish or hope remains of bettering their condition they become indifferent to the most essential concerns of life. The occupation of farms of too reduced a size, from not furnishing constant employment to the family, fosters that extreme love of ease and pleasurable modes of passing time too common in Ireland. and while it is so destructive of industry is equally destructive of morals and if it does [not] tend to promote ignorance, it assists but little in its removal. A portion of information is essential to cherish moral conduct, industry and successful husbandry.

Progress of the evil

Unfavourable to industry and morals

Capital is as indispensable as skill and nothing so powerfully operates to prevent its accumulation as the sub-division of lands and increase of population. Not only are the gains too inconsiderable to allow of such accumulation but the supernumeraries of the families who must live on the industry of the others swallow up all that can be procured and when sickness or bad seasons occur there is nothing in store to make up the deficiency (saving banks can avail little under such circumstances, when there is no means of employing them, see Appendix page [301]). Indeed the capital of the greater part may be properly said to consist of the *landlord's due* as the prompt and regular payment of rent would totally incapacitate them

Prevents accumulating capital

from longer occupying their holdings: hence the ruin which follows where this is rigorously enforced or casualties occur to prevent their making the usual payments. The distinction between *English* and *Irish* tenants is well known, the latter being allowed one year in arrears or owing what is termed the *dead gale*, and attempts to render them English tenants in this respect have been generally injurious in the end. When land is in the possession of persons only a few degrees above mendicity, and greatly deficient in the requisite information or the means of conducting agriculture with success, it is not surprising that the quantity of food provided is so far below what might be from equal labour on the same soil under better management.

The want of a *horse* where *lime* is essential to ensure successful cultivation and must be brought from a distance, is great indeed, as well for this purpose as for drawing home *turf*, carrying produce to market and especially for labour. Those who cannot keep a horse or horses must of course want until those who do possess them have their own lands tilled, and thereby often lose the best part of the season, and the crops rendered later and more uncertain than those of their more fortunate neighbours around them. And a cow is indispensable to procure manure in order to ensure an adequate supply of potatoes, for the occupiers of small holdings without such assistance are obliged to buy part of their subsistence, frequently a large share, which requires a proportional part of their gain by manufacture, and between the old and new crops often suffer great hardship and hunger. In fact no tenant ought to be allowed to hold, at least to get a lease, who does not possess a cow—the butter of which is so important to assist the rent—to ensure a supply of potatoes [and] the subsequent crops of grain and pasture. It is the frequent want of *livestock* which renders bad seasons so severely felt by the lower class of tenants. The flattering pictures of Irish abundance which p. 268 were drawn by Arthur Young and others about some thirty or forty years ago, are now infinitely less general and as the consumption of the population is now rapidly becoming equal to the average supply, the melancholy and distressing consequences of scarcity when this supply falls under the average is, and will be more and more dreadful. A total or very general failure of the potato crop must be more injurious than that of any other on which the population are less dependent because when subsistence is reduced to the lowest scale, as it is when potatoes form the chief food, there is no substitute which can be easily resorted to, as may be the case where wheat and other grains are in common use. And it is this which in all time to come will create additional misery in Ireland when a failure of the potatoes, more or less extensive, takes place; a proportional share of the resources of the tenantry are absorbed to procure subsistence and of course nothing or less produce remains to pay rent.

The interests of landlord and tenant are too nearly allied and intimately connected to be long at variance without manifest loss to both. The direful consequence of the too rapid increase of population to the tenantry themselves, has been discussed at large, and that this must be injurious to the proprietor is too obvious to require much further illustration; whatever disables the tenant and abridges his comforts and abilities to industry must ultimately, if not immediately, lessen the rental. When the usual supply of crops cannot be raised and the whole or greater part of the other gains from manufacture are required to procure subsistence, it is evident rent cannot be paid. Hitherto privations and high prices have enabled such reduced tenants to pay rents with greater or less punctuality but as the increase of population is not only more rapid than the increase of food under good systems of rural management, it must be more deficient and extend with greater rapidity when the very same cause which augments the population, also tends to lessen the quantity of food produced; each succeeding year will leave less for the landlord, until the whole will be engrossed. That this *ultimatum* is not so very distant as to excite little present alarm is obvious since it has actually been long in operation. This is proved from the late adverse seasons which were more severely felt in Ireland than among the rural population in Britain which is infinitely less dense. So great a scarcity may not again speedily occur but every five or six years is commonly more or less deficient and when it is considered that the population will be increased in proportion to the length of time which may intervene, a less severe scarcity will produce equal if not greater calamity.

Thus poverty and the necessary consequence—ignorance and discontent—which result from the *minute sub-division* of lands, the temptations to idleness and hopeless despondence (while they render parents careless in making any comfortable provisions for their *own* old age, or the future situation of their children) powerfully influence the conduct of the latter, as industry is the acquirement of early life and becomes strengthened and habitual by years. Inferior desire for additional comforts, merely a desire to exist without consideration of future consequences, leads to premature and improvident marriages to which the sub-division of lands furnish the chief facility. When a son marries he gets a portion of his father's holding or looks out for a partner who can obtain it from her father, and even the want of this prospect is little bar to connections of this kind. Hence the possession of a cabin and a *patch* of land is the great object of every individual and from the number of competitors the rents are proportionally high, being not regulated by the *real value* of the holding, nor by the ability of the parties, but the urgency of their wants, And in this way the population is increased beyond the *capital* of the country employed in agriculture, and always leaving a large part of most families as supernumeraries, who must subsist on the produce of others' labour to which they have no power of contributing, or on the share of produce which ought properly to belong or fall to the landlord. A greater number of hands must be employed to perform a less quantity of labour, and that more imperfectly, from the inability to have it better, from the want of proper implements etc.

p. 269   Even live stock must often be wanting or maintained at an excessive expense. One half of the generality of occupiers who are still able to retain one or more cows have to purchase the whole or a considerable part of the fodder for winter and this forms a very common drawback against paying of rents. When the general interest of landlords and happiness of the country are placed in so alarming a predicament it surely ought to excite attention, to adopt what may appear most likely to effect a change.

Small farms: why particularly unfit for the Gosford estates   The Reporter may not have been able to illustrate this most important subject with sufficient distinctness but it is not the least important and he will now proceed to state why he conceives it particularly so as applied to the Gosford estates. In the remarks on the mineral formation of these estates it has been repeatedly noticed that the *soil* is naturally deficient in calcareous matter, and (in page 234) that the prevailing soils on them are difficult to manage, and ill-adapted to be held in occupation by poor tenants without the skill or ability to labour them sufficiently. In a rich *calcareous* soil, in little need of extraneous and distant manure, poor tenants or those holding very inconsiderable portions may be able to occupy them with considerable advantage, but when the circumstances of the country are quite dissimilar the case is very different, and more particularly where *fuel* is remote, to obtain which even for the consumption of a small family is often a very material item to a poor tenant. Unless the upper part of Baleek manor, the greater part is remote from turf and will every year be more so. A due supply of this necessary article is indispensable to promote the manufacture of linen and the burning of *lime* which tenants who might contrive to draw and burn it themselves, could not find opportunity of money to purchase it ready burned else-where.

In attempting to remedy or check the evils which have been just recited, many difficulties occur, some of which may appear insurmountable. Sons and daughters marry and are retained in the houses of their fathers, and by degrees get into the occupa-tion of part of their lands, and any attempts to remove them must be painful in the extreme. Having no property but the interest in their lease or holding, it is but natural that parents should wish to part this amongst their children, instead of giving all to one or a few, and any endeavour to change this mode of proceeding must excite much unpleasant feeling among the unfortunate sufferers. But when it is taken into account that this division, so reasonable in appearance, is productive of future misery to those concerned and of certain loss to the landlord who is equally bound to secure his own interest, the occasion of temporary distress may be the means of preventing much greater in future. An assurance that no sub-division would be allowed might perhaps tend to lessen the solicitude to obtain land without considering of their ability to pay rents, and might also tend to create a greater degree of provident care and exertion to procure other means of settling and disposing of the other branches of their family, or the farm might be disposed of and the produce divided among them. The diffi-culties which do exist may deter many from making any attempt to surmount them, but there are other persons who still enter-tain objections to such attempts from a conviction that they may prove injurious. Prepossessions of this kind may be traced to the mistaken ideas which have been long entertained with regard to the fancied advantage of an abundant population: conceiving that it cannot be too abundant. And perhaps it cannot under certain circumstances but it requires little force of argument to prove that half a dozen industrious persons, well fed and accommodated, are capable of more exertions than double the number wretched and discontented, as they are certainly more likely to contribute to the strength and wealth of the country and to furnish a surplus for the payment of rent. In some peculiar situations the occupiers of very small portions of land may for a time be found to pay rents better than others around them holding larger portions but although this may be the case in partial instances, yet the tendency must be ultimately productive of the same injurious consequences. The evident decrease of the linen manufacture already noticed, will oblige

p. 270 the tenantry to become more dependent on agriculture and this
must be ruinous to landlords, unless the farms are of a size to
be occupied so as to afford a surplus for rent. Much has been
urged in favour of the beneficial effects of the *linen manufacture*
being connected with agriculture as in Ulster (and compared
with the effects of overgrown manufactures carried on in towns,
on morals they are correct) and it has, as already noticed
(page 251), tended to augment rents. And perhaps could the
system be restricted within due limits it would be of permanent
advantage to landlords but it tends powerfully to a minute
sub-division of the lands which must to a moral certainty prove
injurious to the interest of the latter. And this will be more
speedily the case as the profits of this branch of labour become
lessened, either from the reduced state of manufacture or the
increase of population requiring a greater share of labour to
procure subsistence. And this is in fact already the case in a
remarkable degree so that the advantages hitherto derived
from it or their being continued in peculiar situations, decide
nothing in favour of the general policy of the system.

Having attempted to illustrate the causes which have tended
to the rapid increase of population and the injurious sub-
divisions of lands, and the evils resulting therefrom, it remains
to suggest what occurs as the most practicable and judicious
means of checking or removing them in a way least injurious
to the tenantry and the landlord. This is imperative but ought
to be considered with care as injudicious attempts might not
only prove abortive but prevent any being successful hereafter.
Some have considered any means of correcting the evil impossible or impracticable at present, some consider that evils of this
kind will work their own cure (fortunate indeed it is that such
evils do sooner or later operate in this way); but then it is
obvious that unless timely remedied it must be with great
distress, and loss to landlords. There is no human probability
that anything can soon naturally occur to check the increase
of population in this country or to provide for their future
employment or support unless by consuming the whole or
greater part of the produce of the soil, and so depriving the
landlord of the share he might derive from a less dense population possessed of greater skill and industry. Any great mortality
which might materially lessen the numbers must for a time
deprive landlords of any return, where lands must be for some
time vacant and few possessed of means to again occupy them
with advantage. But in the meantime the pressure of population
will be the constant occasion of arrear, whatever the *nominal*
rent may be. Under such circumstances indigence must daily

increase while any exertion of private or public benevolence will not be able to alleviate, for were the stream of charity to flow even or abundantly, though it might produce some partial relief it could effect no remedy. The ability to give can by no possibility be competent to supply the wants of indolent and unemployed, increasing thousands. Giving would indeed but aggravate the evil which the power of earning can only remove. Giving, while it debases, generally slackens industry and any attempts to better the condition of the rural population which have not for their object not merely encouragement to industry but also to check the increase of population and better the condition of those which already exist, will only in the end be injurious. Unless great pains are taken to render the tenantry respectable a desire of greater comfort will not tend to check the too rapid increase of population: but how any artificial check can be made to operate is a difficult problem.

Any hasty innovation would involve a great part of the lower and most numerous class of tenants in incalculable misery and bring so much embarrassment on landlords that it is difficult to afford any immediate and substantial melioration to the *former* without loss to the *latter*. Unless the mutual interest of both are consulted they cannot be expected to be adopted or to succeed. Were the lands to be at once thrown into what might be elsewhere deemed profitably large farms, beside the capital required to be in the possession of the occupier a great expenditure on the part of the proprietor would be also necessary, at least in the first instance, to the evident reduction p. 271 of his income. To procure such persons would be totally impossible in Ireland and to think of obtaining them from any other country is absurd since a change of this kind might be effectually resisted by the present tenantry; and even could such be procured, in what way could so many families be disposed of, which under such an arrangement must be dispossessed of their holdings and shelter. It is not possible to conceive the heartbreakings and calamities which would attend so great a change in their condition, which could not be assuaged by any prospective benefit capable of being shown to the present generation or future promise of advantage to their posterity. In fact so many helpless wretches without house, without food, and deprived of all prospect of obtaining them any more, reduced to despair and animated with all the sentiments which distinguish a people in despair, a rebellion would be unavoidable of a new description, and such as in all the varieties of human calamities never occurred before. But still, as the evils result from *moral* causes they admit of correction, if not of removal. Perhaps they have been already allowed to proceed too far to be speedily removed. All that can be at present effected is to check their further progress: their removal must be a work of time.

Rents when too high may be lowered with advantage so as to encourage perseverance but beyond what is necessary for this they will only tend to slacken industry and exertion. They cannot have the smallest tendency to prevent the sub-division of lands: on the contrary they will rather encourage it. Leases are also essential to improvement but if granted without any restriction they will not tend to alter the same system. It might be difficult, perhaps impossible, to alter the size of the holdings throughout the estates or to remove the present occupiers where they may be considered too small. But any further sub-division should not be allowed on any account—and against which they should be strictly bound in the leases now to be granted—each person being served with a printed notice to this effect, stating that on any division being made the penalties will be rigorously enforced. A similar notice should be kept constantly and conspicuously posted up in the office where the rents are received and as there is no document so carefully preserved and attentively perused as the receipts granted for payment of rent, it might essentially serve to impress the indispensable importance of attending to observe the regulations against sub-divisions, if a memorandum to the same effect was printed on such receipts. And those who occupy old leases [see page 322]* and articles should also in like manner be immediately served with a similar notice that any division which may take effect after this time will not be recognised when the leases shall expire: every existing division having been carefully surveyed and marked on the maps, and any which are hereafter not found so recorded not to be recognised. In the remarks on leases (page 262) it was suggested that a clause should be inserted against alienation to any except to a child, grandchild, or wife, and then only to pass into the occupation of *one* individual, but no objection ought to be made against the holding being left to the whole family when it is intended to be disposed of and the proceeds shared. But the obligation to pass into the occupation of *one* person only, ought to be strictly enforced unless in cases where a house and cow's grass might be reserved for the life of a widow etc., or at least every facility should be afforded to provide for their families otherwise than by sub-dividing their lands. It might be of utility in the notice just mentioned to state briefly but distinctly the

---

*Marginal annotation.

proprietor's object in preventing the future sub-division of lands, tending as much to their own ultimate benefit as to his.

But until the great body of the tenantry is made sensible p. 272 that the source of their chief misery arises from their predilection for improvident and premature marriages, encouraged by the too common and minute sub-divisions of lands, the trouble of preventing it will be considerable and often attended with distressing occurrences. In steadily adhering to the resolution of preventing it, which ought not to be given up in any case, as that would lead to dissatisfaction in others where the same indulgence might not be granted, a suitable and well-directed education cannot fail and will perhaps be the first and most effectual means of inculcating the advantages of industry and a desire for superior comforts resulting from a cheerful compliance with the laws and regulations of society, and resignation to the situation in which they may be placed by providence. A radical and fundamental change and a thorough reformation of habits and opinions cannot be speedily brought about and must require due time and slow and gentle operations: hence the interest of landlords in attending to promote schools on their estates (see further, page 286).

A considerable part of the population consists of cottagers or cottiers holding cabins and small patches of land at will from the occupiers who hold from the proprietor. They have been greatly lessened in number during the late adverse years, having with their families become paupers at large, from which state they are seldom far removed. They will soon again become too numerous, often rather encouraging than aiding the industry of the tenants they hold from, and assisting materially in consuming the turf bogs, which now in most places require to be husbanded for the use of the tenantry alone. They also increase the pauperism of the country and add to the public distress in times of scarcity and disease and besides, they most powerfully tend to promote the sub-division of lands, offering rents for the payment of which they seldom possess adequate means. If tenants are prohibited from sub-dividing their farms, they will resort to the system of granting *cot-takes* to their children who may happen to marry, and by this means insensibly creep into the occupation of a share of the farms and in so far defeat the intention. Therefore it is important that every tenant be prevented from sub-letting or in any way granting cot-takes without written liberty. Cottiers are frequently essential for the due occupation of farms of a more considerable size or where the occupiers have not sons etc., to assist them. A reference to the Tabular Report and a com-

parison of the extent and population will show where such
liberty may be granted and this will require particular attention
if the system of checking sub-division suggested be thought
worth adopting. Indeed there is no part of estate management
which will require so vigilant attention as the enforcing of this
system, but there is none which will better reward the trouble
of so doing.

It is not only necessary to prevent the holdings being further
sub-divided but also to promote their *enlargement* in order to
ensure the comfort and, as far as possible, the respectability
of the tenants. Perhaps this can be most effectually and advantageously effected by encouraging the more opulent tenants to
purchase or take such lands as are relinquished or given up by
the more indigent occupiers, but restricting them from again
sub-dividing unless where they purchase or take an additional
holding to retain it as a separate farm for one of their children.
There are several substantial tenants on the Gosford estates
who enjoy old leases and are industrious, who could afford to
occupy more land with advantage to themselves and the
proprietor and such augmentations when advisable and
practicable should be promoted. In this way the tenantry
might be gradually improved, care being observed to preserve
them so. Indeed there is little doubt but it would prove successful and the result advantageous. The Reporter has had experience of this kind on some properties on which he has been
p. 273 employed. And when the occupiers of the more considerable
farm are from indigence, old age, etc., no longer able to occupy
the whole, no portion should be let separately but the entire
let to a more substantial tenant.

An inquiry arises out of the preceding remarks on what *size*
of farms are best adapted to the nature and situation of the
lands and the character, skill and capital of the tenantry; and
on this subject a few observations will suffice for although the
Reporter has urged the losses arising from the minute sub-
division of lands, he has not lost sight of the important consideration that to attempt any change or innovation which
such circumstances may not warrant would be absurd and
injurious. Large and small farms are only comparative epithets:
in this part of the country from twenty to fifty acres is considered a large farm, elsewhere it would be reckoned exceeding
small. From the dependence of the tenantry on manufacture
the generality have in a great measure hitherto paid for accommodation to carry on the particular details of this business.
But this is not universally the case and the Reporter has
repeatedly urged the necessity of looking forward to less

dependence on manufacture as it is not now so profitable as formerly and most likely to be less so. As a means of preventing the loss which its decrease must otherwise occasion to landlords, however advantageous the connection of agriculture and manufactures have hitherto been considered or however prejudicial it may be hereafter, it cannot possibly be altered but by a process exceeding slow.

It is a more arduous task than the speculative and inexperienced may be aware of, to alter the general economy and arrangement of an estate with profit and credit, as much must depend on its natural and acquired circumstances. Its situation, soil, present state of occupation, or system of management, and the present size of the farms require to be maturely studied and duly weighed before any effective steps can be safely taken. If this is done from sufficient data and a hearty desire to promote the permanent good of the estate, plans may be considered and set on foot for its future improvement, which will only require attention and perseverance to be accomplished and ultimately successful. Where the art of agriculture is still in its infancy farms must be small because there is neither capital to cultivate nor skill to manage large occupations. As capital increases and skill improves farms become large and at last attain a *size* calculated to return the highest rent to the proprietor, and with advantage and comfort to the occupiers.

Discussions on the size of farms as a branch of political economy have been numerous but to little practical utility as the declaimers or parties have been either advocates for large or small farms; although it must be evident that whatever scale of occupation may be best adapted to the given situation, extremes should be avoided, [and] such a gradation exist which is essential to encourage industry, frugality and emulation, which are the sinews and nerves of society and would otherwise lose their stimulus and are best laid on by a gradation of farms. Farms of an excessive size or too much above the means of the occupiers must be unbeneficial to all, but the frequent recommendation of small farms to be cultivated by mere manual labour seems to be erroneous in idea and one of the many weeds which have sprung up in the luxuriant garden of philanthropy. On lands naturally of a friable and of a rich quality, in a few situations the plough may be abandoned and cultivated entirely by the spade but in the present state of agricultural skill and industry they must be limited, and in all other situations they are inapplicable with advantage. From the crowded population [and] the want of capital and skill it is not likely that farms can for a great length of time be augmented in Ireland to the size common in the best improved districts in Britain.

But the rural economy of Flanders etc., is a proof that very considerable improvements may be effected on comparatively small farms. In Ireland even where manufacture is called in aid of agriculture the gains of the former are now rarely sufficient to render tenants wholly independent of the return of the latter for the payment of rents. Unless they possess a sufficiency of land and means to keep a cow they must suffer much from the want of the produce of butter to assist in paying rents, and p. 274 of the manure to enrich the ground; and when potatoes are scarce none or only a limited quantity can be spared to fatten pork, so essential an aid to pay rent. There is no part of the estates that can be long occupied without the essential aid of animal manure: as the land from exhaustion must be constantly getting less productive the occupiers will not be able to obtain a sufficiency of food, flax, etc., and their gains from manufacture (however industrious and self-denied) will not be sufficient to procure the deficiency and to pay rent. It has already been stated (page 233) that the lands from being naturally deficient in calcareous matter require lime etc., to be rendered sufficiently fertile, and as it has to be brought from a distance a horse or horses must be kept for the purpose as well as for bringing home turf etc., which is now also become distant from many of the farms. A horse cannot be kept advantageously without a sufficient breadth of land for by endeavouring to keep a horse without such extent, a large proportion of the tenantry are greatly embarrassed, being only able to keep one cow in addition or to purchase a considerable extra quantity of provender, which is a serious drawback on their gains. The same necessity occasions a stinted supply of this and also of pasture during summer, so that the cow yields an inferior quantity of milk and butter and the horse can only perform a scanty portion of labour and besides he must be kept idle from inability or want of employment a great part of the time.

If lands are continued in such small allotments tenants must continue poor and dispirited, and the lands must continue in a hopeless state of perpetual unproductiveness for every effort to excite a spirit of industry under such circumstances will seldom prove successful. Until the farms are enlarged and the mode of occupation more or less changed, as the circumstances of the case may require, the country can never be put into a successful state of progressive amelioration or the lands be made to yield nearly the quantity of human subsistence that they are naturally susceptible of being brought to afford, and the proportional rent accruing therefrom. In fact, unless vigorous efforts are made to introduce a more advantageous system the results will be more and more unfavourable to landlords, as has been already urged. Where the tenants occupy a sufficient extent of ground (with adequate means and industry) to keep two cows and a horse, they contrive to pay rent with comparative ease because they can afford to dispose of a considerable quantity of butter, pork, flax, and even of grain, and some of potatoes; and in assisting others with horse-labour they obtain what may be necessary to purchase additional provender etc., where that may be requisite. But unless there is constant employment for this *one* horse and a person to attend him, an evident waste must be sustained and the greatest possible return cannot be made at the least possible expense.

It is from the regular division of labour that the manufactures and agriculture of Britain have attained to their present perfection and in every case similar principles must more or less regulate the interests of landlords and tenants in Ireland. It rarely happens that the same individual who has to attend to the loom, the plough and the spade is able to derive any considerable gain from either, as some of them must be occasionally neglected. The most profitable connection between agriculture and manufacture seems to be where the occupiers have either sons or can employ other hands to weave constantly, unless at those seasons when they can be called advantageously to assist in rural labour, the farms being sufficiently large to furnish subsistence for them, and their gains nearly adequate or chiefly so to pay the rent etc. A tenant occupying a farm sufficient to employ a pair of horses and to keep two or more looms going by his sons, apprentices or journeymen can pay a higher rent, and live better than one holding a less portion, and the occasional death of a cow etc., will not so readily disable him from paying such rent. The whole or most considerable part of the produce is consumed without being taken to market and the chief part of the flax wrought up, affording employment to all the branches of the family incapable of being otherwise profitably occupied; and in case of any temporary p. 275 or permanent check to manufacture he enjoys a resource (more attentive management of his land) which is latterly out of the power of a tenant holding a small portion.

It is therefore recommended to endeavour by every possible means to increase the number of farms affording employment for a *pair of horses* as much as possible. Perhaps for a long

12

period this will be found the most profitable mode of occupation: as capital, skill and enterprize increase the farms may be extended, and this further change should be looked forward to as the most desirable ultimatum. Encouragement to the more substantial tenants to add to their farms when opportunity serves, without liberty to again sub-divide, has been already suggested as the safest and most practicable means of effecting this end. Where the situations of the tenantry are so very dissimilar it would be absurd to specify any determined size of farms. None should be less than sufficient to maintain a cow or if possible two cows, and the extent of land necessary for this must depend on the quality, say three, five or ten acres. To keep two cows and a horse double this quantity, and to keep a pair of horses etc., with any tolerable advantage from thirty to fifty acres; and as large a proportion as possible should be of the latter kind. The number of indigent tenants who will be obliged to relinquish their holdings may afford ample opportunities of augmenting the size of farms but the more opulent who are already resident on the estate or those who might be desirous of removing from others, cannot be expected to make additions or to expend money so as to occupy them with profit unless due encouragement is held out.

A proprietor may be anxious to afford such encouragement but may either be at a loss to know how to extend it, or may not afford such ostensible evidence of it as will suffice to convince the public that he is in good earnest. It has been already noticed that the real substantial interests of the tenant and the landlords are or ought to be the same: unreasonable rents are destructive to the tenant's prosperity, ruinous to his capital or preventing the accumulation of any, and entailing a double loss on the landlord by a defalcation of rent and in the deterioration of his estate. Moderate rents under fair terms and covenants secured by lease are the principal means of securing their payment and the progressive improvement of the lands. But other encouragements may be used with success especially

THE CHARACTER OF THE ESTATE

For estates like men have their *good* or *bad* characters—which it is of vast utility to establish and preserve. No man who has even a small capital to lose will readily take up his residence on an estate of known or reported bad character; on the contrary when once an estate has acquired the character of a good faith and proper treatment of its tenantry men possessed of means will be anxious there to gain a footing. Besides, setting income at nought it surely is incumbent on a landed proprietor to pay some attention to the character of his estates for what can well add more to the permanent respectability of rank and fortune than a respectable tenantry. It has been well-observed that in a state of civilised society and property one of the great arts of life is to teach character and interest to go hand in hand, and on ordinary occasions to endeavour to turn every incident as it fortuitously occurs to their mutual advantage. If a tenant of capital and improving spirit be found upon an estate, give him due encouragement for the purpose already explained; on the contrary, if another be found to possess refractory habits, to swerve from his engagements, or to injure the lands in his occupation, it is but common prudence to take the first legal and fair opportunity of dismissing him and of supplying his place with another who is better qualified to fill it, not more with a view of rescuing his particular farm from further injury, and making an example of him in terror to others of similar habits, than to preserve and heighten the character of the estate. Hence the utility of such survey as is detailed in this report, in attempting to develop the government of an estate (as already noticed, page 13).

There are few estates on which there are not more than a p. 276 sufficiency of tenants who are ready to break through their obligations without the encouraging example of a superintendent, and it is extreme folly to do anything to induce well-disposed men to join their number. On the contrary it is no more than common prudence to fulfil with scrupulous exactness every covenant, agreement and every promise, which may have been made to the meanest tenant on the estate, in order to inspire others with the same principle and to divest bad men of every pretext for carrying their evil intentions into effect.

Nor is it in mere matters of *good faith* alone that the pro- Encouraging good prietor or managers ought to set an example to the tenantry: tenants endeavours should be used to liberalise their minds by good offices and acts of kindness. There are numberless favours which can be bestowed on them without any or much loss, and very many with eventual advantage to the estate. In fact a spirited and improving tenant should be refused nothing that he can reasonably ask; nay, voluntary favour should be conferred on him, not merely as a reward for the services which he may individually render the estate but to induce its other tenants to follow his example, and to make known to the whole that their conduct is observed and distinction made between good and bad occupiers. If, on the contrary, there is no distinction made between those who are improving the estate and those who are running it to ruin, or perhaps from whim encouraging the latter and discountenancing the former, the consequence need not be traced. Tenants who are able to improve are also able to impoverish and when disgusted by improper treatments will destroy the lands and take the first opportunity of moving to another estate under rational management. And thus every part of an ill-managed estate tends towards ruin until in process of time none but slovens and adventurers who want a temporary residence can be found upon it. When fair-dealing and encouragement is uniformly afforded, higher rents will be more cheerfully paid and at the same time improvements carried on, than lower rents under different management.

On the choice of tenants   A choice of proper tenants is of great importance, particularly at a period like the present when so many of the occupiers must relinquish and be changed. Reasonable rents and a substantial tenantry are certainly the most desirable objects of attention where the permanent prosperity of the proprietor and the occupiers of the lands is fairly taken into consideration. In fact, choosing tenants is little less important then fixing rents. It is evident that the qualifications of a good tenant are *capital, skill, industry and character*. Tenants possessed of the two former are comparatively rare in this part of the country; yet there are some to be found who still possess a share of the gains of former years and where they can be obtained in place of the more indigent they supplant, are to be considered as valuable acquisitions, not only from the hope of recovering arrears but from the permanent improvements they may be expected to effect and the punctual payments of rent they may ensure. *Skill* is yet limited in extent and must be the work of time, to which nothing will so essentially contribute as the dissemination of education, endeavours to establish a respectable tenantry, and to afford them due encouragement. *Industry* is indispensable and may exist without either of the former although with limited effect. An industrious and frugal man will strive with difficulties and get on with less money than a man of contrary qualifications but if he has not a sufficiency of *livestock* to work his land and raise manure, or money to purchase them under ordinary circumstances, he must long live in poverty and on the first attack of misfortune or the failure of crops probably sink under the weight of his accumulated burden. Where *skill* and *capital* are not only wanting but also *industry*, the case and payment of rent is hopeless: but without industry, capital and skill would be unavailing in rural labour when so much depends on seasons and the weather.

p. 277 Idleness is a vice of the darkest hue and every instance of negligence is not only injurious in itself but operates as a bad example and serves as an excuse for the half-industrious with which every estate is more or less encumbered. The moral character of tenants is also important for many will be found sometimes possessed of considerable capital and industry who nevertheless do not merit encouragement. Seeing the intimate connection which necessarily subsists between proprietors and occupiers and how advantageous it is to preserve good order upon an estate, thereby giving freedom to the exertion of its tenantry, it becomes a matter of some importance in choosing a tenant to enquire into his social character, particularly as it relates to habits of sobriety and to a peaceful or a quarrelsomeness of demeanour, as one drunken, gambling person may debauch a townland and an ill-tongued, plotting, litigious fellow keep a whole district in continual animosity.

Tenant right is one of the many peculiar considerations **Tenant right** affecting landed property in Ireland. That a tenant making improvements or enjoying the advantage of a lease and wishing to dispose of the same should expect some adequate remuneration is not surprising, and ought not to be objected to on the part of the proprietor (if the incoming tenant is suitable) whatever clauses may exist against alienation, because it might form an obstacle to improvement if no such advantage could not be derived from them if disposed of. All that is necessary to provide against is the introduction of improper tenants and that mischievous traffic of letting and sub-letting until a farm rented at a *fair* rent passes through one or more intermediate tenants, each deriving a profit rent, until it comes into the occupation of persons too overburdened to make any improvement. But a claim of tenant right where no lease exists and where no improvements have been made is unknown in any other country, and although it cannot at once be done away or in every case wholly unrecognized, yet it ought to be discountenanced as much as possible as nothing has more powerfully tended to retard improvement by its forming an obstacle to the easy introduction of a better class of tenants, and engrossing the capital which ought to be expended in the improvement and occupation of the land. The pressure of population is either the chief cause or effect of this right, and while money was abundant and prices high, sums were universally paid merely for this right which would have formed a sufficient capital for the improvement of the lands. A tenant possessed of some means, in his anxiety to obtain the possession of land, expends the whole and perhaps all his credit can obtain in addition, and he comes into occupation reduced in both means and credit, incapable of making any effort to improve or perhaps to pay rent; and the money so disposed is productive of little benefit, as it either furnishes the means of emigration and is so lost to the country, or is oftener squandered by that improvidence which occasioned the sale of the holding.

ENCOURAGEMENT OF TENANTS

It is easier to conceive than particularise all the ways in which a proprietor may encourage improving and industrious tenants. In addition to granting *leases* at *fair* rents much may be done in a general way and perhaps not a little by definite *premiums*. The latter will at least serve to evince the good intentions of the proprietor towards them: they have generally failed in effecting the intended object in Ireland, viz. the introduction of better systems of management, most frequently from not being adapted to the peculiar circumstances of the country and tenantry, and by attempting too much at first, have failed in effecting almost any beneficial alteration. With a view to ascertain and point out the application of premiums on the Gosford estates it is necessary to inquire into the present systems of tillage and in order to ascertain in how far and in what manner they may be improved. It may be supposed that tenants will naturally adopt what they find to be for their own interest and they will uniformly do so to the extent of their

p. 278 skill and the encouragement afforded. But when that skill is limited and deficient it may often answer an important end to induce them to follow a better. The great obstacle to improvement is the temerity [timidity?] of tenants. That which is held out may not answer the intention and of course occasion so much actual loss to them but when a *premium* is afforded which in case of such failure would either wholly or in part cover such probable loss, there is an additional stimulus to make the attempt. And besides tenants are often afraid to make improvement for which they possess both *skill* and *means* from want of confidence that they will not be taken undue advantage of against themselves.

Excessive cropping   Where agricultural *skill* is deficient the common error on tillage lands is *excessive cropping*, successive crops of grain being taken so long as the land will produce any, and then in this exhausted state thrown out for pasture; and when recovered again subjected to the same process. And even when considerable attention and expense are bestowed to enrich the land by manures and tillage the same ruinous system is pursued, the effect of these being only to enable the system to be further extended and prolonged. The true art of husbandry may be said to consist in a knowledge how to fertilize lands in the easiest and most effectual manner and to obtain the greatest number of crops with the least possible reduction of such augmented fertility. And [as] this is effected in a judicious *rotation* of culmiferous and leguminous or succulent crops, the advantages of this compared with the contrary system are obvious: the one is constantly productive, the other only occasionally and even then inferior as to profit—after the first and second crops of grain they become so inferior as to scarce repay the expense of cultivation; and when the land is thrown to grass, weeds so occupy the surface that the grass produced is very trifling or of inferior value; and when the lands are again brought into tillage the roots and seeds of weeds prevent the crops of grain from being so productive as they would be under better management, and without the intervention of green crops properly cultivated and cleaned the weeds are only imperfectly destroyed. Indeed, had it not been for the natural fertility of the lands in Ireland and their aptitude to produce grass spontaneously the lands must have long since been less productive: and in particular, the necessity of procuring a sufficient or a due supply of potatoes has been the chief stimulus to procure manure, which is very generally collected with considerable pains but almost universally again exhausted by excessive cropping with grain, and thus accumulating a capital to be again dissipated, instead of its being allowed to remain in store, or only partially lessened, so as to form a capital stock for future reproductions *ad infinitum*. Under the exhausting system the supply of pasture and fodder is both coarse and limited, tending to retard the growth and profit of live stock, whereas under the enriching system the supply of herbage for the support of stock *both* during *summer* and *winter*, not only is increasing the profit on them but wonderfully augmenting the quantity of manure to keep up the same advantageous system. Under the one it is scarcely possible to prevent lands becoming constantly less productive: under the other care will render them increasingly productive.

The lands now under consideration are occupied in too small portions and the tenantry too deficient in capital to effect much, or skill to continue therein, to think of introducing the improved systems of agriculture. Yet much may be done. Whatever will be found tending to increase the extent of potato crops will be readily adopted. Hence the means of augmenting the supply of manure becomes important, and to prevent its being improperly exhausted it is necessary to promote and encourage the cultivation of artificial grasses with a view to check the evil of excessive cropping and also to augment the quantity of pasture and fodder: and these will again tend to augment the supply of manure to preserve and extend the same system.

Draining　　Draining especially on lands of a cold and retentive nature ought to form a *precursory* improvement, as on this being properly attended to, the success of all future operations must essentially depend. There is often more benefit derived from draining a field than would have been both from dunging and liming it: indeed the latter will not avail or will be of inferior importance and permanency without the lands be sufficiently dry. In the course of the preceding observations the importance p. 279　of draining has been repeatedly urged and the particular cases in which it is more immediately so adverted to. Beside the portion of arrears which are recommended to be liquidated by allowance for draining, premiums might be held out to others who are not in arrears. There are few general drainages in which many are mutually interested as the general hang of the country and hilly surface prevent any great stagnations of wet and from the great uniformity of the strata the same system of drainage is evident and generally applicable. Considerable attention has been made to open drains but they are in many cases too shallow, and covered drains are very generally wanting through the fields.

Fencing　　Enclosures and fencing. No farm can return an adequate rent unless properly enclosed and fenced. Fences are not only useful in affording shelter but necessary in confining *live stock* and protecting arable and meadow crops from their depredations. With the aid of proper fences an equal capital will make a larger return with less expense and loss and the embellishment they confer is far from being unworthy of notice. Beside saving the trouble and expense of herding [they] tend to prevent the early habit of indolence which it fosters. Without sufficient fences artificial grasses cannot be sufficiently cultivated as they will not otherwise be protected from cattle, especially during winter when on clayey soils the poaching of their feet would be most injurious. The lands have been generally sub-divided into small enclosures from the necessity of providing for their drainage but the ditches or shoughs are in many cases too shallow or not cleared so often as requisite, and their utility as fences is seldom complete unless by temporary expedients of stopping the numerous gaps with loose stones or bushes. In some of the upper part of the estates thorns would not thrive and in many places where they have failed more attention to place the good mould about the roots, to weed them, and protect them for a few years at first would have ensured success. Furnishing hedge plants to the tenantry, as has been sometimes done with advantage, might become too expensive as applied to so large an extent of property, but premiums for the different species of fences might be afforded (see page 318).

Lime and other manures. The nature and properties of the clayey or argillaceous soils which prevail on the Gosford estates have been already noticed (in page 233) and the vast utility of the judicious application of lime to soils naturally defective in calcareous matter. No *lime* occurs in the primitive formation on which the estates rest, except on the lands of Argonnell (see page 232), and although the quarries are at a considerable distance yet the lime is of an exceeding rich quality. Lime

Want of turf or fuel to burn it is likely to form the chief obstacle to its more extensive application, together with the prepossessions and injuries resulting from the *abuse* of this valuable source of fertility, and hence the utility of endeavouring to introduce better systems calculated to ensure the full advantage being derived from its application (see page 278). Perhaps the remoteness of the supply may be of some utility in preventing its being too extensively applied under the present imperfect systems of tillage and, as a greater part of the lands are of rather a shallow description, a less quantity is sufficient to produce effect. Clay soils cannot be profitably occupied without the assistance of lime: if properly applied it changes their nature and gives a degree of permanent fertility to them which can be imparted by no other manure. In bringing in new or *maiden* soils of this kind the use of lime is found to be so essential that little good can be done without it. *Lime* is also peculiarly beneficial in improving boggy or moorish soils by making them produce good herbage where nothing but heath and other unpalatable grasses grew formerly. [On] boggy soils enriched by other manures crops of grain will often set out with every appearance of success but on putting forth the ear they proceed no further and dwindle away in fruitless abortion, producing little beside straw: the same soils after getting a sufficient quantity of lime will produce good grain and in good seasons bring them to maturity in all future times, if the ground is kept under proper culture and the climate adapted to the crop.

Lime chiefly acts as a stimulus and by its injudicious application and abuse may prove very injurious, for where it duly p. 280

operates the whole powers of the soil are put into the state of requisition and may be forced to act till the very soul of vegetation is exhausted. It is scarcely practicable to restore fertility to land even of a good quality which has been thus abused: at least a considerable period must elapse before it can be restored to its original fertility. But thin moory and boggy soils after being exhausted by lime are not to be restored: lime alone will not restore fertility to lands worn out by excessive cropping; and when applied a second time to boggy soils it is only a useless expenditure of labour and may even sometime produce mischief. When the effects of lime have disappeared on clay soils etc., it might be supposed that a repetition of the dose would be equally beneficial in restoring the exhausted fertility, as on the first application; but from very general experience it appears that *unmixed lime* added a second time to the same soil even after an interval of many years is injurious to vegetation. And hence it seems in all cases necessary where lime has been applied before, to apply it again in much smaller proportions, and always in the form of a *compost* (generally with dung), a practice which in almost every case will be found advantageous. These remarks which are fully supported by facts, lead to important inferences and further corroborate the opinions already stated (in page 239) that much of the mountain lands formerly brought into cultivation by means of lime are no longer found to be equally productive, and that on lands of a stronger description the abuse of lime has been highly injurious, now rendering the crops infinitely less valuable. All lime granted to the tenantry in upland situations ought to be restricted to the tracts yet to reclaim. And [I would] further point out the great importance [of] introducing systems of management calculated to prevent the abuse of lime and to restore such lands as have been already so abused, because otherwise the profits derived from their occupation will be inferior to what was formerly derived on the first application of the lime. During the wet years of 1816-1817 all lands highly enriched and otherwise rendered friable absorbed the greatest quantity of moisture rendering the crops worse than on lands of an inferior quality, which from being compact more effectually resisted the wet: and as lime was the chief means employed to render the land friable, a prepossession has in many cases originated against its utility. But the success in common years will remove this mistake.

A more lasting prepossession arises from its abuse by excessive cropping, which a more judicious use of it can only remove. The land being allowed to go to grass or sown out with it after the *first* or at farthest the *second* grain crop, is the most effectual means of preventing the abuse of lime, as the *rest* which it will enjoy will [not] only produce more profitable pasture but fit it for farther crops of grain after such rest; and although the same number of successive grain crops may not be produced or obtained the quantity produced both of grain and grass will be infinitely greater and the staple and fertility of the soil preserved. Over a considerable part of the estates, particularly on the upper part of Beleek manor, the more the lands are improved by liming the more inferior are the crops of flax; and this would also be obviated by taking no more than one or two grain crops after its application, the flax crop being taken after breaking up from ley or grass.

In all the applications of lime it ought to be kept as near the surface as possible and intimately mixed with it because it has a natural tending to go down into it in the course of tillage, and when kept near the surface will operate with most beneficial effect, particularly in producing better and more abundant herbage. Necessity, the most useful monitor in the infancy of every art, has already taught many of the tenants to adopt an application of lime in a way likely to be beneficial, viz. applying the lime with the potato crop, or where the lands have been long under tillage and formerly either burned or marled, in mixing it with fresh soil before spreading it on the land. The argillaceous subsoil being dug up either out of pits, or in the process of sinking drains, and exposed for some time to the influence of the weather (the longer the better), if mixed with fresh-burned lime and allowed to remain so until carried out, thus making an artificial marl—renovating the soil by this acquisition of fresh mould and furnishing fresh materials for the *lime* to decompose and operate upon, so as to restore fertility even to very exhausted lands. Where lime is scarce and the soil not so strong as not to be easily injured by it, or where the tenantry are apt to use it injudiciously or to crop p. 281 excessively, it may be used with more advantage and safety thus mixed and in various other composts.

If a sufficient quantity of *lime* were employed and mixed with alternate layers of clay or clayey sods, combustion would take place and the clay be charred or burned to ashes, which would further promote fertility, and beside[s] render the *lime* more easy to spread with advantage, and would convert the clay into a substance little less efficacious. An excellent compost might be made of *lime*, *clay* and *bog-earth* or turf-mould (see Appendix No.   * (page 310): bog mixed with lime alone has rarely been found to answer.

---

*Blank in text.

Burning

Paring and Burning. The process of paring is not followed on the estates nor would its introduction be productive of advantage on lands so long under excessive tillage. Burning of bog etc., is practised and might be rendered more beneficial than what it is under the present system: it is one of the best practices of husbandry on suitable soils but may fall into discredit as being injurious in bad hands; and when too much of the best manures are applied and injudiciously used they are liable to the same objections. And exhausting courses of crops may be ruinous on all soils, unless on *siliceous* sandy soils and *rich moulds* which do not occur on the Gosford estates.

Where beneficial

Burning cannot be prejudicial if properly applied: on these moory soils such as occur on the uplands and the thin limestone soil as on Argonnell, burning is most liable to abuse but even then less excessive cropping and cultivation of artificial grasses will render it advantageous. Burning is one of the most advantageous modes of bringing in and improving all soils where the surface consists of a coarse sward composed of bog or other inactive substances, the ashes furnished serving as a stimulant to the dormant power of the soil. But prejudices have arisen from this abuse which led to the enactment of *abused* laws against its being adopted in any case: had they been directed to the mode of cropping after employing it, if they failed in effecting the intended object they would at least have been more rational. Where bog or turf-mould is burned either to reduce the depth of bog or to be afterwards applied to a field of a different sort of soil or quality, the effects of ashes used in this way are precisely the same with those of lime, though their operation is more violent and therefore sooner over. The first crop is commonly luxuriant but unless dung is afterwards administered the soil will rather be exhausted than enriched by the application of such ashes; and in all cases they should be as speedily as possible laid down or allowed to go to grass, the growth of which they are better calculated to promote than that of grain, both mixed with the soil and spread on the surface as a top dressing, particularly for *clovers* etc., especially on stiff and cold soils.

Burning clay is little practised in this district but might be more so with advantage and the common objections against burning do not apply to this practice. The speculative objections are that it reduces the depth and staple of the soil, and that it destroys the vegetable and animal matter in it. But it has been proved that where there is an excess of inert vegetable matters their destruction is beneficial, the carbonaceous matter remaining in the ashes being more useful to the crops than the vegetable fibre from which it was produced; and in cases where the texture of the earthy ingredients are permanently improved there is more than a compensation for this temporary disadvantage. The practice of burning sods or part of the green sward on clay soils has been long practised in Ireland, and is one of the few instances in which the agricultural practices of Scotland have been benefited by those of this country, where it is rapidly extending, the ashes produced being found excellent, particularly for turnips; and from experiments lately made it is said that lands of the same quality have been found even more productive with *burnt clay* than with stable manure. By this the power of cropping may be extended beyond what could otherwise be practicable, particularly in the vicinity of bogs where fuel is accessible, where this resource is cheap and **p.** 282 inexhaustible. On all extensive districts which are out of the reach of the lime and are destitute of good marl and other adventitious assistance, *paring* and *burning* the sod while in a green state and by a slow smothered fire will always reward the labour. The process of burning renders clay soils less compact, less tenacious and retentive of moisture, and when properly applied tends to render wet, stiff and cold lands dry and warm; and the soil in place of being thinned by the burning is in fact thickened because a portion of the subsoil is brought up and is impregnated and brought into action, whereby the staple is deepened and its productive powers increased. A portion of vegetable *alkali* which is so highly beneficial to the growth of plants is thus procured, besides the advantages of the burned clay on other soils. But the effects of burning although instantaneous are not of long duration: a dressing of dung soon becomes necessary. The great object in using stimulants is to use moderate cropping afterwards, otherwise what with justice might have been considered as a meritorious improvement may turn out to deserve a contrary character. To burn clay a portion of fuel is requisite and it unfortunately happens that in these parts of the estates where this practice would be most beneficial, that article is scarcest. Perhaps more ingenious methods of burning clay may be discovered: some of these already known and practised are mentioned in Appendix (page 310).

Marl occurs in many places on the Gosford estates parti- Marl cularly in the Manor of Coolmalish, under the small bog in Carricklane and boggy meadows in Glassdrumond etc., but in most of these places where it does occur, is either under the bed of the adjacent streams or in hollows where there is an imperfect outlet for the water and of course difficult to raise.

About fifty or sixty years ago when improvements seem to have been for the first time vigorously pursued in this part of the country, a very considerable part of the lands was marled and from the *excessive cropping* which succeeded the lands were so materially injured that a strong prepossession against its use has taken deep root: and this will account for its not being now employed where calcareous manures are so necessary and expensive. The operations of lime and marls depend on principles very different. Quick-lime tends to the more rapid decomposition and solution of the vegetable and animal matters in the soil as well as to neutralise other substance in it: *marl* will only improve the texture of the soil in its relation to absorption, acting merely as an earthy ingredient. The value of marls is nearly in proportion to the quantity of lime or calcareous earth in their composition, taken in conjunction with their distributability or the ease and completeness with which they mix with the soil. *Clay marls* which generally occur in argillaceous districts are often very weak and impure and it is highly probable that a very moderate quantity of lime would at a less expense answer the same intention. The *artificial* marl already noticed may have obviated the necessity of recurring to the natural marl which is to be found. Marl should not be used until it is ascertained that the quality is sufficiently rich to be worth the cost and labour of raising and spreading it (see Appendix page 311). On the   * part of the argillaceous formation (on which so large a portion of the Gosford estates rest) which extends across the County of Down, the use of marl has been after long disuse again begun to be introduced to practice, with considerable success. It ought to be spread early in the season so as the weather may mellow it down before ploughing or planting potatoes thereon, which is perhaps the best method. The quality of the land and of the marl must determine the quantity to be employed. But marls are often followed by bad consequences.

p. 283 There are many kinds of impure and mixed marls such as sandy, clayey, loamy, and stony marls according as these varieties of soil are incorporated or mixed with the principal substance. These sorts, of course, are inferior to the *pure* marls, but the stony kind is considered to be the best because its efficacy is more lasting though the *fat* and crumbling kinds enrich or operate more speedily. The hard marls, however, in every case operate for the greatest length of time and are often followed by bad consequences to the soil unless good management with regard to cropping is exercised during the

---

*Blank in text.

period of operation. After being long excessively fruitful and productive the soil will gradually become so sterile and barren as scarcely to be worth cultivating, in which case the greatest exertion can hardly procure a return of fertility. In this respect the effect of over-cropping land that has been marled is precisely the same as takes place with lime: an uncommon exertion is made occasioning a proportionate debility, though were good husbandry studiously practised the exertion would neither be so excessive in the first instance nor the after-consequences so mischievous. In numerous instances land has been reduced so much as to be thought little better than useless, by the effects of lime and marl. Both however are excellent agents in forwarding agriculture though often their agency has been misapplied and used for mischievous purposes. Under a correct rotation of cropping and with a suitable supply of dung neither lime or marl is injurious. Reverse the circumstances and the contrary effect must necessarily be produced.

Bog-earth compost. There are few methods by which the quantity of manure may be so easily augmented as by the judicious use of bog-earth or mould, where it can be obtained. From the scarcity of fuel many of the turf bogs are so closely cut as to leave scarce any bog-soil, especially on the manor of Coolmalish. But several bogs still remain affording scarce any turf for fuel but would furnish a considerable supply for compost to the adjoining farms and every facility ought to be given for obtaining it for this purpose. And many of the meadows which have been formed on boggy bottoms might be lowered with advantage, or at least without injury and so furnish a supply of excellent materials for a compost to enrich the claylands adjoining, if taken so as not to leave pits as is done in cutting up those meadows for fuel, as already noticed (page 235).

By employing *bog-stuff one load* of dung will serve to change from $2\frac{1}{2}$ to $3\frac{1}{2}$ loads of this stuff into excellent manure. It would undoubtedly be found of very essential importance particularly on the very tenacious soils which occur on part of Coolmalish manor (as mentioned in page 234) and indeed on almost any part of the estates. In the counties of Donegal, Londonderry, Tyrone, etc., it is imperfectly employed on the basalt and schist soils extensively and with great success, and the Reporter has had considerable experience of its great utility in restoring soils which had been from the use of lime and marl (followed by excessive cropping) reduced to a state scarcely capable of producing anything. In conversing with the tenants on the Gosford estates he found some degree of prepossession against the use of *bog-earth* in composts, which have originated from its improper application or abuse. The common mode of employing it by such as have tried it, is drawing it to the dung-stead but from being imperfectly mixed with the dung or too much trampled on to be sufficiently fermented, or when the fermentation has been allowed to proceed too far as to consume the materials by fire *fanging*[1], this kind of manure has got a character it does not merit, because when not sufficiently fermented the antiseptic properties of the bog are not changed, which not only prevent its decomposition but communicate its quality to the soil, encouraging the growth of sorrel. And scarce any two substances can differ more in their qualities than bog-earth as it naturally occurs and after it has been properly warmed and fermented: in the one case it is one of

p. 284 the most infertile substances in nature and in the other highly fertile and until so altered should not be applied to land. The common argument against it is from rendering the succeeding crops of corn chaffy and light, is the same as against marl etc., and will occur in all cases under the *exhausting system*. But when the lands are laid out to grass after the first crop this objection is obviated and its utility in promoting the growth of profitable herbage is allowed by the tenantry, who consider it as being ill-calculated to enable them to continue the mistaken and unprofitable mode of several successive grain crops. Surely what would tend so amazingly to augment the volume of manure with advantage must be important: in Scotland as good crops of wheat have been raised from it as from dung alone. In the Appendix (page 308) the mode of preparing it is described at length and might be abridged and simplified so as to be better understood by the tenantry. As a top-dressing for meadows it can scarcely be equalled and for this purpose alone is important.

From the want of properly constructed and arranged *farm-buildings* the quality of dung made is much less than it might otherwise be. The *urine* which is capable of being employed so advantageously especially in composts, is almost entirely lost or but turned to inferior account. In Britain considerable attention is now bestowed to take advantage of this fertilising liquor but its management seems to be understood and most vigorously followed in Flanders. Its vast importance may be learned from the following facts. In Flanders the liquid manure chiefly prepared from urine is relied on beyond any other, especially for their *flax* crops at the rate of about 2,480 gallons

---

[1]Fanging=Catching hold (O.E.D.)

beer measure to the English acre. The produce of the urine of eight horses and thirty-six head of cattle, housed winter and summer, manure twenty-one English acres in the best manner; and on a small farm on which the livestock consisted of two horses, three cows and two yearling heifers, the urine alone with three hundredweight of rape-cake dissolved in it, and the aid furnished from the privy, manured three English acres of rye and turnips. Proper cisterns are formed for this purpose into which the urine is conveyed by proper channels and into which the rape-cake is put and also the cleanings of privies. This important article to the farmer has been duly attended to in Britain. It is calculated that the urine of a horse from its being so much lighter is more valuable than the dung he produces, and that the urine of twelve cows is sufficient to top-dress two English acres of meadow, the urine of each cow being worth about eighteen shillings per annum. Urine is advantageously employed by throwing it over the dunghill or as a compost with bog-earth etc. It is said that bones sprinkled with urine are dissolved by the fermentation thereby excited: a profitable method of preparing it is mentioned in Appendix (page 309). Manure cannot be collected or properly employed unless the farm buildings are properly constructed and arranged —see '*Remarks on Designs*' in the Appendix (page 329)— and this leads to notice *Farm-Buildings* in general as a means of improvement.

The farm-buildings and cottages in this part of the county of Armagh are much more substantial and comfortable than in many other parts of Ireland. But they certainly admit of further improvement and if any timber is granted towards the erection or improvement of buildings on the Gosford estates it may be under some stipulated obligation to employ it to the best advantage. Too much interference, however, in this respect is not recommended—tenants often know best what is for their own advantage—or at least it is frequently dangerous to attempt too great innovations of which they themselves cannot see the propriety or utility. One great defect in the common cottages or cabins is the want of separate bed apartments for the different members of the same family and this defect even extends to *farm-houses* of a more respectable description. This is particularly attended to in the designs given in the Appendix.

The plan of the farm-yard inserted in the Appendix (page 333) is inserted to show what would be most convenient and p. 285 commodious to the *first* class of occupiers, the most consider-able of whom are engaged in the linen manufacture.

Livestock   The *livestock* may be advantageously improved by affording
the tenants the use of improved breeds but this too may be
abused and a partial amendment on the common stocks of the
country is more to be recommended than attempts to introduce
stock of too high a breed for which the pasture and keep would
not be sufficient.

Farming Societies   Farming societies have been already noticed (in page 21) as
being too often relied on to effect essential improvement in the
rural economy of a country but they may be certainly rendered
of essential service (see an instance page 18). This perhaps
more from the opportunities and inducements which such
associations afford of bringing landlords and tenants frequently
and intimately together and under a feeling of mutual goodwill,
from the flattering countenance which is extended to the
unostentatious occupation of the farmer, that they tend to
promote improvement than even any diffusion of agricultural
knowledge, in which they are generally barren or often rather
injurious in attempting injudicious methods of introducing
good systems of husbandry or in attempting crude and inapplicable ones. In attempting to establish a farming society
much previous consideration is requisite to adapt it to the
habits, feelings and practices of the neighbourhood so as to
render it permanent or really useful and as so many rules for
the regulations of such in almost every district may be consulted
in framing such for any particular one, it is not considered
necessary to enter into further details here.

Ploughing matches   *Ploughing matches* generally proceed from and are promoted
or supported by farming societies and when any disposition
appears to introduce them, they ought to be encouraged.

If one great utility of public agricultural associations is to
bring landlords and tenants more frequently together under
such circumstances as tend to their mutual advantage, it must
be obvious that the intimacy between an individual proprietor
and his tenantry must be of much more essential advantage,
and has this superiority that it is not so much dependent on
adventitious circumstances and the will and caprice of others
as upon his own will and pleasure. For it can scarcely be
supposed, even after all due allowance for the absurd prepossessions of human nature, that any landlord who really
wishes to act fairly towards his tenantry, would in vain attempt
to conciliate their good will, or to serve and gratify both himself and them by his personal countenance and attention. It is
indeed almost indispensable that industrious tenants should as
frequently as possible be taken notice of: some small indulgence
or gratuity or other marks of distinction may serve as powerful

excitements to the individual and operate as an inducement to the exertions and industry of others; occasional visits and personal commendations from a proprietor or agent will often do much. It is in this way that premiums can only be of advantage and without this they ought not to be attempted, unless the proprietor or his agents have it in their power steadily to follow up and carry the arrangement into effect. In fact, unless they can make this a source of amusement the mere cold and partial efforts of prudence or mere good wishes of intentions will not suffice. After all, as it is long before persons of limited experience and observations and who have little which they can afford to hazard at a venture, can be brought to see the utility of many excellent plans, any permanent and rapid effect need not be calculated upon. It is only in a highly improved country that new methods of tillage etc. are speedily adopted. In page 277 the subject of premiums has been already noticed in order to point out the utility of considering the defect of the present systems of occupation and tillage which has been done at considerable length, and also further discussed in Appendix (page 317) where a scheme of premiums is given which are considered applicable to the present circumstances to the Gosford estates.

The only *market* connected with the estate under the control of the proprietor is the one held in Markethill which has latterly been greatly augmented, much to the advantage of the town and neighbourhood, and is likely to increase, particularly if further aided and encouraged. Large quantities of yarn and flax are disposed of and in the event of building a new inn or market-house, lofts should be provided for storing and paying the latter in. Some kind of a market-house is much wanted to afford shelter to the persons bringing *meal*, etc. for sale, as well as shambles for the exposure of butcher meat. Markets

p. 286

It is the opinion of some of the linen buyers, several of whom reside in the immediate neighbourhood, that a linen market might be established, particularly as Mr. Bernard McKee can now give cash accommodations and he will be best able to give such advice as may be most likely to carry so desirable an object into effect—than which nothing would more essentially tend to increase the extent and trade of the town and consequent advantage to the vicinity.

In Scotland there are *General Regulations* to which all the tenantry are bound, and of which they are frequently informed by printed circulars, and to which are sometimes added admonitions and encouragements. The miscellaneous kind of occupation and management which prevails in Ireland does not General regulations perhaps render this so necessary nor could it be so advantageous but still it is presumed there are various particulars of which the tenantry ought to be fully aware and frequently brought under their notice. Those should be as brief and distinct as possible, and no regulations mentioned unless such as can be and are intended to be adhered to. As there is no document so carefully perused in general and so often recurred to as the receipts for rents, the whole or as many as possible might be printed on the back of these (see a scheme of this kind, Appendix page 322).

Seneschal   The appointment of a *seneschal* to the different manors is necessary for the purpose of having proper persons appointed to view trespass etc., and to enforce the regulations of the estates (see page 322).

Office   As much inconvenience has been sustained from the loss of many documents etc., relative to the estate it is highly requisite that an *office* should be procured, in which they could be properly arranged and preserved.

There are few subjects of territorial improvement in Ireland on which it is advisable for a *proprietor* to *expend capital*, beyond the precincts of a demesne, merely with a view to profit, for any improvement made on lands to be again let to tenants will not as in other countries bring an adequate rise of rent, as the tenants would not be prudent enough to preserve or take due advantage of them without the risk of abuse.

The subject of planting forest trees is discussed in the Appendix (page 306).

Bogs   Some of the *bogs* as noticed in the Additional Remarks to the Tabular Report (see page 104) may be profitably improved by lowering the outlets so as to drain them further for cutting turf and when they are not leased to the tenants, will repay the expense to the proprietor by the additional rents which they will then afford.

Roads   There is no new line of road apparently of essential importance to the local convenience of the property. The partial improvement of roads and lanes, where wanted, has been noticed in the Additional Remarks on each townland.

Rivers   The chief improvement of which the rivers and streams seem in most cases to be capable of, is fixing the boundaries with adjoining estates, not so much for the recovery of land as to put an end to the constant and irritating disputes with their neighbouring tenants, particularly along Cregans, Dirlet, etc. (see pages 110, 121).

Schools   Perhaps there is no means of improvement although slow so likely to be ultimately effectual and efficacious as the *education* of the rising generation, and as the Earl of Gosford is persuaded of this it is unnecessary to enter into a review of the mistaken arguments which have sometimes been adduced against it. An additional school is still wanted somewhere about Lisdrumchor for the accommodation of the middle parts of Baleek manor, and perhaps one about Lisnegat etc., and p. 287 another at Hamilton's Bawn. In addition to the schools which his Lordship or the societies may establish or support, grants of timber and other aids might be advantageously extended to such additional schools as the tenants themselves may find it for their accommodation to establish.

RETROSPECT AND CONCLUSION

After so lengthened and perhaps so tedious a detail it may be proper before taking leave of the subject to take a *hasty retrospect* of the whole, with a view to leave the mind impressed with the scope and intention of the arrangements which have been suggested.

In the Prefatory Remarks some observations were made on the importance of attending to the improvement of estates in Ireland, and on the present urgency of such attention; also some illustrations of what *individual* proprietors may effect, and of the importance of general reports in devising and promoting the necessary arrangements to carry such intentions into effect.

Having detailed the present circumstances of each farm and occupier as the *ground work of improvement* General Observations have been added in which an attempt has been to digest and apply the facts therein recorded in a practicable manner.

After noticing the natural and local circumstances of the estates, the circumstances of the tenantry as connected with their character etc., and present situation, and of the effects of war and of peace, as well as the more temporary effects of *adverse seasons* and contagion, have been adverted to; in the course of which a comparison was drawn between the effects of the peace of 1782 after the American war and of the present peace (see page 252 and see pages 253, 254). Some conjectures have been hazarded of the probable restoration of trade and situation of the tenantry in future, and (in pages 256, 257) the probable future price of produce, with a view to urge the importance of an *abatement* of rent as a means of improvement of primary importance; the arguments for and against this measure, and the various means of liquidating arrears which have been attempted. And in order to take that enlarged view of the subject of rents, which its great importance obviously warrants, the subject of the *appreciation* and *depreciation* of money has been noticed (in pages 248, 249); from which it is presumed it will appear that an *abatement* of rent is not only indispensable but more a *nominal* and *actual* reduction, from the increased value of money, and that *so long as money continues to rise in value, that rents must continue to fall in proportion.* The increased value of money above the former period during the late war is variously estimated from thirty to fifty per cent.

The rapid increase of the rural population in Ireland is too intimately connected with the subject to be omitted and full illustrations have been given of its ruinous results and tendency in promoting the minute sub-division of lands; and on the utility and means of checking this and augmenting the size of farms, particularly as looking forward to a less dependence on manufacture to pay rents. But this is not recommended to be carried beyond what the circumstances of the country warrant and what may be really practicable [and] it is hoped under the firm conviction that no sudden innovation can be made with advantage, so that important as this measure is considered to be, yet it is not intended to be carried to an extent beyond what circumstances may point out as the most advisable. It is not therefore to be considered an attempt to introduce or attain the system of excessive large farms, which has latterly been so prevalent in Great Britain, as to augment the *size* of *farms* so as to enable the occupiers to keep a horse or horses for their tillage and drawing lime, fuel, etc., from a distance; and especially to check the system of sub-division which has and will continue to work misery to the tenantry and loss to the landlord. Hence the obvious importance of encouraging opulent and industrious tenants to increase the size of their holdings when practicable or when other more indigent tenants are removed; and of attending to the character of the estates, so that tenants of skill and industry may be induced to embark their capital in improvements. The improvements of draining, fences, etc. have been noticed and some suggestions offered for their advancement, and the use and abuse of liming, burning, marling, etc., have been illustrated with the ruinous effects of *excessive cropping*, to point out the importance of introducing a better rotation of cropping; and hence the great utility of promoting the cultivation of artificial grasses, the various kinds of composts and   * which may be brought

p. 288

---

*Omission in MS.

to assist in this, and of improved **farm-buildings** for facilitating the increase of manure etc.

When the Reporter was first employed in drawing up his remarks on the Gosford estates a greater variety of opinions was prevalent relative to the circumstances of the country and their effects on the agricultural interest. Many who then violently opposed an abatement of rent etc., as unnecessary or injudicious, have now been convinced of the contrary, and when it has been withheld where so necessary, abundant proofs may be found of the ruinous consequences of withholding it. Had this been then as obvious to the generality as it now is, it would not have been necessary to enter into many of the details which may have rendered the Report in some respects tedious. But if the embarrassment may not be yet over, and it is at present very questionable indeed if things are yet at the *worst*, or that money has yet reached the extent of its appreciation, many of the facts and reasonings employed may be of future utility and will then, perhaps more than even at present, justify and bear out the opinions which have been hazarded. When the *new valuation* was made things wore a better aspect or at least people were more generally unwilling to believe that they would come to the present state, and being reluctant to rest solely on his own opinion the Reporter made *that* valuation *much higher* than he otherwise would if he had taken a less cautious method—and certainly the ability of the tenantry is now much less—so that the fears he hinted with regard to the difficulty of recovering *arrear* without injury to the future ability of the tenants to pay current rents is fully confirmed; and he now with the same freedom records his firm persuasion that it cannot without such a remarkable change as is not at all reasonably to be expected. And if the *circulation* continues so limited and the linen manufacture to decline *his valuation cannot be paid*. If such valuation was now to be made it would be much under the rates then fixed. And he believes that any reluctance which has been shown to take out leases by the generality has been from a well-founded conviction of their inability to pay the rents settled on.

Having in the meantime had considerable opportunity of observing the effect of the various plausible modes of attempting to *liquidate arrears*, either by having works and labour performed on the grounds of the proprietors or on *their own farms*, he is now decidedly of opinion that any departure from *money payments* is rather injurious to the great body of the tenantry than otherwise and ultimately of little real benefit to either party because while employed for the proprietor so much labour is abstracted from the cultivation and management of their own lands and occupations, by which they might be able to earn more or less. Labour in this way is given with so much reluctance that it is done imperfectly or in a way little advantageous to the proprietor and it has uniformly happened in nine cases out of ten that when tenants have been so allowed to clear up rent, they have ceased to make exertions in other ways and to trust to this indulgence for their payments in future. If only those in arrear are so indulged and employed the more industrious and opulent who have paid in cash begin to grumble, as they very reasonably conceive that any indulgence which is afforded to the indolent and those behind ought

p. 289 to be also extended to them, and to become qualified for or have as they suppose a fair and equal claim, intentionally fall into arrear. This has actually been the case in numerous instances.

Another mode of clearing off arrears has been to allow tenants for works and improvements made in their own farms— and this appears to be a more rational plan—but it must be here kept in view that the more common occupations only leave a certain portion of time at disposal for *extra* improvements, and thus to derange or overdrive this may be also injurious. Thus if a tenant be obliged to make say for instance a certain extent of *fences*, to apply a certain quantity of lime, or to execute any other work which might really be an improvement and more or less beneficial. But if in doing this he actually expends so much of his *time* which is his capital, and which could he spare it he might not perhaps be able to expend to more ultimate advantage, yet it may be more than he can afford and prevent him attending to more ready returns to pay his current rent. In fact it is too much to be apprehended that any mode whatever of paying up or clearing off arrear will either immediately or remotely injure the ability of tenants to pay even an abated current rent, with any tolerable punctuality, and if the present arrear is only cleared up at the expense of another accumulation the actual advantage requires no demonstration.

The reluctance to *forgive* arrear has not always been so much from the actual loss of so much *cash* in the meantime as the fear that this indulgence might encourage accumulations in future, in the expectation of similar indulgence. And perhaps under any other circumstances than those which so peculiarly distinguish the present period from all which has preceded, this might be a correct argument but when not merely great political changes have entirely altered the relations of Europe

and embarrassed every branch of industry, but when the
inflictions of providence in adverse seasons and contagion
have deprived the tenantry of part of their stock—and all this
has been effected by causes over which the tenantry could have
no control—a very sufficient reason is furnished to account for
this indulgence. And if the lands are again let at rents in
proportion to the price of produce and possible gains of the
tenantry it will be the fault of those entrusted with the management of the estate if the tenants are allowed to incur future
arrears. Unbiased good sense and the prudential conduct which
regulates transactions between man and man will clearly point
out that it is the real interest of a landlord to enact no more
than his tenant can afford to pay, and it may be boldly stated
as a duty to share in what is actually the dispensation of
providence. The future receipts from an estate with an arrear
hanging over for a series of years, not to mention the bar and
discouragement and inability to effect improvement, must
different be, compared with one whose tenants have been put
upon what is commonly called *clear ground* with only the
current rent to meet. This has now been done in many instances
and where it has been so done there has been no cause of
regret on the part of the proprietor.

These opinions and remarks are here given with a freedom
which a selfish fear of giving offence might withhold, and which
a wish to be really useful could alone apologise for. Having
thus discharged a conscientious duty the adoption or rejection
is left to those whose best interests are more immediately
involved. The Reporter now takes leave of the subject, fully
sensible how deficient it must be in many particulars after his
best exertions but he at the same time humbly trusts not
unworthy attentive consideration.

Signed   William Greig   May 1821.

[*Page* 290 *is blank.*]

III IMPROVEMENT OF THE TOWN OF MARKETHILL

*[Originally planned by Greig as part of the section on Additional
Remarks on the Manor of Coolmalish it overran its space and
was continued after General Observations on page 291.]*

p. 209   In offering a few observations relative to the *improvement* of
the *town* of *Markethill*, the Reporter premises by stating his
decided opinion against the propriety of a *proprietor* expending
his *own capital* in forwarding an object of this kind, unless
such aid towards the erection of a market-house etc., as will
be noticed hereafter. Since his acquaintance with this town he
is happy to have it in his power to remark the very great
improvement which has taken place in the increased extent
and importance of the *market*, and latterly of the erection of
additional buildings, so that the encouragement from the
proprietor is not considerable, and affords a prospect of a
suitable return for such attention as may be judiciously
bestowed in forwarding its further advancement. The great
inconvenience arising from the want of a market-house has
been already noticed (in page 286) and if it be not the wish of
Earl Gosford to expend a considerable sum for the purpose of
mere ornament, it is presumed that a moderate sum say £200
to £250 would furnish suitable accommodation particularly
if built in connection with an inn or any other of the buildings
which may be erected in a suitable situation. As the town is
not likely to extend very much beyond its present bounds it
is most desirable that the stand of the market-house should be
as central as possible and it is therefore suggested that the
market-house be erected between No. 191 and No. 196 where
the tenements are presently held at will. If built in connection
with an inn, apartments might be obtained over the market
space below or a loft for storing or paying flax, which would
be of essential service both to the inn-keeper and merchants in
the event of a linen market being established, a moderate rent
being charged for this loft. And the rear of a market-house on
this plan would afford additional accommodation of yard and
garden to the inn. Or if the steepness of the ground and cost of
gravelling were not objections a space might be obtained for
the *flax market* off the street as in Tanderagee. The shambles
for butcher meat might also be obtained backward, but not
too remote from the street, leaving the space next the street for
meal, *potatoes*, etc.

p. 210   As *Roundtree's* tenements No. 190 and 189 with the houses
built by Captain Kay and Nos. 198, 199 and 200 are considerably farther back than those on Nos. 191 to 197 and 201 it

would be most desirable for the accommodation of the market, etc., as well as for improving the regularity and appearance of this side of the street, that the other buildings were built on the same *line* of front. All those so projecting except Nos. 197 and 201 are held at will, and in the event of the others being re-built it is probable the owners of these two would also ultimately re-build on the same line of front, or they might be removed as is common in such cases by a county presentment, being in a mail-coach line of road.

But while it is considered desirable thus to widen the street and improve the appearance of the houses, it should not be forced beyond the ability of the occupiers for if they are obliged to expend too large a portion of their capital the future loss might be considerable, and this is an error very commonly incurred in the improvement of many towns. So that even although this improvement can only be slowly effected, it is better that it should be so, or even not at all, than involve persons of limited means but whose industry and business has long been of some importance to the place. Perhaps persons might offer who would re-build the tenements-at-will in this way, if the present occupiers were unable or unwilling, but this also requires caution for the idea of a perpetuity often induces persons to embark on speculations of this kind without adequate means, to their own ruin and disadvantage of the town. For in almost every place many instances may be found of persons who have undertaken building on which they have expended all their capital and credit, and when completed remain without either to trade upon, to the manifest loss of themselves and the public. And surely persons of known industry who may pursue their business and avocations in buildings of perhaps an inferior or unhandsome appearance are more desirable tenants and useful members to the community than *untried* adventurers, whose capital may not be superior and whose industry and prudence may be greatly inferior. So that caution is recommended in affording encouragement to persons wishing to take tenements to build, especially if they are to supplant the older residents.

[*continued on page* 291]

In any case their character and means ought to be fully p. 291 known and as the tenants-at-will pay higher rents than they will do if re-built at the cost of the occupier, this sacrifice of income ought not to be made unless likely to be ultimately advantageous. At the same time a partial sacrifice of income in the meantime must be sometimes given up to obtain an object which may ultimately be repaid with interest, as any judicious moderate sacrifice may be expected to secure. It is not so much the *mere rent of town tenements* or the additional rents obtained for town parks (although this last is of considerable importance) as the benefit derived by the vicinity in affording a *better* because a more convenient *market* for produce, and enabling the tenants at large to pay higher rents than might otherwise be the case.

As the town is mostly confined on *three* sides by the demesne, the wood, and Gray's perpetuity there is not much scope for its being considerably extended, and if more space existed it is not likely that its extension to a much greater size would be either practicable or desirable. When the *new road* is finished the present old road at Mr. McCalla's tenement No. 83 may be let for building on, some arrangement being made to straighten the north side with Mr. McCalla as dotted on the plan.

Nos. 185 and 186 at present held under leases of lives and occupied by *low* houses, when the lease expires might also be let for building and in case of a further demand for tenements of this kind on which such buildings as *Stevenson's new houses* etc., ought to be erected, two or three additional tenements might be obtained off the common, although the present bare and barren quality of the rear might be an objection. It has occurred to some persons that instead of extending the buildings here, those on tenements Nos. 185 and 186 ought to be removed and thrown into the *fair-place*, changing the Glassdrumond Road as dotted on the plan, and placing a market-house or sheds at the corner. But the Reporter is of opinion that this alteration is not advisable, because, as the ground likely to be occupied by the first class of houses is very limited and cannot be otherwise extended, that instead of its being curtailed in this place it ought to be extended. And for the reasons already given it is not desirable to place the market-house so far from the centre of the town. The *fair-place* may be extended otherwise, even if part be laid out for tenements as already suggested, by taking in as much as may be wanted from Captain Barker's field adjoining. And further, from the steepness of the ground the space occupied by Nos. 185½ and 185¼ could not be conveniently occupied as a market place and would not appear so sightly as if built upon; and so much loss of rent without any adequate advantage.

If the *fair-place* was to be thus extended into Nos. 185 and 186, it was also thought that part of the front of No. 228 at the south end of the present *fair-place* might be let for tenements of a secondary class. But this does not appear feasible because the greater part of the rear is a *bare basalt* rock or the rubble of the rock formerly quarried there, and so not likely to afford useful gardens without going to such an expense as few would be willing to incur. But the most material obstacle is the *new mill-race*, which is too near the road-side to admit of the houses being built between the same and the road and if they were built on the west side, unless the race was arched over, it would be both unsightly and dangerous and this could only be remedied by an additional expense joined with the cost of improving the rear that no tenant would be likely to incur, so that this part might still be retained in the fair place.

As the space between John Stevenson's (or Steenson) *new* tenement No. 183 and the *new* mill lane is bounded on the front by this race which would be very expensive to arch over in this place, and render any buildings erected thereon unavoidably damp and unwholesome, it is not supposed that any person would be inclined to take it to build on the same front with Stevenson's houses. But as the space down the Mill Lane p. 292 between this race and the Mill holding is nearly double the length of the front so rendered useless for building, it is estimated that at half the rate, sixpence per foot, it would produce a rent nearly equal: this lot is marked 282 on the plan. And as there is a space between the stream which bounds Gray's tenement and the *new* Mill Lane, houses of a secondary class might be built thereon with small back yards towards *Water Lane*, having gardens in front on the opposite side of the lane, between it and the mill-race (see plan). Tenements for houses of an inferior class on leases for lives or forty-one to sixty-one years might be let along both sides of the Glassdrumond Road at from sixpence to eightpence per foot front with a suitable rear for gardens (see plan). There is scarce any scheme can be mentioned so likely to benefit the town and be at the same time advantageous to the proprietor and encourage the building of new tenements as appropriating more land as *town parks*, taking care to apportion it out as generally as possible so as to prevent too much being in the occupation of one individual, either to the owner's neglect of business or to the inconvenience of others who may want the accommodation of land. This may be done by appropriating additional portions of Coolmalish, Drumlack, Edenkennedy etc., as already noticed in the Additional Remarks on these townlands (see pages 200, 201), all of which may be supposed to bring a higher rent than from farm occupation to persons not resident in the town.

The new *mail-coach road* will facilitate the access from Newry especially if the presentment be obtained for reducing part of the hill by cutting and filling, according to the design and section already laid before the grand jury. If the *old road* be stopped up a pass must be opened to the Seceder Meeting-house. Perhaps as the access is impracticable by Water Lane (which is little better than the bed of the stream) this may be obtained by the new Mill Lane by either continuing it through the bottom of Stevenson's tenement or, to save the cost of two arches across the *tail-races*, allowing John McCalla compensation for taking it through No. 226.

The mail-coach road which William Greig laid out for the Post Office some years ago (which went round the town of Markethill) would have been prejudicial to the town if carried into effect because it would have taken the great thoroughfare out of the main street and there is no probability that a new street would have been built to make up the deficiency.

The *fair-place* may be enclosed with a wall or ditch and quicked and furnished with one or two gates so as to confine the cattle from the road and street. Perhaps the fairs may be augmented by suitable premiums.

With regard to the *ornamental* improvement of the town it may be remarked that from standing on a site so elevated it does not appear to so much advantage as if it were more concealed, the rears being at present the most conspicuous from the approach[es] from Newry and Armagh. From Dundalk it appears to most advantage, from this point of view partially hid by grown trees which remain on this side, and this may be adduced as a proof of how essentially trees planted around it on the other sides would improve the appearance, and these are the cheapest and most beneficial means of ornament.

The plantations of the demesne being now extended close to the town on that side, all that is wanted on the opposite side of the entrance from Armagh is some masses of planting. Perhaps the gardens Nos. 62, 105, 106, and 103 on the maps might be planted and perhaps garden No. 202 at the rear of the session house; and timber sallows, alders, etc., planted profusely around the mill-pond and as far as possible and in and around the bottoms of the gardens on the banks of the mill-race. And the plantation already made at No. 61 ought to be continued around the south brow of the hill through Nos. 97, 98, 99 and 96 which would also essentially tend to improve the appearance from the Newry road. The town looks
p. 293 bare and exposed from the Newry road and will appear more

so from the new road but this may be much remedied and the appearance greatly improved by the following small mass of plantations, viz. the old road when shut up between the oak wood and Seceder Meeting-house, and perhaps if this congregation were supplied with trees they might be induced to plant their yard (No. 227½ as coloured green on the plan). The space marked A at the new corn mill being contained between the two *tail-races* and thereby well protected from cattle and of little use for any other purpose ought to be planted; also the space marked B.C.D.E.F. all of which will tend to conceal the mill, etc.; part if not the whole of Lewis Robinson's garden (No. 181) which will be cut off by the new road as coloured green. If 185½ and 185⅓ are not laid off for building tenements the steep space G.H.I. ought to be planted, also K.I. with some skirting off Captain Barker's field. And as the common and fair-place are bare and very unsightly opposite the new entrance from Newry, a belt might be planted along the new mill race to fence in and conceal it, as coloured green on the plan M. to N. And these last would also improve the appearance in coming down the street towards Newry. As the new office and distant view of Mullaghbrack church will terminate the view from the street at the north end and this would be much heightened if a vista be made to bring the principal tower of the new castle also into the same view, which might be done without exposing the town to the castle unless from the top where it cannot be concealed.

A proper *day* school-house is much wanted in this town and if the inhabitants would contribute towards the erection of one, Earl Gosford would render an essential aid by giving some spare corner on which it might be built, and perhaps adding a grant or aid of timber etc.

[*pages* 294-7 *of the MS are blank*]

IV APPENDIX

p. 298   *Manufactures*

Connection
between
agriculture and
manufacture in
Ulster

Although the business of the *farmer* and *manufacturer* can only be carried on with the greatest ultimate advantage to individuals and *landed proprietors* as *distinct* pursuits, yet the *linen manufacture* from being employed in working up the rude produce of even an inferior quality of soils, from being so much a *domestic* manufacture and affording employment to the young and aged of both sexes, and from requiring only a small portion of capital and simple machinery (unless in the finishing processes of bleaching, etc.), is perhaps capable more than any other species of manufacture of being profitably carried on in connection with agriculture at least by the occupiers of small farms. From the minute *sub-division* of *lands* among the occupiers which various causes already noticed (page 262) have tended to produce, it is evident that the *linen manufacture* has hitherto essentially tended to raise or to keep up the value of lands in Ulster, particularly in the county of Armagh, as without the assistance and gains derived from the produce of flax the present rents could not be punctually paid by the generality

Linen manufacture
now less profitable

of tenants, occupying farms of so inconsiderable a size and with so small a portion of skill and capital. Hence the urgent importance of endeavouring to encourage and promote its extension and preservation. And this is more particularly the case at present as the *linen manufacture* has been for several years *evidently* on the *decline*, at least so far as relates to the gains of those employed in preparing the green cloth and yarn for the market; being frequently so inconsiderable as only to afford a trifling remuneration for the labour of either the spinner or weaver scarcely exceeding from half to two-thirds of the average gains during the preceding ten or fifteen years; and whether from the recent introduction of cotton cloth into general use, the competition of other nations in the foreign market, or both, no very flattering expectation can be held out of its again regaining its former lucrative advantages. In suggesting any remedies for this alteration which has and is still materially affecting the ability of many tenants to pay rents, it may be mentioned that many of those having large families of females have not *wheels* in sufficient number to employ them all. This may be at least remedied in part by a judicious distribution of wheels granted by the Linen Board among the most necessitous, or by others which the Earl of Gosford might consider advisable to get made as premiums to the more industrious only.

In Scotland *double* spinning-wheels are in common use, by which from one-fourth to one-third more work may be done than by single wheels as used in Ireland. The Irish *Linen Board* are at present encouraging the introduction of the former into Ireland and the attempts lately made at Londonderry etc., have already been tolerably successful. A person competent to teach the use of the double wheel might perhaps be obtained from the Board or some of those places to conduct a school in Markethill or its vicinity, the Earl of Gosford aided by the Board to defray the expense attending its introduction, procuring a few double wheels and the cost of altering the common ones. But their introduction into common use is not likely to be very speedy owing to the prejudices, the indolence or the inability of many to procure wheels, but it is probable that the attempt would be ultimately successful.

Double spinning-wheels

But although the *want* of *spinning-wheels* is far from being inconsiderable, the want of a sufficient number of *looms* is perhaps still more severely felt than the former among the more indigent class of tenants, spinning-wheels costing only from fourteen to eighteen shillings, looms from three to four pounds each. Many of the tenants on the Gosford estate who have been taught to weave are without *looms*, and several others having many sons, from the want of *looms* have not the means of keeping them properly employed. Among some of the industrious there are many instances of *looms* being occupied constantly day and night by individuals of the same family alternately, at least during the adverse seasons of 1816 and 1817.

Looms wanted

A considerable number of those who have not *looms* of their own are in the practice of hiring looms at the rate of about a pound or a guinea per year. Those in a very few years paying out for this use a sum equal to the prime cost of the loom being a serious drawback on their earnings, *looms* or *timber* to assist in their construction would furnish *premiums* to the industrious, in several respects more suitable to the present circumstance of the country than any other, at least among the indigent occupiers of small farms (see further, page 303).

On granting looms

Separate workshops for weaving have been erected by several of the tenants and encouragement ought to be afforded towards the erecting of others by *grants* of *timber* for *roofing*, more especially if those erecting them entered into an obligation to set up and occupy at lease *two looms*. For those having two or more looms employ apprentices or journeymen in addition to their own family, by which employment is afforded to the females and children and the most profitable mode of disposing of the *flax produce*, the consumption of potatoes and other

p. 299
Weaving shops

14

produce without carrying them to a distant market. As a considerable portion of time is occupied in the purchase and preparation of yarn and sale of the cloth one person can with little additional trouble attend to these for several looms; hence the chief advantage which their having several sons or ability to employ others, derives from the linen manufacture.

Female weavers

There are few sedentary employments usually followed by men which are so well calculated to be also engaged in by females as that of weaving. In many [of] the manufactures of England and Scotland numbers of females are employed even in the laborious work of weaving *sail-cloth*, and in the counties of Down and Antrim numbers are now to be found profitably employed in weaving both *linen* and *cotton*. One or two instances of this also occur on the Gosford estates and with a view to encourage other females to learn this branch of business, some premium or gratuity might be perhaps bestowed with the hope of future advantageous results.

Cotton manufactures encouraged

Whether the opinion that the *linen manufacture* has been for several years past less flourishing than it formerly was, and that it is therefore necessary to provide for its farther decline, be correct or not, numerous facts warrant the opinion that considerable advantage would accrue from a more extensive introduction of *cotton weaving* among the tenantry. This has been for several years fully proved in the counties of Down and Antrim, and also in part of the *county of Armagh*. The *linen manufacture* from being so little liable to fluctuation and to be affected by changes of fashion might be supposed more permanent than most others, yet the competition of other nations in the foreign market, and the superior cheapness of *cotton* articles for many purposes of home consumption for which linen was formerly employed, is quite sufficient to account for the reduced prices of linen cloth. Certain it is that the gains usually derived from *cotton weaving* are generally superior to those arising from the manufacture of linen. All manufactures dependent on foreign demand must necessarily be subject to fluctuations and occasionally depression but the manufactures of *plain white cotton cloth* to which these remarks are chiefly meant to apply, are not liable to the same fluctuations in the weaving department as the fancy articles which so immediately depend on fashion.

Perhaps the manufacture of the *soil only*—in other words, farming alone—when pursued with sufficient skill and capital must be considered on the whole as ultimately more advantageous to the proprietors of estates. But as it is beyond their power to change, unless very gradually, the peculiar circumstances of a country in which the tenants for a long period and for a variety of causes, have generally become dependent on the *impolitic* junction of manufactures and agriculture for the means of paying the current rents, necessity obviously points out the propriety of taking the best advantage of such a connection and endeavouring to remedy what cannot be entirely changed without immediate injurious consequences.

The superior advantages which the weaving of *cotton* seems to possess over that of *linen* are the following, viz.

Linen looms cost from three to four pounds each, *cotton ones* from only thirty to forty shillings each, so that many persons who are unable to purchase the former might more readily procure the latter; or, those who might only be able to purchase *one linen* loom, could for the same sum purchase *two cotton looms* and thus provide better for the employment of their families. Boys of a younger age and females may be employed in the lighter labours of the *cotton loom* and thus be enabled to contribute to their support several years sooner than if employed weaving linen.

Superior advantages of cotton weaving to the tenantry

p. 300

But whatever advantage might accrue to *landed proprietors* from the introduction of the weaving of *cotton*, it would in most cases be totally beyond their power to effect it in situations where nothing of the kind had been previously attempted with effect by manufacturers of *capital* and *skill:* at least any risk of capital on the part of proprietors would be inadvisable as likely to be unprofitable and abortive. But wherever skill and capital is attempted by others every encouragement and facility ought to be afforded, and more particularly as this can in most instances be done without any great sacrifice of income on the part of the proprietor of the lands and with the prospect of increasing the value of land, which is always consequent on the establishment of *extensive* manufactures, as they afford employment to numbers of the more indigent, more or less furnish a nearer and surer market for the produce of the more opulent tenants.

Proprietors cannot establish manufactories

Hence it is gratifying to advert to the *peculiar advantages* which the *estates now under consideration enjoy in this respect,* from the establishment of the *extensive cotton manufacture* at *Glenanne* on the townland of Lisdrumchor by *Mr. Atkinson,* which is carried on with a liberality and enterprise highly creditable to him. The buildings, machinery and other erections which are conveniently erected in a most substantial manner, must have cost at least from ten to fourteen thousand pounds and a very considerable amount of floating capital required

Cotton works at Glenanne important to the estate

to keep them so constantly and extensively employed as they have hitherto been. This may be considered as the most *complete* and extensive *cotton* manufacture so far inland in any part of Ireland, and the Reporter considers it likely to be ultimately so advantageous to the adjoining estates that he feels warranted after much consideration and inquiring to recommend it to attention, and to offer what he conceives the most practical means of rendering it more generally beneficial to the tenantry, and of increasing their ability to pay rent. That this is capable of being effected to a considerable extent will appear from the following details.

Extent of the Glenanne cotton works   The number of persons employed immediately in the *Glenanne cotton works*, as spinners, bleachers, and labourers is about 150: one half men, the other half women, girls and boys, whose wages (with some exceptions of learners) from four shillings to twenty-five shillings per week according to their age, ability and employment. A good many of these are tenants on the Gosford estates or their cottiers, as Mr. Atkinson gets all the yarn wove up by country weavers. On the first of January last
            * he had looms at work in 316 different houses in an extent of ten to fifteen miles in every direction from Glenanne, but chiefly towards Portadown where he first established the cotton trade twenty years ago. In no house are there less than two persons employed, that is a weaver and a winder who attends the weaver. In many there are three or four looms with attendants in proportion so that it is considered not much above the truth to estimate two weavers and one winder to each house on an average, which makes 948 employed in this department alone, besides the 150 employed at Glenanne, 1,098 in all.

And the works are still on the increase. A very inconsiderable number of the weavers hitherto employed are tenants on the Gosford estates from the slowness with which new pursuits and habits of industry are adopted and from the difficulty of procuring looms. But there remains little doubt that it would take root very fast among them if they had looms; this is ascertained from the frequent applications which are made at Glenanne for looms. Mr. Atkinson says he had about two hundred made many years ago for his own tenants about Portadown, and of which he sometimes brings a few up to this part of the country as they can be spared from thence. Where a population exists beyond what the cultivation of the lands requires, employment in other pursuits becomes imperatively

---

*Blank in MS.

necessary for the inability of tenants to pay rents in many cases is chiefly owing to them having families so numerous as to consume the whole or greater part of the produce of their farms, and being without the means of otherwise employing them so as to defray the cost of subsistence. By furnishing employment for such supernumeraries they would not merely be relieved from this serious drawback but be put in possession of the means of augmenting their incomes, and in the present circumstances of the country no other employment is so likely to ensure so desirable an object as that of the aid which may be p. 301 derived from the extension of cotton weaving here recommended. At all events the object to be obtained is daily becoming more and more imperative and as the prospect of success is so flattering it merits an attempt, which may be done without incurring any considerable outlay. Some cotton looms might be procured and given out as already suggested for *linen looms*, and every inducement held out to tenants having several sons to encourage one or more being taught to weave cotton.

On procuring looms

The readiness with which the generality of the tenants, particularly those occupying small farms, enter into obligations to pay money and the remissness with which they are fulfilled, from indigence, improvidence or want of honesty, holds forth little encouragement for a proprietor to expend money with a view of benefiting them or of being repaid. But if a *scheme* could be devised by which *looms* could be furnished, as those who are without any are obliged to *hire* them at an exorbitant rate, it would be very beneficial. If looms were provided by merely paying the usual rate of hire they would in a few years have paid up the entire cost and then have the looms free; or they might be paid up by monthly or quarterly instalments, until cleared off. All looms stamped by the officer of the Linen Board are not seizable for debt, so that if not repaid according to agreement there would be little risk of recovering them again.

Saving banks, however beneficial their tendency, are not likely to be adopted among the indigent class of small tenants whose earnings differ from common workmen and labourers in being so uncertain, and indeed their gains are so inconsiderable compared with the constant demand of rent, that they have rarely anything to spare for such deposit. It is not improbable that in order to procure looms they might be induced for a time to make stated deposits of money to obtain them. In Scotland societies or, as they are more commonly termed, *clubs* have been long common among the lower classes for the purpose of

Clubs for procuring looms

obtaining articles of household furniture etc., and in this country for obtaining watches. In Bangor in the county of Down a carpenter from Scotland some years ago commenced *clubs* for various articles of furniture, which has been the means of inducing numbers of both sexes in that vicinity to deposit small sums for this purpose, rendering their houses convenient and comfortable, and even neat and showy, which might not otherwise have been the case more than elsewhere. Perhaps something on the same plan might be the means of enabling persons without looms to obtain them.

The following is the common mode in which the clubs or associations here alluded to are conducted. Each member agrees to pay weekly or at any other stated time, a certain sum so that within a limited period he shall have paid the full amount of the articles he is to receive. He must either be trustworthy or be able to provide sufficient security that he will continue punctually to pay the stipulated quota, because he may have a chance to receive the article at or soon after he commences paying, as lots are drawn at such times as the tradesman making the article can have one of the kind furnished; and whoever draws the prize gets the article then ready-made, and as soon as each is ready for delivery until they are all completed, when the member who has at every previous drawing got a blank gets his article also. The chance of getting the article even before the whole cost shall have been paid, is a powerful inducement to become a member and has so little of gambling or any tendency to mischievous combination that it is presumed no objection need be urged against it on those heads. The payments of the members furnishes a capital for the tradesman to carry on his business so as to have the article ready at the time fixed on: something of this kind under proper regulations might be the safest mode of procuring looms with less inconvenience and distress to the persons contributing than otherwise. And if the Earl of Gosford was to give say from a penny to twopence for every shilling deposited it would furnish an additional encouragement, such premium however being restricted to those paying the late valuations or of an industrious character. The same scheme might be extended to procuring spinning-wheels, single- or double-handed, and other necessary articles.

p. 302

On flax and flax mills

The importance of extending the cultivation of *flax* on the Gosford estates has been already stated in page   * and con-

---
*Blank in text.

nected with the same subject the following remarks on flax mills and the further encouragement of flax are now added.

In many parts of Ulster the entire process of preparing *flax* for the hackle is still performed by mere manual labour but in the county of Armagh etc., the laborious work of scutching is performed by mills of which kind there are *four* on the manor of Baleek and four on Coolmalish.

But in order to prepare the flax for these *scutching mills* the laborious, tedious and of course expensive operation of breaking is necessary. In Scotland this is universally performed by *mill machinery* as well as the operation of scutching, and in order to point out the great importance of introducing those into use in this part of Ireland the subject is introduced into this report. There are one or two of the more improved flax mills in the county of Down and one near the village of Clare in the county of Armagh. In Scotland there are above four hundred such flax mills which have undergone little improvement for the last twenty-five years. The want of capital and enterprise may account for their not being long since introduced into common use in such a flax-growing country as Ulster, as the Irish Linen Board have at length directed their attention to the introduction of improved flax mills into Ireland. If they were only calculated to save the expense of labour in the work of breaking the flax for scutching, [it] might perhaps be considered of secondary importance in this country where the population is so much in want of occupation. Yet the saving of manual labour in scutching has been found to be of importance in the county of Armagh, a proof that labour is more in demand there than in other parts of the country where the common scutch mills, rude as they are, have not been yet introduced nor any material inconvenience found from the want of them.

The improved or Scotch flax mills are calculated to scutch a greater quantity and in a better manner than those of common use in this country: the flax is also broke for scutching by the former which saves the process of *toasting* or *fire*-drying so generally injurious to Irish flax. The scutchers in the Irish mills are merely *vertical arms* fixed at right angles to the axletree; in applying the flax to these the workman has not sufficient command over it, and [it] is so dangerous that it requires great care to prevent serious accidents. The improved mills have the scutchers placed *horizontal* and enclosed in a circular box, or drum, unless an opening into which the workman introduces the strick of flax to be scutched, and by which he has a complete command over it while under the operation; and he may

Improved
flax mills

as he thinks proper shift it so as to prevent any part getting more than is requisite, as occasion may require, using both his hands free from any danger. One person can only be employed at one set of scutchers in the Irish mills whereas from four to nine persons may be employed by one set of scutchers on the Scotch mills. The process of breaking is performed on the latter by three fluted rollers which beside breaking the *woody part* of the flax plant effectively, does not injure the fibres of the flax so much as when done by means of wooden mallets or beetles. But the chief defect of the Irish flax mills is that the flax must be previously broken by hard beetling, and in order to expedite this operation and render it less laborious the flax must be *toasted* or *dried* quickly by fire: this is done to render the woody part of the flax brittle, and without which hand beetles would not be powerful enough to bruise it sufficiently. It is this process of excessive fire-drying which is so injurious to the flax and is not necessary when the improved flax mills are used, [that] renders them of such importance. The following details show that although the injury and loss sustained by fire-drying are not much adverted to, they are *nevertheless* so very considerable as to render the means of obviating them an object of great importance.

Fire drying flax
injurious

Flax which has been *much fire-dried* before breaking and scutching comes to the hackle with its fabric or quality greatly injured, and its quantity less than it might be under different management, the effect of the fire being to *dry up* and destroy
p. 303 the natural sap or oleaginous matter out of the fibre, or filaments, on which the strength, softness, elasticity and even durability of the flax so essentially depends. And the adhesion which keeps the filaments together is also discharged and prevents finer yarn being spun from it, particularly by spinning mills, where the motion of the spindles is very rapid. The flax also by thus losing the *oily* matter becomes *hard* and renders the fibre easily broken in hackling, occasioning too great a proportion to go tow: parcels of Irish and Scotch flax apparently of the same quality hackled to a same size for spinning, left a balance in favour of the latter of about twenty-five per cent. It is the unanimous opinion of the flax merchants and manufacturers in Scotland who have dealt or used Irish flax, that the present mode of *fire*-drying flax in Ireland is most injurious for besides the oily matter being extracted, [there is] the *gummy* substance of the plant which makes the woody part adhere to the fibrous and which it is the intention of the fermenting process of steeping to dissolve and extract: and as it is impossible from the situation of flax in steeping but that a part

will be more or less imperfectly done, when flax having some part of this gum remaining on it is exposed to the action of a quick fire, the woody and fibrous parts are again so closely united that to effectually separate the one the other must be destroyed. In this way part of the wood adheres to the fibre and when the flax come to the hackle it not only tends to increase the quantity of tow but from running up into knots renders the tow of far less value. This difficulty of separating the woody part from the filaments or fibres is not found to be by any means so difficult where fire-drying is not used. In the opinion of the Reporter there is still another injury occasioned by excessive fire-drying, viz. the outer bark which the same gummy matter already mentioned attaches to the outer surface of the filament, is in like manner apt to be again hardened to such filament by the action of the fire, rendering the flax harder, of a bad colour and difficult to bleach. This scruff remains in too great a quantity and in such a case the flax is attempted to be remedied by the process of hard cloving; but [this] is seldom applied to the flax which is exported, and hence the complaints of manufacturers in Britain that much of the Irish flax and yarn is hard, bad coloured, and difficult to bleach.

It is not so much the humidity of the climate of Ireland which renders this process necessary, as has been supposed, but merely to enable the operation of breaking to be done more easily by hand beatles or mallets. The climate of Scotland is not in any remarkable degree less humid than that of Ireland and it is never found necessary to use this process in that country.

It is the opinion of persons conversant with the flax trade from Scotland, who have visited Ireland, and of those who have gone to Scotland to make enquiries on this subject, that the Irish farmer by the method of excessive fire-drying, hand beetling, and the imperfect scutching—but particularly by fire-drying—is losing at the rate of from fifteen to twenty per cent in *weight*, and that the flax is from fifteen to twenty worse in *quality* than if otherwise managed. For when Irish flax in Scotland and England is not worth more than from £50 to £55 per ton, their own flax sells at from £75 to £80. Yet it is also their opinion that the Irish flax if properly handled in those operations and process and less fraudulently made up for the market, is better than any from the Baltic and might be rendered equal to any from Holland or any other part of the world.

It is rather surprising that the attention of the Irish Linen Board should have been only so lately aware of the utility of introducing the Scotch flax mills and two-handed spinning-wheels into Ireland. They now intend to give the inside machinery of *five* of those mills, to be erected in Ulster, to persons who have a sufficient fall and supply of water and who will undertake to build a house proper for them to be put up in.

The machinery of such mills cost from £70 to £120. If Earl of Gosford was to obtain a grant of one of those it might be worth making an arrangement with Henry Patterson, the tenant of the scutch mill on Drumnahuncheon, with widow Byers who has a scutch mill at Drumnegean, or with Steenson the tenant of Markethill mill, to build or alter their mill-houses for the purpose of erecting such machinery therein.

p. 304

The machines for dressing flax invented by Mr. Lee and which lately excited so much attention in Ireland and on which the Linen Board expended considerable sums with a view of introducing them into use, are found to be of little utility and perhaps their failure may, like most other unsuccessful attempts at improvement, have a tendency to discourage the introduction of others. But they doubtless have had one good effect of calling the attention of that Board to flax mills, and being disappointed in one attempt, have been induced to look out for mills likely to answer so desirable an end.

Mr. Lee's flax machinery

Mr. Lee's system of preparing flax without steeping would be found difficult in a climate usually so wet and damp after the season of pulling flax. That which has been steeped, being deprived of its natural moisture and outer bark, may be readily dried. They [the machines] are beyond the means of most tenants to purchase; would occupy more house room than they have to spare; [and] are very liable to get out of repair, as the least deviation from the square occasions the flax to be cut by the sharp edge of the machine. The inconsiderable quantity of flax which a person can dress with them in the day compared with other mills and machines, and the difficulty of disposing of the flax when dressed, being too fine for the common linen manufacture and totally unfit to dispose of in the markets, being in part wrought into a substance resembling cotton without possessing its elastic properties which facilitates the operation of spinning.

Mr. Lee's breaking machines might perhaps be found useful in preparing steeped and dew-retted flax for the scutch mills: any breaking machines which would wholly or in part obviate the necessity of toasting or fire-drying would be productive of great advantage.

Plantations of forest trees

Although the high price of land will not warrant the pro- p. 305
priety of its being occupied with plantations of forest trees,
with any prospect of a more profitable return, yet it must be
remembered that the better the soil is on which they are planted
the quicker will be the growth and the return will be valuable
in proportion. Hence it frequently happens that plantations of
this kind formed on lands of a very inferior description of
soil cannot be planted with forest trees with any tolerable
certainty of ultimate profit. As the attempt cannot be made
on a large scale without a very considerable expenditure the
matter ought to be well considered before such is incurred.
Indeed, the expense of enclosing, planting, renewing and protecting plantations of forest trees on inferior soils in exposed
situations generally amounts to the fee simple purchase of far
superior lands in more genial situations. In considering the
utility of forest planting in this report profit is the chief object
kept in view, mere *ornament* in this particular case being a
secondary consideration.

A belt has been planted around the inside of the park at
Baleek but either from them being injudiciously planted or not
properly protected from cattle, have not made the progress
which the situation seems calculated to ensure. This might be
extended and properly fenced, leaving the remainder for
pasture; and as such might be an advantageous appendage to
Gosford demesne as an outlet during summer for young livestock. The original intention of the park seems to have been
for the purpose of ornament, perhaps as the site of a hunting
lodge, and in case there may be any probability of its being
still so appropriated any additional plantations might be disposed with this subject in view. The park has been enclosed at
a very considerable expense and as no good object could be
obtained by its destruction, its preservation merits attention
and care. For this purpose a confidential person should be put
to live in the lodge. A strip of land was reserved around the
outside of the wall to allow of access to repair it and to prevent
any operations of the adjoining tenants which might tend to
injure it. It is still reserved for this purpose and not surveyed
into their farms.

The common (No. 8) at the east end of the village of Baleek
consists of a clayey soil of considerable depth and as it is at
present totally useless, should be planted with *larch* and *ash* etc.
after being properly enclosed. Part of the steep glen (No. 7)
on A. Johnston's farm adjoining this and which is incapable
of being tilled is also recommended to be planted. There is also

waste ground formerly occupied by Robert Black with an intention of building on it. He has given it up and as it is too steep and wet to be ever profitably occupied as a garden, [it] might also be planted chiefly with *alders*: it is already mostly enclosed. These three portions of plantation would tend to ornament the village and with a view to improve its present bleak appearance at the west and part of the ground No. 26, lying between the new and old road at Pat McParlane's land, might be planted with this intention. Part of John Chamber's farm overhanging this is so steep and rocky as to be capable of little improvement: one acre or more of this might be enclosed for planting (see [Additional] Remarks No. 53 page 86 and No. 41 page 89).*

There is no extensive portion of ground untenanted on the estates on which plantations of forest trees could be made with a sufficient certainty of success to warrant so great an expenditure of capital as their formation would unavoidably require.

The ground on Upper Corromannon usually known by the name of 'the waste farms', both from the situation being sheltered and the soil so rocky as not easily to admit of being all tilled, seems the best adapted for planting. This is now, however, all let to tenants except a few acres which is lately planted. In case this portion may be found to thrive well the plantation might be extended and the lands held at will until this is fully determined on, or a clause of resuming them inserted in the leases on paying the tenants for such improvements as they might make in the meantime. If forest trees are found to thrive they would pay better than trifling rent for the occupation of tenants. More than one half of this ground, however, consists of deep turf bog of little value for any purpose save turf cutting (see [Additional] Remarks No. 78 page 90).*

The ground not occupied which seems best adapted for forest planting is the cut-out bogs, particularly those along the p. 306 lower side of the road leading from Baleek to Forkhill through this townland of Baleek at farms Nos. 7, 8, 13, and the high ground at Nos. 19½ etc. These portions are sheltered and if properly drained and fenced might be planted with advantage, and the latter although high might answer; and they are not likely to be worth scarce any other improvement. Yet unless Earl Gosford may feel particularly desirous of extending plantations on this quarter, the attempt in either case is not warmly recommended.

Flow-bogs can seldom be planted with advantage unless of a dry and compact quality in low and sheltered situations. The

---

*Not included in this volume.

flow-bogs in Baleek which are not occupied for turf-cutting, from being of a quite contrary quality and not very well sheltered cannot therefore be recommended as worth attention for forest planting until they are cut out. When drained as recommended under the head of 'draining flow-bogs', a portion might be tried as suggested in other doubtful situations.

The portion of ground which occupies the summit of Baleek and denominated mountain (No. 11) merely consists of flow-bog of various depths resting immediately on the bare rock unless towards the north-east end where some portion of gravelly clay intervenes. The sketch of its section (No. 1 page 333)* will convey an idea of its situation. In some places the rock is barely covered, in others to a considerable depth, with bog between the points or parts of the rock which jut up to the surface forming small basins occupied with spongy flow bog scarcely capable of being drained. The entire of this bog is formed of decayed sphagnum etc., the most difficult to reclaim and the least valuable of any species of bog. The Reporter is decidedly of opinion that this entire tract, unless two or three acres at the north-east end adjoining McCardel's holding under the brow of the hill, is totally unfit for being planted with any expectation of a sufficient return for the capital which it would require, or indeed for any other purpose unless the cutting of turf after being drained. But as this has been considered capable of being planted and in case the proprietor may choose to risk the expense of an attempt as an experiment, the following remarks are offered with the view to assist such effort.

The difficulty of procuring shelter forms a great obstacle to planting even on soils of tolerable quality in exposed situation, but when the situation is defective both in soil and shelter the attempt is hopeless; and in so humid a situation subject to be frequently enveloped in fogs, even should the trees thrive for a few years and attain a correspondent height they will be apt to become covered with moss and stunted. Enclosing this will require to be done with a double sod wall made with great care and well-coped with sward to prevent its bursting with the drought of summer, or be as little as possible injured by the frost to which it will be very liable, and will require frequent repair as no hedge plant can be expected to grow unless the common purple sallow etc., which should be planted and would prevent the bank from crumbling. A dry stone wall unless where the bog is too deep to get a proper foundation, although expensive in the first instance, would be ultimately the cheapest.

*Illustration not included in this volume.

Draining this will require to be minutely attended to, not only to draw off the stagnant water [but] also to provide for the escape of rain and snow water to which so elevated a situation is subject. In planting so elevated and exposed a situation, to provide for shelter for the young plants is scarce less indepensable than draining, as without it they cannot be expected to thrive. This is frequently done by sowing lines of broom a few years before planting but as there are few parts of this tract on which broom would grow or at least attain sufficient height, rude single walls of sod four or five feet high would be very advisable: they may be erected for about two-pence or threepence per yard, placed so as to break the force of the prevailing winds. The only objection to these is the extent of surface which must be stripped in procuring materials for such walls but they should be made at least 200 to 250 feet asunder in belts running from north to south; and if these zone belts were planted in succession beginning at the lowest and most sheltered part, at intervals from five to eight years they would furnish shelter by which the summit might be planted with most hope of success. Mr. Bell on the land of Sturgan in the vicinity of Baleek and nearly at as high an p. 307 elevation as the tracts just noticed, has formed a considerable plantation which seems to thrive but the strata is granite with a dry subsoil, a soil of considerable depth with a fine southern aspect, very different from the cold retentive schist rock covered with bog and hanging to the north-east.

It is not considered advisable to recommend plantations on the lower parts of the estate unless such as may [be] added to the demesne which should chiefly consist of *oak*, *ash* and *elm* as they will be ultimately of more advantage and infinitely more ornamental than firs and larch. The greater part of the grown timber detached through Coolmalish manor is in a state of decay and might be sold or disposed of. The grove on Cor-drumond ought to be cut down and might be again replanted as it is too steep for tillage and is very ornamental.

If extensive plantations are formed on Baleek or elsewhere they ought to be effectively fenced and drained and a sufficient number of cottages placed around them for their protection, any risk of depredation not considered as any objection to their formation when other circumstances render them advisable.

Although the Reporter has not found himself warranted in recommending the formation of extensive plantations on the estates unless what may be connected with the demesne with a view to profit, he is of opinion that every means and encouragement ought to be afforded in order to induce the tenantry to

plant forest trees on their farms. For it is not merely the effect
which trees have in rendering the aspect of the country more
agreeable, but the shelter they afford and thereby insofar
improving the climate; the advantages they are of in enabling
the tenantry to erect better houses, and to be better supplied
with implements than they otherwise would be; and also the
sums which they may yield to the proprietor without any
considerable expenditure.

There are few timber trees planted by the tenantry above
twenty years growth. The trees which have been latterly given
out to the tenants for planting were chiefly firs and are not
generally thriving, not so much from the want of care on the
part of those who received them but from their being of too
great a *size* and of kinds not adopted for being planted detached
in hedgerows.

Planting timber trees in hedgerows is seldom a judicious
method as the injury done by their roots and shade generally
more than counterbalance any benefit derived from their
shelter. In a country imperfectly enclosed or in exposed situations hedgerows seldom come to be profitable. Most of the
trees latterly planted through the farms are firs, which should
only be planted in masses, particularly the larch which requires
the shelter and confinement of a number planted together to be
drawn up to yield useful timber. As a hedgerow tree in almost
every situation it is either stunted or distorted and besides is so
impatient of the numerous injuries it must unavoidably sustain
in the bark when exposed to the attacks of cattle and other
accidents that it rarely recovers again. Larch and other firs,
but particularly the former, are the best adopted for the higher
part of the estates and other exposed situations but more should
be given out to those who will engage to plant them in masses
in the angles of their gardens, and some encouragement might
be held out to induce them to do so. Where shelter only is the
object sycamore will grow quickly in very exposed places.
Alder and *birch* will also grow where exposed, the former in
wet and boggy situations. But wherever *ash* is likely to thrive it
should be planted in preference to any other kind: it sustains
cropping and injuries better than almost any other tree and is
useful for almost every purpose, and for some one purpose at
any period of its growth, that no tree is so likely to bring a
profitable return, more particularly as it is likely to continue to
rise in price from the injudicious preference which is so
generally now given to *firs* and other quick-growing timber.
Of the trees given out to the tenants larches in masses have been
well planted and protected by a few (see pages   *).

---

*Blank in text.

Ash plants, etc., of a sufficient size might be given out to those making new fences for although hedgerows are not recommended as advantageous, yet as there is little risk of them being so generally planted as to occasion injury, they may be encouraged where likely to be made and [taken] care of. Trees in masses might be so disposed as to shelter the buildings around which they are planted.

The tenants should be encouraged to plant and to register them. It generally leads to good buildings and other improvements as it gives the tenant an additional interest in the farm and an additional motive to improvement, and may thereby render it worth a higher rent, or in due time to give a higher at the expiration of the lease. The proprietor may also have it in his power to make an advantageous purchase of the trees which will be worth more to let stand for future growth than if cut down for sale when half grown; and if the tenant should cut them down on leaving the farm—an occurrence so rare in Ireland—any expense in clearing the ground will be counterbalanced by so long a rest from tillage. Considerable plantations for tenants occupying farms of so small a size have been also well planted and fenced and registered by some of those holding leases (see pages   *).

p. 308

Composts

The advantages of *bog-* or *peat-earth compost* having been already noticed (in page 283) the following practical directions for its preparation etc., may be of some assistance in promoting its introduction among the tenantry on the Gosford estates.

Let the bog earth of which compost is to be formed be thrown out of the pit for some weeks or months in order to lose its redundant moisture. By this means it is rendered the lighter to carry and less compact and weighty when made up with *fresh* dung for fermentation and accordingly less dung is required for the purpose than if the preparation is made with bog taken recently from the pit. The bog taken from near the surface or at a considerable depth answers equally well.

Take the bog-earth to a dry spot convenient for constructing a dung hill to serve the field to be manured. Lay the cart-loads of it in two rows and of the dung in a row betwixt them. The dung thus lies nearly on the area of the future compost dung hill and the rows of bog should be near enough each other that workmen in making up the compost may be able to throw them together by the spade. In making up let the workmen begin at

---

*Blank in text.

one end, and at the extremity of the row of dung, which should not extend quite so far at that end as the rows of bog on each side of it do. Let them lay a bottom of bog six inches deep and fifteen feet wide, if the grounds admit of it. Then throw forward and lay on about ten inches of dung above the bottom of bog, then add from the side-rows about six inches of bog, then four or five of dung, and then six more of bog, then another thin layer of dung and then cover it over with bog at the end where it was begun at the two sides and above. The compost should not be raised above 4 ft. or 4½ ft. high, otherwise it is apt to press too heavily on the underparts and check the fermentation. When a beginning is thus made the workmen will proceed working backwards and adding to the column of compost as they are furnished with the three rows of materials directed to be laid down for them. They must take care not to tread on the compost or render it too compact and of consequence, in proportion as the bog is wet it should be made up in lumps and not much broken.

In mild weather seven loads of common farm-dung tolerably fresh made is sufficient for twenty-one loads of bog-earth, but p. 309 in cold weather a larger proportion of dung is desirable. To every twenty-eight loads of the compost when made up it is of use to throw on above it a load of ashes either made from coal, bog or wood or if these cannot be had, half the quantity of *lime* may be used, the more finely powdered the better. But these additions are [in] no wise essential to the general success of the compost.

The dung to be used should either have been recently made or kept fresh by compression as by the treading of cattle or swine or by loads passing over it. And if there is little or no litter in it a smaller quantity will serve provided any spongy vegetable matter is added at making up the compost as fresh weeds, the rubbish of a stack-yard, potato-shaws, sawings of timber, etc. And as some sorts of dung even when fresh are much more advanced in decomposition than others it is material to attend to this, for a much less proportion of such dung as is less advanced will serve for the compost provided care is taken to keep the mass sufficiently open either by a mixture of the above mentioned substances, or if these are wanting by adding the bog merely, that is first making it up in the usual proportion of three to one of dung and then after a time adding an equal quantity more or less of moss. The dung of this character of greatest quality is shamble dung, with which under the above precautions six times the quantity of bog or more may be prepared. The same holds as to pigeon dung and other fowl

15

dung and to a certain extent also as to that which is collected from towns and made by animals that feed on grains, refuse of distilleries, etc.

The compost after it is made up gets in to a general heat sooner or later according to the weather and the condition of the dung: in summer in ten days or sooner, in winter not perhaps for many weeks if the cold is severe. It always, however, has been found to come on at last and in summer it sometimes rises so high as to be mischievous by consuming the materials fire fanging.* In that season a stick should be kept in it in different parts to pull out and feel now and then for if it approaches to blood heat it should either be watered or turned over and on such an occasion advantage may be taken to mix it with a little fresh moss. The heat subsides after a time and with great variety and according to the weather, the dung, and the perfection of making up of the compost, which then should be allowed to remain untouched till within three weeks of using when it should be turned over upside-down and outside-in and all lumps broken. Then it comes into a second heat but soon cools and should be taken out for use. In this state the whole except bits of the old decayed wood appears a black free mass and spreads like garden mould. Use it weight for weight as farmyard dung and it will be found in a course of cropping fully to stand the comparison.

Let it be observed that the object in making up the compost is to form as large a hot-bed as the quantity of dung employed admits of and then to surround it on all sides so as to have the whole benefit of the heat and effluvia. Bog nearly as dry as garden mould in seed time may be mixed with the dung so as to double the volume and more of it. Workmen must begin with using layers but when accustomed to the just proportions, if they are furnished with bog moderately dry and dung not lost in the litter they throw it up together as a mixed mass and they improve in the art so as to make a less proportion of dung serve for the preparation.

The addition recommended of ashes or lime to the compost is thought to favour the general perfection of the preparation and to hasten the second heat. The lime laid on the above dung hill is rendered mild by the vapours that escape during the first heat.

Compost made up before January has hitherto been in good order for the spring crops but this may not happen in a long frost. In summer it is ready in eight or nine weeks and if there

---

*Fanging=Catching hold (O.E.D.).

is an anxiety to have it soon prepared, the addition of ashes or of a little rubbish of old buildings or of lime slaked with foul water applied to the dung used in making up will quicken the process considerably.

Lime has been previously mixed with the bog but the compost prepared with the mixture or with the simple bog seemed to produce equally good crops. Bog prepared with lime alone has not been found to answer as a good manure.

Compost of bog earth, lime and clay   p. 310

The value of this kind of compost is evident from the following facts, viz.

In the year 1786 about three hundred tons of bog-earth was collected and formed into an oblong square seventy or eighty feet long, from fourteen to eighteen feet broad and six feet high. To this was added two hundred and forty bushels of quick or unslaked lime which was introduced by cutting trenches across the bed of bog and covering up one trench with the bog which was thrown out of the other. When the whole lime was covered up a considerable quantity of water was added and in two or three days the bog took fire. About one hundred and fifty tons of wet clay in lumps were then thrown on at random. At the end of four or five days the bed was covered up with clay sods and it remained untouched for eleven months at the end of which time when it was carried to the field the heat was so great that it could scarcely be handled. The compost thus prepared was laid on nine English acres of grassland, sown with clover and rye-grass three years before. The grass was greatly improved and the land was not broken up for six years afterwards. The field was several times in corn and grass, and the grass was always cut and never pastured without receiving any manure till 1810.

Methods of burning clay

In the month of March trenches about three feet deep and two and a half feet wide may be formed in the ground to be improved, the turf or surface-soil first taken off and equally spread on the ground but the clay dug out laid in heaps by the sides of the trenches to dry. The burning to commence in May, a few loads of the worst clay employed as a circular floor or foundation about a foot thick to prevent the burning of the surface of the earth under the heap. Three or four billets of wood are placed upright in the middle of the floor and leaning against each other, and round those and over the whole floor small faggots and brushwood are intermixed and raised to the height of about six feet: where turf is the only fuel which can be conveniently procured, iron supporters might be used in place of the upright billets of wood. In either case construct a turf wall at least three feet thick around the heap of wood etc., and of the same height; three or four openings about two feet wide and two feet high and at equal distances might be formed over the bottom of the kiln by placing three or four sticks across the top of each. Throw a quantity of dry turf on the top of the pile and then kindle the fire with wisps of straw at all the openings, and when the whole pile is on fire shut up the vent holes with turf. Supply the heat with the necessary quantity of turf and clay which is to be regulated by the smoke emitted: when it is abundant an addition of clay is required but when diminished, air must be admitted by forcing a sharp stake through the crown of the heap. When the heat is raised to a convenient height and the fire has nearly reached the top, rake down the red-hot ashes and cover them immediately with turf. Before the sod wall is entirely consumed it must be replaced by a new one which confines the heap and by often pulling it almost flat prevents its burning too fast. A heap of sixty or seventy feet in circumference produces five hundred cart-loads of ashes. The fire must be carefully watched at all times. Sometimes it burns so fast that the labour of five or six men is required to supply it with clay. A dry season is the most suitable for this kind of work but a wet season only retards it a little for large fires after two or three days burning are not extinguished by rain and the ashes are of a superior quality when the process of calcination is slow and gradual.

Another method of burning clay is practised in the following manner, viz. To form an oblong enclosure of fifteen feet by ten of green turf sods and raised to the height of three or four feet. In the inside of the enclosure air pipes communicating with openings at each corner of the wall are drawn diagonally and formed of sods placed on edge and of such a width as can be easily covered with another sod. A fire is kindled with wood or dry turf in the spaces between the air pipes and the outer wall. The whole kiln is then filled with dry turf and when it is well kindled the clay is thrown upon it in small quantities. The pipe on the weather side of this kiln only is kept open, the other three being closed up unless it should be necessary from a change of wind to re-open one of them. As the kiln is filled with clay the outer wall must be gradually raised and kept at least eighteen inches higher than the top of the clay to protect the fire from the action of the wind. When any breach is made in the outer wall by burning it must be immediately repaired. The wall may be raised to any convenient height for throwing on the clay and the kiln may be increased to any size by forming a new wall on the outside. The proper management of a kiln of this description depends on the exclusion of the air by the outer walls and the attention that is given to have the top always lightly but completely covered with clay. The masses of clay p. 311 are of various sizes, some as large as a man's head, and it burns better by being dried for a day or two before it be thrown on the kiln. The operation of burning sods etc., is also likely to be much facilitated by a very cheap and simple contrivance, viz. a portable furnace made of old cart iron hoops of the following shape:

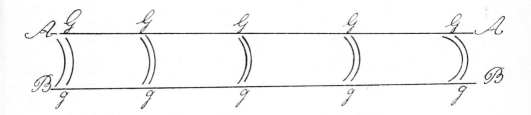

The two pieces of hoops A and B are made straight to lie on the ground and the half hoops g/g/g/g are fixed to them by rivet nails. They are about four feet long each and so light that a boy could run about with two of them in each hand. Turf being laid along the sides and over the top, they keep an opening through the hoop for air to make the fire burn. Before this invention it was very difficult to get the turf sufficiently dry in so moist a climate and the process was extremely expensive and uncertain but this simple apparatus keeps the turf always open and ready to receive air by means of which a few hours of dry weather makes it fit for burning. The expense of these turf kilns is but trifling and by their means when once the small quantity of turf is set on fire a great deal of it may be burnt in one day.

The analysis of marls

In order to ascertain the proportion of calcareous earth which they contain. The following is one of the simplest and easiest methods, viz. Dry a fair sample of the substance to be proved. Pound it and mix the whole uniformly. Put one hundred grains of it into a common four ounce vial. Cover them an inch or two deep with clear water which has been boiled. Pour into the vial a small quantity of the *marine acid*, pure spirit of salt. When the effervescence has ceased add more and continue to add it until shaking the vial no farther hissing or fermentation takes place. Fill a goblet or large drinking glass lightly with clean straw giving the surface of this a smooth dishing form and cover it completely with a piece of common blotting paper (that which is used to dry fresh writing) the precise weight of which has been previously ascertained. Pour the liquid part of the contents of the vial upon the paper and when that has passed through it add pure water to the earthy matter left in the vial, shake it and wash out the whole upon the paper, afterwards repeatedly washing the gross matter on the filter with warm water to prevent any part of the calcareous earth from lodging among it or in the pores of the paper. The water having finally drained through, remove the paper with the dross or residue which remains upon it and place them on a piece of strong paper or pasteboard to dry either in the sun or at the fire. When they are thoroughly dry weigh them carefully. From their joint weight deduct that of the paper and then subtract the remainder from the gross weight of the materials, namely one hundred grains. The second remainder is the quantity of calcareous matter or chalk which the original substance contained and which having united with the acid has passed off with the liquid state through the pores of the paper.

If the quantity of calcareous matter be not equal to one-third of the whole or thirty-three per cent the marl is weak. If it be equal to two-thirds it is good marl and may generally be spread over non-calcareous soils with great profit. There are no other accurate means of ascertaining the strength of marl than those of solutions and filtration. Even the marine acid used as a test is fallacious in the extreme. The degree of effervescence which rises from its application as such, depends infinitely more on the combination of the materials than on their component parts. It is therefore highly imprudent to enter upon a work of any extent with calcareous fossils until their qualities have been accurately ascertained by analysis.

[*Page* 312 *is blank.*]

No. of farm on map	Page of General Report	No. of Addit. Remarks	No. in Rental	Names of Lessees etc.	Townlands	Acres at commencement A	R	P
23, 24, 25	27	16, 18	316, 317	Samuel McKnight	Upper Baleek	31	0	0
20, 22	27	14, 15	318, 337	William Newell	,, ,,	40	0	0
17, 18	27	12	342, 343	Edward and Hugh McElroy	,, ,,	21	1	10
7	31	37	294	Archibald Johnston	Lower Baleek	17	0	0
1	33	55	388	Andrew Ross	Upper Corromannon	14	2	0
4, 5	33	58, 59	393, 394	Alexander Thompson	,, ,,	32	0	0
9, 10	33	63	360, 361	Widow Burns	,, ,,	12	0	0
12	33	65	359	Samuel Bridges	,, ,,	24	0	0
18	33, 34	70	368	Hugh Mooney	,, ,,	30	2	23
19, 23 25	35	74, 76	395, 397	Pat Walsh	,, ,,	26	0	0
				Edward McGuy	Middle Corromannon			
				Walter McCoy Patton	,, ,,			
					Lower Corromannon			
				H. and M. Andrews	,, ,,			
				James Kenner	,, ,,			
				Terence Brady	Carrickannany			
				William Patton	,,			
				Daniel Bennett	Carrickgollogly			
				Margaret Brady	,,			
				John Ferguson	Upper Cregans			
				Thomas Scott	Lower Cregans			
				W. and A. Slieth	,, ,,			
				Samuel Warnock	,, ,,			

Number of Souls resident: Souls	In what year	Acres to each then	State in 1818: No. of shares	No. of souls	Acres to each	No. of years in which they double	Remarks
7	1801	4½	4	20	1½		divided amongst three sons and one daughter
9	1801	4¼	5	12	3½		divided amongst four sons and one daughter
1	1801	21	2	6	3½		two brothers purchased
5	1801	3½	3	9	1¾		two shares given to two daughters
6	1801	2⅛	3	15	1 nearly		divided amongst three sons
5	1801	6½	2	13	2¾		divided amongst one son and daughter
6	1801	2	2	7	1¾		divided amongst herself and one son
5	1788	5	3	15	1¾		divided amongst son of lessee and shares sold
6	1788	5⅛	4	17	1¾		divided amongst widow and daughter and two shares sublet
8	1801	3⅛	3	17	1¾		divided amongst two sons and one daughter

[*Pages* 314 *and* 315 *are blank.*]

Premiums

The following premiums deduced from the remarks which have p. 316
been already made on the present situation of the lands and
tenantry should be granted under the following regulations, viz.
No person to receive more than two premiums in the same year
nor for the same premium more than once in six years, because
without this limitation those who were most substantial and
industrious might always continue to engross them constantly.
Any person using any deceit or fraudulent representation etc.,
with a view to obtain them otherwise than in the manner pre-
scribed, to forfeit what may have been surreptitiously obtained
etc., to forfeit all claims to premiums and countenance in
future. As the premiums are intended to promote improvement
it might not be proper to exclude those who are far in arrear
from being claimants but unless they have paid up to some
particular period, say November 1817 or some other term to be
fixed on, that in the event of their becoming entitled to any of
the premiums then the amount of such premium to be allowed
in rent: but when they are cleared up the rent to such term
they are to receive the amount in money etc., if required. All
those holding leases and articles granted before 1800 to be
allowed one-half the amount of the respective premiums, the
full amount only being paid to those holding at the late valuation.

It is of importance to arrange the premiums so as to meet the
circumstances of the different classes of occupying tenants.
Perhaps this may be done by classing them in the divisions, viz.
those paying £10 and under of yearly rent; those paying above
£10 and not exceeding £20; and those paying above £20 yearly.
Those occupying more than one holding or leases in the same
or adjoining townlands to be considered as one holding. But
as the rents will in some instances approach very near or very
little exceed the sums here specified as separating the different
classes, some partial deviations may be found necessary in
adjudging the premiums.

The Reporter having been at some pains to enquire into the
results which have been produced from the premiums etc.,
which have been granted on several estates in Ireland, thinks it
necessary to remark that he has found a very prevalent idea
among the tenantry of some that the main object of their landlord was to ascertain what the land was capable of producing
in order to raise their rents accordingly; and whilst opinions of
this kind prevail, no matter whether well or ill founded, little
good can be produced. Hence in devising objects for reward or

distinction it is necessary that care should be taken to avoid as much as possible whatever might be construed into this being the object of the proprietor.

Scheme of Premiums

p. 317 [*This is laid out in tabular form in eight columns. In the first column the kind of improvement is numbered and in the second it is specified. In the third it is described in detail. This is followed by four columns (in none of which is any figure entered) and they correspond to the three classes of tenants named in the previous paragraph, and to the total amount to be expended. The final column for 'Remarks' was also left vacant. The obvious intent was for the agent to fill in the premiums to be awarded, with the conditions in the column headed 'Remarks'.*]

1. *Fences with whitethorn hedges.* To the occupying tenant who shall within one year make and properly finish the greatest extent of new fences. Not less for the first class than   perches Irish; for the second class   perches; for the third class   perches and who shall have planted the same with sufficient whitethorn quicks. Note: the ditches to be at least   feet wide and   feet deep; the plants to be laid (and not dibbled in) on a bed of earth properly prepared and sufficiently covered with mould before the   day of April   and carefully weeded at least twice during the two succeeding summers.

2. *Drains.* To the occupying tenant for the greatest extent of hollow, covered or French drains made and properly finished within one year. Not less for the first class than   perches Irish; for the second class   perches; for the third class   perches. At least   feet deep and at least   inches wide at bottom. To be filled   inches with stones etc. (to be viewed before and after filling).

3. *Liming.* To the occupying tenant for the greatest quantity of lime laid on arable land within one year. Not less than   barrels per acre; and the land to be sown out with clover or grass seeds at least with the second crop of grain or flax after such liming (if sown out with the *first* grain or flax crop the premium to be increased one-third but if sown out with the third crop only half the premium to be allowed).

Note: The lime may be laid on pasture to be ploughed down the same season for oats etc., or on ground for potatoes; either mixed with clay, mould etc., or before the planting or first shovelling.

4. *Clover and Grass-seeds.* To the occupying tenant for the greatest quantity of clover or grass-seeds sown on potato ground, with the *first* corn crop. Not less for the first class than   acres; for the second class   acres; for the third class   acres English measure. If sown with second corn crop after potatoes one-third less premium, if the occupier has not claimed the premium for liming.

5. *Building.* To the occupying tenant who shall build the best   p. 318 dwelling house and finish the same in a substantial, workman-like manner within two years according to a plan to be approved of; if covered with slates premium to be doubled and one year additional if lofted: money or timber to the amount of   .

6. To the occupying tenant who shall within one year build the best barn or stable (with the same allowance for slates and lofting as above) and at the same time enclose the best yard for cattle, pigs, dung, etc. (including a sufficient gate), money or timber to the amount of   .

7. *Reclaiming bog etc.* To the occupying tenant who shall within one year reclaim and bring into cultivation the greatest extent of bog, mountain, etc., which has never been cultivated before. For the first class not less than   perches; for the second   perches; and for the third   perches English measure. The ground to be properly drained and planted with potatoes, with ashes, lime or dung, etc., for the two first years and afterwards sown with oats or flax, and to be sown out with grass-seeds with the first or second crop of oats. If planted with ashes or mud only, the premium to be one-third less, if with lime to be at the rate of not less than   barrels per acre.

Note: This premium not to extend to spent bog let in addition to leases granted before the year 1800.

8. *Planting.* To the occupying tenant who shall plant the greatest number of forest-trees in one season. For the first class not fewer than   hundred; for the second class   hundred; for the third class   hundred, if ash and oak (only half the premium for other trees); to be planted in or around gardens or where they can be properly protected from cattle   p. 319 etc. If afterwards destroyed or injured through neglect the premium to be forfeited and refunded. Occupiers receiving the plants from Earl Gosford free of expense or who may register such as they purchase themselves only [to] be entitled to half premium.

9. *Increasing the size of farms.* To the occupying tenant who shall add to his present holding the greatest number of acres by

purchase etc., from the former occupier or owner of the lease in the same or adjoining townlands within one year. For the first class not less than   acres; for the second class not less than   acres English measure.

10. *Industry etc.* To the occupying tenant having his children, houses, gardens, etc., in the neatest and most decent order.

Note: No occupier to be entitled to this class of premiums who shall not once at least within the preceding year have whitewashed his house inside and outside, and kept a paved or gravel way or footpath in front at least   feet wide free from any dung hill or dirt and who has not a place or yard enclosed (otherwise than in front of his house) for his cattle, pigs, turf, dung hill etc.

As whitethorns cannot be expected to thrive on some of the upper parts of Baleek and Corromannon etc., the following additional premiums may be afforded.

11. *Earth and stone fences.* To the occupying tenant who shall make and build the greatest number of perches of earth fences with stones within one year. For the first class not less than   perches Irish in length; for the second class   perches and for the third class   perches. The wall or dyke to be at the least   feet high, the bank at least   inches broad at bottom and   inches at top properly coped with sods or large stones; and when the ground will admit, to have a ditch at least   feet deep and   feet wide at the top.

p. 320

12. *Sod or earth fences.* To the occupying tenant who shall make the greatest number of perches Irish of earth or sod fences within one year. For the first class at the least   perches; for the second   perches; for the third   perches. The fence to be faced with sods, properly coped, and if not so faced to be planted in the front with a row of sallows, elder or alder plants as for whitethorns.

[*Page* 321 *is blank.*]

General Regulations etc.

p. 322 The Earl of Gosford being desirous to promote the prosperity of his estate and the comfort and respectability of his tenantry, has ordered an abatement to be made in such rents as exceed the valuation lately made by his surveyor and also that those holding at will who appear to be sufficiently industrious to continue in the occupation of their farms [are] to get leases at such valuation that they may be encouraged to improve the same.

And further with a view to promote this desirable object with advantage to them, he expects that all those who are desirous to merit his good opinion and countenance will attend to the following regulations, as those who do not see that such is for their mutual advantage need not expect either encouragement, countenance or the renewal of their leases when they shall expire, viz.

1st. That as much injury has arisen both to the proprietor and the tenantry from the sub-division of farms, by not only rendering the occupiers less able to make improvements or pay rents but also lessening their respectability and comforts, for which reason the Earl of Gosford is resolved not merely to strictly prohibit this in all the leases which he will grant but enforce the clauses and penalties against alienation (without permission in writing) in such of the old leases as are yet unexpired, so that no occupier transgressing herein need plead ignorance or expect indulgence or exemption from the penalty and its consequence.

Those having families to provide for are therefore warned and entreated to make timely and prudent provision for them otherwise than by giving them portions of their own holdings, either by apprenticing them to trades separate from farming or obtaining other holdings for their accommodation.

Every facility and encouragement will be given to those wishing to add to the size of their holdings by purchasing from their neighbours in the same or adjoining townlands, but without any permission to again sub-divide or separate them.

2nd. Those who do not think proper to have all disputes which may occur relative to trespass, boundaries, lanes, etc., equitably settled by proper persons appointed for each town-land at court leets, or who may not be willing to have all other disputes between tenants connected with the occupation of p. 323 their farms etc., left to the decision of honest and respectable neighbours, mutually chosen, will be considered as of a quarrel-some, troublesome and litigious disposition who, with those of a dissipated or indolent character, will not be held deserving of encouragement or countenance; whilst particular respect will be observed towards sober, industrious and improving tenants.

3rd. Those who improve their farms and keep their fences, houses, etc., in good repair, and who protect such timber trees as may be growing or planted on or about their holdings will meet with suitable indulgence; for the encouragement and advantage of whom the premiums and rewards which accompany this address are especially intended, as well as for those who may find it in their interest to follow the same praiseworthy and profitable example.

A careful and minute examination has been made of the present state and condition of each farm and occupier and a report thereof laid before the Earl of Gosford and his agent, and in future a register will be regularly kept of such improvement as may take place and of the peaceable and industrious as well of the improper conduct of the tenants.

But in making the present or future valuations no advantage has or will be taken of whatever improvements or outlay which may be made by tenants in buildings etc. On the contrary, the lands will be more readily let to improving tenants on terms even more favourable than to their neighbours who may not have made the same improvements.

The following may be printed at the bottom or on the back of the rent receipts:

Rents received on Tuesdays only from 10 to 3 o'clock.

Take particular notice that the penalties will be rigorously enforced against those who alienate or dispose of their lands without permission in writing, as in future sub-divisions will not be allowed either during the leases or on their expiration. At the same time encouragement will be afforded to those who may be disposed and have opportunity of adding to the size of their holdings.

[*Pages* 324-328 *are blank.*]

p. 329 [*Page* 329 *is illustrated on plates* 1 *and* 2, *pages* 230 *and* 231.]

p. 330   Plan etc. No. 1 is intended to show the interior arrangement of the best description of common cottages or cabins in this part of the country, the principal defect of which is the want of separate sleeping apartments, which it is conceived may be obtained without much additional expense as shown in plan No. 2 which also will be at the same time more commodious and comfortable. If the situation is exposed the ends may be carried upright and not hipped, as in the annexed elevation. The dimensions may be varied to suit the wish or intention of the proprietor or occupier. Perhaps a grant of timber etc., towards roofing might induce those about to built houses of this scale to adopt the plan here recommended and so introduce it into more common adoption.

p. 331 [*Page* 331 *is illustrated on plates* 3 *and* 4, *pages* 232 *and* 233.]

Plans Nos. 2 and 3 are adapted for the residence of labourers. p. 332
If [it is] to be occupied by a weaver [it] may be extended [so]
as to afford space for a loom or looms, which would render
No. 2 more uniform in the elevation. No. 3 would be sufficiently
sightly for such cottages as may be found necessary about the
demesne and their erection may be encouraged as recommended
for Nos. 1 and 2.

[*Page* 333 *is illustrated on plates* 5 *and* 6, *pages* 234 *and* 235.] p. 333

From the small size of the holdings and agriculture being p. 334
generally followed in connection with manufacture etc., the
judicious arrangement of a farm yard is rarely to be met with
in this part of the country. Keeping the intention of augmenting
the size of farms as much as possible in view a judicious
arrangement of this kind will become more important. But as
from the circumstance of the country, want of capital, etc.,
this can only be carried to a certain extent, say from 20 to 100
acres or thereby, and as there are many reasons to render
attention to manufacture still desirable as affording occupation
to a part of a numerous family which cannot be otherwise
readily and easily provided for or otherwise employed, a
weaving shop etc., is included.

There are two bed apartments on the ground floor and two
or even four more may be obtained on slight lofts over these
and the weaving shop. The living room or kitchen will require
to be roomy. The large pantry adjoining will be necessary as
dairy, store, etc. This is formed under a lean-to the roof of
which is continued along the back of the building and will
afford shelter for cleaning vessels—drying yarn, etc.

If a larger description of dwelling-house is required the end
next the potato house may be extended so as to afford space
for a sitting parlour, or the whole may be raised to two stories
and in that case ought to be covered with slates.

The offices houses are calculated to afford all the requisite
accommodation for this kind of an establishment with convenience, security and cleanliness.

The prospective elevation No. 2 is intended to show the
appearance and effect of the buildings according to the annexed
ground plan and the view No. 1 of the dwelling-house extended
so as to afford the parlour etc., mentioned as above.

PLATES

16A

Common Cottage or Cabin

N⁰ 1

Elevation

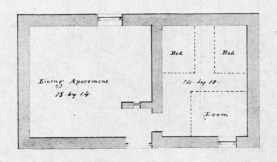

Living Apartment
15 by 14

Bed | Bed
14 by 10

Room

Ground Plan

Plate 1

230

Improved Cottage

N<u>o</u> 2

Elevation

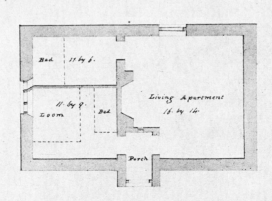

Ground Plan

Plate 2

231

Improved Cottage N.º 2.

Elevation

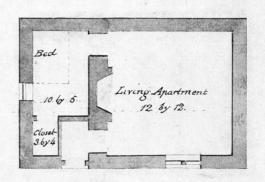

Ground Plan

Plate 3

232

Improved Cottage Nº 3.

Elevation.

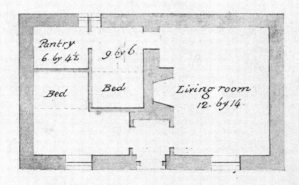

Ground Plan

Plate 4

233

Improved Farm House & Yard

Elevation Nº 1

Elevation Nº 2

Plate 5

234

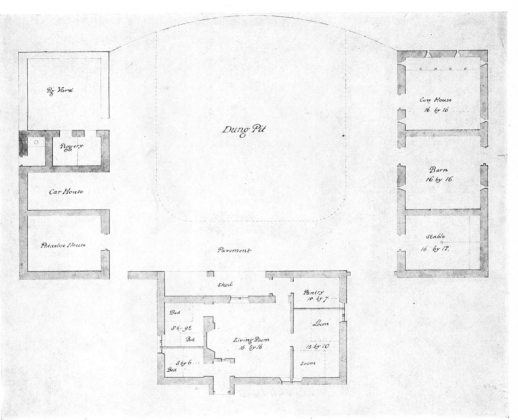

Pig Yard

Piggery

Car House

Potatoe House

Dung Pit

Pavement

Cow House
16 by 16

Barn
16 by 16

Stable
16 by 12

Shed

Bed
8 by 9½

Bed

Bed
8 by 6

Living Room
16 by 16

Pantry
10 by 7

Loom

13 by 10

Loom

Plate 6

235

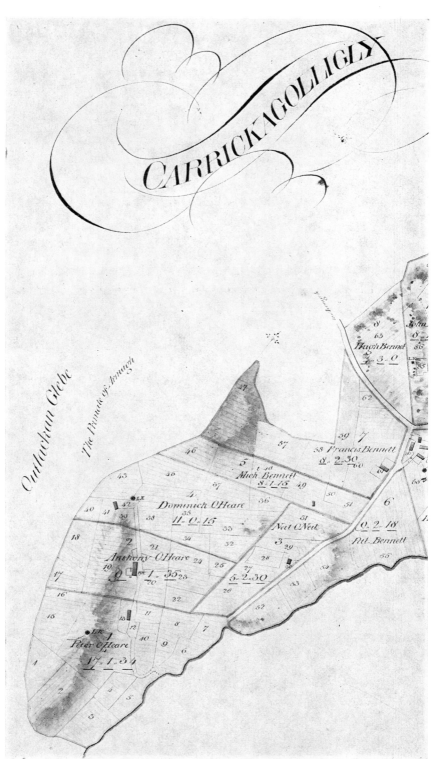

CARRICKAGOLLIGLY

Peter O'Heare

Plate 7

105 Moses Andrew purchased from Samuel Anderson the Lessee and gave part to his son Hugh — they are very industrious and improving tenants, and when the lease falls ought to be re-leased as now divided between Moses and Hugh Andrew

105½ James Kinner &c the lease of this farm was taken out by James Kinner

Carrickgollogly

106 The lands of this townland though rocky are in general of a good quality and tolerably dry subsoil, allowance for fences and liming are most applicable for its improvement — and white thorn would thrive on the greater part, also ash timber.

107 Peter Heare this farm is at present in very bad condition but might be greatly improved by draining but the occupier seems not to have industry, skill or capital to effect any material improvement, a large portion of the arrears (which it is presumed are considerable) ought to be allowed for drains carried round the base of the hill passing the fences which separate fields Nº 123 from 14.   Section Nº 6 page 339 will illustrate the necessity and utility of this.

108 Anthony Heare having a less extent of ground than Peter may be supposed more equal to the profitable occupation of it — it is also better drained — but allowance of area ought to be granted for this purpose.

237

Index

No distinction has been made between the introduction and Greig's test

240

Index

Cess
  parish, 68
  county and vestry, 74
Chalmers [Thomas], 15
Charity, 115, 159
Children, 37, 38, 41–6, 68
  see also families
Clare, County Armagh, 203
Clauses, see leases
Climate, 99, 113, 114
Clover, 222–3
Clubs, see savings banks and clubs
Clutton, John, 7
Colquhoun [Patrick], 15
Common, 192, 195, 207
Composts, 174, 175, 179–80, 186, 212–5
Consolidation, 33, 36, 61, 66, 94, 159–60,
  162, 166, 223–6
  see also holdings
Coolmalish, manor of, County Armagh,
  20, 21, 23, 37, 38, 40, 42–6, 48n,
  49, 50, 52, 55, 58, 63, 65, 67, 68,
  98–103, 177, 179, 210
Coote, Sir Charles, 19, 32n, 44, 50n, 54,
  56n, 58–9, 63n, 68n
Cornwall, Duchy of, 4
Cottages, see housing
Cottiers, 37, 38, 47, 48, 145, 149, 161, 200,
  201
  and turbary, 150, 161
  census, 38
  cot-take, 161
  role in society, 67–8, 77
Cotton, 133
  bleachers, 200
  consumption, 198
  factory, 46, 66, 199–201
  looms, 46, 199, 201
  manufacture, 16, 152, 198
  spinners, 43
  wages, 198
  weavers, 44n, 46, 198, 200, 227
  winder, 200
Court leet, 225
Covenants, see leases
Cow's grass, 160
  see also cottiers
Credit, public, 133, 169, 183, 191
  see also capital, currency, investment
Crop rotation, 32, 130, 171, 179, 186, 222
Crops
  barley, 130
  clover, 222–3
  flax, 107, 118–9, 128, 129, 152, 165, 175,
    183, 190, 196, 197, 202–6, 223
  fodder, 35, 171
  grain, 109, 110, 112, 152, 165, 170, 173
  grass, 32, 35, 118, 144, 172, 222–4

Crops—*contd.*
  green crops, 32, 35, 171
  hay, 68, 144
  oats, 118, 127, 128, 130, 222, 223
  potatoes, 50, 68, 106, 114, 118, 130, 152,
    154–5, 164, 171, 175, 190, 197, 222, 223
  prices, 111–2, 127–9, 131
  wheat, 130, 131, 180
  yields, 13, 29
  see also arable farming
Currency
  circulation, 17, 125, 128
  paper, 17, 125–6, 133
  metallic, 126

Debt, 201
Demesne, 92, 184, 192, 207, 210
Demography, 21, 37–48, 51, 55–7
Depressions, economic, 111–9, 127, 131
  see also disasters, natural, *and* harvest
    failures
Devon Commission, 7, 34
Disasters, natural, 17, 28, 48, 50, 85–6,
  114–20, 128–9, 139, 154–5, 174, 197
Disease, 48, 115–6, 119, 130, 185
Disputes, 225
D'Ivernois [Sir Francis], 15
Donegal County, 179
Drainage, 29, 33, 75, 99–100, 102, 172,
  186, 210, 222
Driver, Edward, 4
Drumbanagher, County Armagh, 34
Dublin Society, 19
Dungannon School lands, 34

Ecclesiastical Commissioners, 6, 7n
Education, 25, 148, 161, 184–5
Elder tree, 224
Electioneering, 64, 94, 149
Elm, 210
Emigration, 62, 63, 150, 151, 170
Employment, 43–8, 196–201
Enclosures, 172, 207, 209–10
  see also fencing, hedges
Epidemics, 115–6, 185
Estate
  archives, 81, 184
  character of, 166–8
  maps, 71, 72, 160
  office, 160, 184, 195
  papers, 10, 80–1, 184
  regulations, 183–4, 224–6
  surveys, 2, 4–5
Estate management, 1, 2, 4–5, 22–36,
  79–90, 92–3, 110, 185–9
  see also agents, alienation, consolida-
    tion, drainage, evictions, housing,
    improvements, investment, landlord-
    tenant relations, leases, middlemen,

Index

Index

Dd471946 K8 3/76 BL&C Gp55/0/0 S4786

ISBN 0 337 23174 5